TWENTY FIRST
SC

Project Directors

Angela Hall   Emma Palmer

Robin Millar   Mary Whitehouse

Editors

Angela Hall   Emma Palmer

Mary Whitehouse

Authors

Mike Kalvis   Carol Levick   Nick Owens

Elizabeth Swinbank   Dorothy Warren

THE UNIVERSITY *of York*

THE SALTERS' INSTITUTE

Nuffield
Foundation

OCR
RECOGNISING ACHIEVEMENT   OXFORD
UNIVERSITY PRESS
Official Publisher Partnership

Contents

How to use this book

Welcome to Twenty First Century Science. This book has been specially written by a partnership between OCR, The University of York Science Education Group, The Nuffield Foundation Curriculum Programme, and Oxford University Press.

On these two pages you can see the types of page you will find in this book, and the features on them. Everything in the book is designed to provide you with the support you need to help you prepare for your examinations and achieve your best.

Module Openers

Why study?: This explains why what you are about to learn is useful to scientists.

Find out about: Every module starts with a short list of the things you'll be covering.

Ideas about Science: Here you can read about the key ideas about science covered in this module.

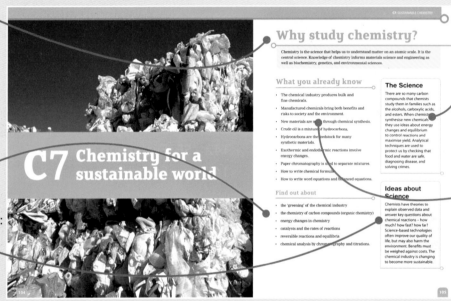

The Science: This box summarises the science behind the module you're about to study.

What you already know: This list is a summary of the things you've already learnt that will come up again in this module. Check through them in advance and see if there is anything that you need to recap on before you get started.

Main Pages

Find out about: For every part of the book you can see a list of the key points explored in that section.

Key words: The words in these boxes are the terms you need to understand for your exams. You can look for these words in the text in bold or check the glossary to see what they mean.

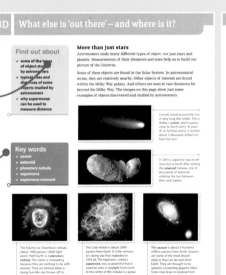

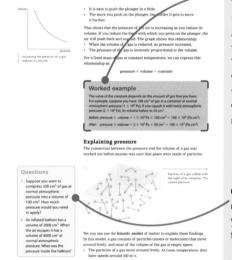

Worked examples: These help you understand how to use an equation or to work through a calculation. You can check back whenever you use the calculation in your work to make sure you understand.

Questions: Use these questions to see if you've understood the topic.

You should know: This is a summary of the main ideas in the unit. You can use it as a starting point for revision, to check that you know about the big ideas covered.

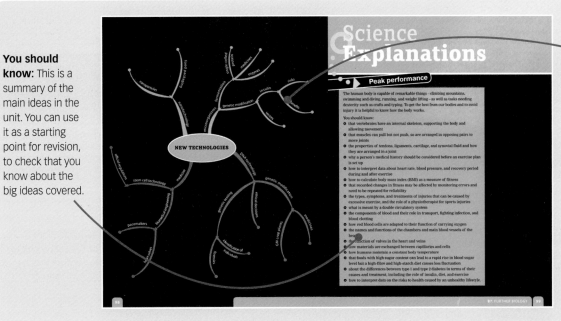

Visual summary: Another way to start revision is to use a visual summary, linking ideas together in groups so that you can see how one topic relates to another. You can use this page as a starting point for your own summary.

Ideas about Science: For every module this page summarises the ideas about science that you need to understand.

Review Questions: You can begin to prepare for your exams by using these questions to test how well you know the topics in this module.

Structure of assessment

Matching your course

What's in each module?

As you go through the book you should use the module opener pages to understand what you will be learning and why it is important. The table below gives an overview of which main topics each module includes.

B7

- Peak performance – the skeletal system
- Peak performance – circulation
- Peak performance – energy balance
- What can we learn from natural ecosystems?
- New technologies

C7

- Green chemistry
- Reversible reactions and equilibria
- Alcohols, carboxylic acids, and esters
- Analysis
- Energy changes in chemistry

P7

- Naked-eye astronomy
- Light, telescopes, and images
- Mapping the Universe
- The Sun, the stars, and their surroundings
- The astronomy community

How do the modules fit together?

The modules in this book have been written to match the B7, C7, and P7 modules, supporting the specifications for GCSE Biology, GCSE Chemistry, and GCSE Physics, respectively, when used alongside the student books for GCSE Science and GCSE Additional Science. In the diagram to the right you can see how the modules fit in the series.

		GCSE Biology	GCSE Chemistry	GCSE Physics
GCSE Science		B1	C1	P1
		B2	C2	P2
		B3	C3	P3
GCSE Additional Science		B4	C4	P4
		B5	C5	P5
		B6	C6	P6
Separate Sciences Top-Up		B7	C7	P7

GCSE Biology, GCSE Chemistry, and GCSE Physics assessment

The content in the modules of this book matches the modules of the specifications. The diagram below shows you which modules are included in each exam paper. It also shows you how much of your final mark you will be working towards in each paper.

Unit	Modules Tested			Percentage	Type	Time	Marks Available
A161	B1	B2	B3	25%	Written Exam	1 h	60
A162	B4	B5	B6	25%	Written Exam	1 h	60
A163	B7			25%	Written Exam	1 h	60
A164	Controlled Assessment			25%		4.5–6 h	64

Route 1

Unit	Modules Tested			Percentage	Type	Time	Marks Available
A171	C1	C2	C3	25%	Written Exam	1 h	60
A172	C4	C5	C6	25%	Written Exam	1 h	60
A173	C7			25%	Written Exam	1 h	60
A174	Controlled Assessment			25%		4.5–6 h	64

Route 1

Unit	Modules Tested			Percentage	Type	Time	Marks Available
A181	P1	P2	P3	25%	Written Exam	1 h	60
A182	P4	P5	P6	25%	Written Exam	1 h	60
A183	P7			25%	Written Exam	1 h	60
A184	Controlled Assessment			25%		4.5–6 h	64

Route 1

Command words

The list below explains some of the common words you will see used in exam questions.

Calculate
Work out a number. You can use your calculator to help you. You may need to use an equation. The question will say if your working must be shown. (Hint: don't confuse with 'Estimate' or 'Predict'.)

Compare
Write about the similarities and differences between two things.

Describe
Write a detailed answer that covers what happens, when it happens, and where it happens. Talk about facts and characteristics. (Hint: don't confuse with 'Explain'.)

Discuss
Write about the issues related to a topic. You may need to talk about the opposing sides of a debate, and you may need to show the difference between ideas, opinions, and facts.

Estimate
Suggest an approximate (rough) value, without performing a full calculation or an accurate measurement. Don't just guess – use your knowledge of science to suggest a realistic value. (Hint: don't confuse with 'Calculate' and 'Predict'.)

Explain
Write a detailed answer that covers how and why a thing happens. Talk about mechanisms and reasons. (Hint: don't confuse with 'Describe'.)

Evaluate
You will be given some facts, data, or other kind of information. Write about the data or facts and provide your own conclusion or opinion on them.

Justify
Give some evidence or write down an explanation to tell the examiner why you gave an answer.

Outline
Give only the key facts of the topic. You may need to set out the steps of a procedure or process – make sure you write down the steps in the correct order.

Predict
Look at some data and suggest a realistic value or outcome. You may use a calculation to help. Don't guess – look at trends in the data and use your knowledge of science. (Hint: don't confuse with 'Calculate' or 'Estimate'.)

Show
Write down the details, steps, or calculations needed to prove an answer that you have given.

Suggest
Think about what you've learnt and apply it to a new situation or context. Use what you have learnt to suggest sensible answers to the question.

Write down
Give a short answer, without a supporting argument.

Top Tips

Always read exam questions carefully, even if you recognise the word used. Look at the information in the question and the number of answer lines to see how much detail the examiner is looking for.

You can use bullet points or a diagram if it helps your answer.

If a number needs units you should include them, unless the units are already given on the answer line.

Making sense of graphs

Scientists use graphs and charts to present data clearly and to look for patterns in the data. You will need to plot graphs or draw charts to present data in the practical investigation and then describe and explain what the data is showing. Examination questions may also ask you to describe and explain what a graph is telling you.

Describing the relationship between variables

The pattern of points plotted on a graph can show whether two **factors** are related.

To describe the relationship in detail you should:
- read the axes and check the units used
- identify distinct phases of the graph – where the gradient is different
- use data when describing the changes.

Gradient of the graph

The **gradient** of the graph describes the way one variable changes relative to the other. Often the x axis is the time axis. The gradient then describes the rate of change.

Look at this graph, which shows the product of a chemical reaction being produced over time. The gradient of the graph gives the rate of the chemical reaction.

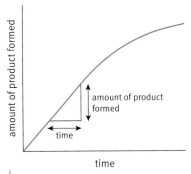

Graph showing how rate is calculated for a chemical reaction.

Look at this graph, which shows the distant travelled by a car over a period of time. The gradient of the graph gives the speed of the car.

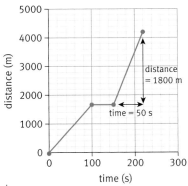

$$\text{speed} = \frac{\text{distance travelled}}{\text{time taken}}$$

$$\text{speed} = \frac{1800 \text{ m}}{50\text{s}} = 36 \text{ m/s}$$

Calculating the gradient of a distance–time graph to find the speed.

Calculating reacting masses and percentage yields

Problem *How much aluminium powder do you need to react with 8.0 g of iron oxide?*

$$2Al(s) + Fe_2O_3(s) \longrightarrow Al_2O_3(s) + 2Fe(s)$$

Work out the relative formula masses (RFM) by using **multiplication** and **addition**.

Reactants:
RFM of $Al = 27$;
RFM of $Fe_2O_3 = (2 \times 56) + (3 \times 16) = 160$

Products:
RFM of $Al_2O_3 = (2 \times 27) + (3 \times 16) = 102$
RFM of $Fe = 56$

To find the relative masses in this reaction **multiply** the RFM by the numbers in front of each formula in the equation. Then convert the relative masses to reacting masses by including units. These can be g, kg or tonnes depending on the data in the question. The units must be the same for each of the values.

$2Al(s)$	$+$	$Fe_2O_3(s)$	$\longrightarrow$	$Al_2O_3(s)$	$+$	$2Fe(s)$
$(2 \times 27) = 54\,g$		$160\,g$		$102\,g$		$(2 \times 56) = 112\,g$

To find the quantities required, scale the reacting masses to the known quantities by using **simple ratios.** Always include the **correct units** when substituting values.

$$\frac{\text{mass of aluminium required}}{\text{reacting mass of aluminium}} = \frac{\text{mass of iron oxide used}}{\text{reacting mass of iron oxide}}$$

$$\frac{\text{mass of aluminium required}}{54\,g} = \frac{8\,g}{160\,g}$$

Rearrange the equation, to find the mass of aluminium.

$$\text{Mass of aluminium required} = \frac{8\,g}{160\,g} \times 54\,g = \mathbf{2.7g}$$

Problem *What is the percentage yield of iron for the same reaction, if 4.9 g of iron is actually produced?*

To work out the theoretical yield of iron, use ratios as before

$$\frac{\text{mass of iron yielded}}{\text{reacting mass of iron}} = \frac{\text{mass of iron oxide used}}{\text{reacting mass of iron oxide}}$$

$$\frac{\text{mass of iron yielded}}{112\,g} = \frac{8\,g}{160\,g}$$

and then rearrange the equation.

$$\text{Theoretical yield of iron} = \frac{8\,g}{160\,g} \times 112\,g = 5.6\,g$$

Use this equation to calculate the percentage yield

$$\textbf{percentage yield} = \frac{\textbf{actual yield (g)}}{\textbf{theoretical yield (g)}} \times \textbf{100 \%}$$

Actual yield of iron given in the question = 4.9 g

Substitute the quantities.

$$\text{percentage yield} = \frac{4.9\,g}{5.6\,g} \times 100 = \mathbf{87.5\ \%}$$

Frequency data

Frequency graphs or charts show the number of times a data value occurs. For example, if four students have a pulse rate of 86, then the data value 86 has a frequency of four.

A large data set with lots of different values can be arranged into class intervals (or groups). Collecting data in class intervals can be done by tallying. It works well to have data arranged in five or six class intervals.

Class interval	Tally	Frequency
60–65	|	1
65–70	||||	4
70–75	卌 卌 ||	12
75–80	卌 |||	8
80–85	卌	5
85–90	|	1
	Total	**31**

A data set of pulse rates from a class of 31 pupils tallied in a frequency table.

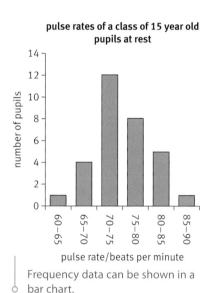

Frequency data can be shown in a bar chart.

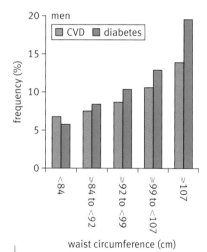

Sometimes frequency graphs have % as the units on the y axis. CVD: cardiovascular disease.

Q Write down a question that can be answered from each of these graphs.

Range and mean

Statistics are used to describe data. Useful statistics to describe the pulse rate data are the range and mean of the data.

The range of this data set can be expressed as 'between x beats per minute (lowest value) and y beats per minute (highest value)'

The mean is the total of all the values divided by the number of data points.

Q Write down two statements about the pulse rate data.

Q If you are comparing the pulse rates of two different classes in your school, why would it be useful to have both statistics (mean and range)?

Controlled assessment

In GCSE Biology, GCSE Chemistry, and GCSE Physics the controlled assessment counts for 25% of your total grade. Marks are given for a practical investigation.

Your school or college may give you the mark schemes for this.

This will help you understand how to get the most credit for your work.

Practical investigation (25%)

Investigations are carried out by scientists to try and find the answers to scientific questions. The skills you learn from this work will help prepare you to study any science course after GCSE.

To succeed with any investigation you will need to:

- choose a question to explore
- select equipment and use it appropriately and safely
- design ways of making accurate and reliable observations
- relate your investigation to work by other people investigating the same ideas.

Your investigation report will be based on the data you collect from your own experiments. You will also use information from other people's research. This is called secondary data.

You will write a full report of your investigation. Marks will be awarded for the quality of your report. You should:

- make sure your report is laid out clearly in a sensible order
- use diagrams, tables, charts, and graphs to present information
- take care with your spelling, grammar, and punctuation, and use scientific terms where they are appropriate.

Marks will be awarded under five different headings.

Strategy

- Develop a hypothesis to investigate.
- Choose a procedure and equipment that will give you reliable data.
- Carry out a risk assessment to minimise the risks of your investigation.
- Describe your hypothesis and plan using correct scientific language.

Collecting data

- Carry out preliminary work to decide the range.
- Collect data across a wide enough range.
- Collect enough data and check its reliability.
- Control factors that might affect the results.

Analysis

- Present your data to make clear any patterns in the results.
- Use graphs or charts to indicate the spread of your data.
- Use appropriate calculations such as averages and gradients of graphs.

Evaluation

- Describe and explain how you could improve your method.
- Discuss how repeatable your evidence is, accounting for any outliers.

Review

- Comment, with reasons, on your confidence in the secondary data you have collected.
- Compare the results of your investigation to the secondary data.
- Suggest ways to increase the confidence in your conclusions.

Secondary data

Once you have collected the data from your investigation you should look for some secondary data relevant to your hypothesis. This will help you decide how well your data agrees with the findings of other scientists. Your teacher will give you secondary data provided by OCR, but you should look for further sources to help you evaluate the quality of all your data. Other sources of information could include:

- experimental results from other groups in your class or school
- text books
- the Internet.

When will you do this work?

Your school or college will decide when you do your practical investigation. If you do more than one investigation, they will choose the one with the best marks.

Your investigation will be done in class time over a series of lessons.

You may also do some research out of class.

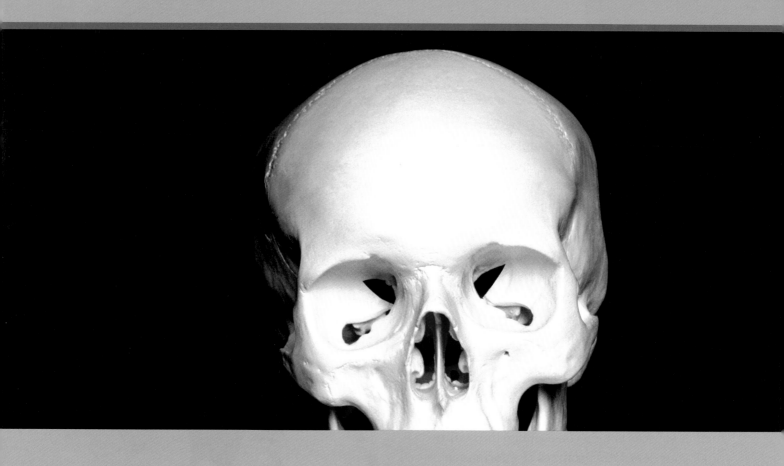

B7 Further biology

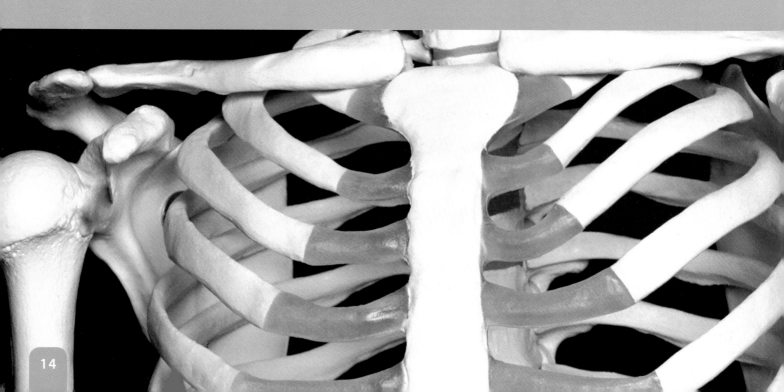

Why study further biology?

Biology is the science of life, and biological knowledge and understanding will be increasingly important for humans and their relationship with the natural world during this century.

What you already know

Further biology builds on your knowledge about the human body, how ecosystems function and new technologies.

Find out about

* how our skeleton, joints, and muscles support our body and allow us to move

* how we can monitor our level of fitness

* how our heart and blood function as a transport system

* how we keep our body temperature balanced

* how exercise and a healthy diet can help prevent illnesses like diabetes

* how natural ecosystems provide us with food, water, timber, clean air, and shelter

* the difference between a linear lifestyle and a closed-loop lifestyle

* the way materials cycle around natural ecosystems

* solutions for fishing and timber harvesting to make them sustainable

* better ways to live in a post-oil world

* using bacteria and fungi to produce medicines and enzymes

* genetic modification of bacteria and plants

* DNA technology, nanotechnology, stem cell technology, and biomedical engineering.

The Science

In 'Peak performance' you will learn more about how human bodies work and how to keep fit and healthy. In 'Learning from natural ecosystems' you will find out how the natural world provides a habitat for humans and a model for sustainable systems. In 'New technologies' you will discover more about modern biological techniques, with implications for human food and medicine production.

Ideas about Science

Data collection and analysis are important in all areas of biology. The validity of conclusions from data needs evaluation. Thinking about cause and effect is important too, and it is often useful to develop scientific explanations. We need to think if new technologies are ethically right. Risks need to be taken into account too.

Topics B7.1–3: Peak performance

Why study peak performance?

Manufactured devices can only begin to imitate the incredible endeavours that every one of us can perform. Human performance is a triumph of intelligence, sense, and control.

To keep at your peak performance it helps if you understand how your body works. Striving for peak performance has positive impacts on your health and well being.

The Science

As vertebrates, we have a jointed internal skeleton, which is moved by muscles that work in pairs. A physiotherapist can help if we have an injury.

We can monitor our levels of fitness accurately using a range of techniques. A body mass index calculation based on our height and mass can quickly tell us if we need to make changes to our diet and lifestyle.

Our heart is a double pump – its muscular walls and valves circulate blood around the lungs and the body. Blood supplies every part of our body with nutrients and oxygen whilst removing waste products.

The conditions inside our body need to remain constant for our cells to function properly. If conditions change from their normal level then our body responds until the balance is restored. If we choose a poor diet and don't exercise, we become vulnerable to illnesses such as diabetes, heart disease, and some cancers.

Ideas about Science

Measurements of performance rely on collecting repeatable and accurate data.

Data on health and performance from a human population lies within a range due to variation between people, and other factors.

Deciding what is 'average' or 'normal' needs to refer to mean values, the spread of the data, and any outliers in the data.

Scientists must be aware that when two factors are correlated, this does not mean one causes the other.

Find out about

✓ **the skeletal system**

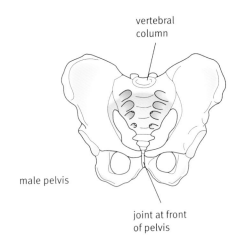

male pelvis

vertebral column

joint at front of pelvis

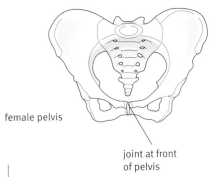

female pelvis

joint at front of pelvis

The adult human male and female pelvic girdles look different. The female's pelvis is shallower and wider for childbearing. This fact will help an archaeologist or forensic scientist to establish the gender of human remains.

Peak performance in activities needing physical strength and flexibility rely on a system of soft tissues supported by a tough and flexible **skeleton**. **Muscles** provide movement at joints and maintain posture.

As well as supporting your body, your skeleton:
- stores minerals such as calcium and phosphorus
- makes red blood cells, platelets, and some white blood cells in bone marrow
- forms a system of levers with muscles attached, which allows the body to move
- protects internal organs, for example, the pelvis protects the reproductive organs.

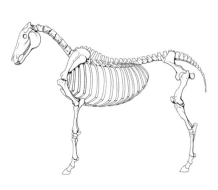
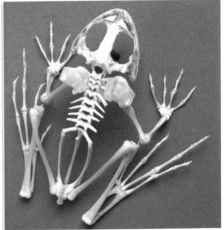

Vertebrates have bones inside them – match the creature to the skeleton.

Living bone

The skeleton is not just dry bone. Its tissues, such as **bone** and **cartilage**, are made of living cells. Blood brings nutrients and oxygen to the cells.

Bone is continually broken down and rebuilt, which allows a child's bones to grow in size. Even an adult's skeleton is continually changing. Weight-bearing exercises such as jogging stimulate bone growth, increasing its density. Inactivity makes bone less dense and weaker.

Key words
- ✔ skeleton
- ✔ muscle
- ✔ bone
- ✔ cartilage

Questions

1 List four functions of the skeleton.

2 Describe how exercise changes bones.

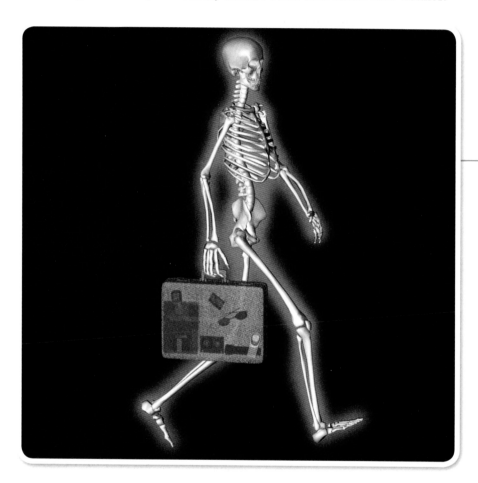

The human skeleton has over 200 bones. Most will move, but some are fixed in position, for example, those in the skull. Skull bones are flexible during early development, but fuse together soon after birth.

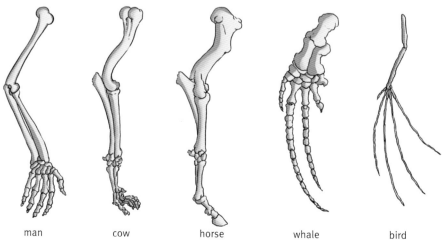

man   cow   horse   whale   bird

It is interesting to think that all vertebrate skeletons are developed from the same original plan. Can you spot the same bones in each creature? A horse walks round on single 'fingers' with big 'finger nails' as hooves.

Find out about

- ✔ **how movement is produced at your joints**

Holding the bones together

Any sport or physical activity involves movement where two or more bones meet at a joint. Ball-and-socket joints, at your hip and shoulder, are the most versatile. These joints move in every direction, like a computer joystick. Hinge joints, such as the knee and elbow, move in just two directions – backwards and forwards.

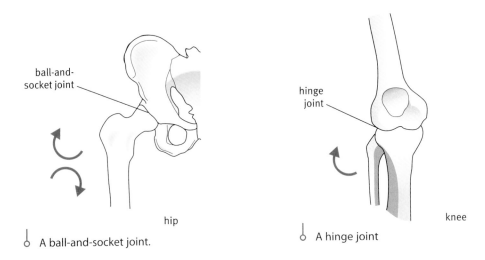

ball-and-socket joint

hip

⌕ A ball-and-socket joint.

hinge joint

knee

⌕ A hinge joint

Tough elastic bands, called **ligaments**, hold the bones in place and limit how far the bones can move. Smooth cartilage stops bones from grinding against each other as they move. It forms a rubbery shock-absorbing coat over the end of each bone. This stops the bones from damaging each other. Cartilage is smooth, but friction could still wear it down. To reduce this as much as possible, the joint is lubricated with oily **synovial fluid**.

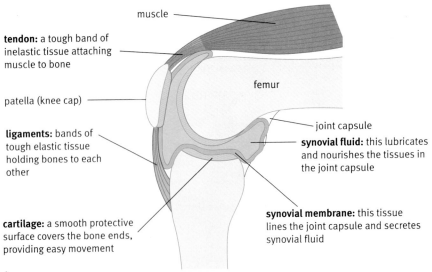

muscle

tendon: a tough band of inelastic tissue attaching muscle to bone

patella (knee cap)

ligaments: bands of tough elastic tissue holding bones to each other

cartilage: a smooth protective surface covers the bone ends, providing easy movement

femur

joint capsule

synovial fluid: this lubricates and nourishes the tissues in the joint capsule

synovial membrane: this tissue lines the joint capsule and secretes synovial fluid

⌕ The knee joint. Like most joints in the body, this is a synovial joint.

How muscles move bones

Inelastic **tendons** transmit the forces from muscles to the bones. Muscles can only pull a bone for movement at a **joint**. After contracting, the muscle is stretched again only when the bone is pulled back by another muscle. So at least two muscles must act at every joint:

- One muscle contracts to bend the joint.
- The other muscle contracts to straighten it.

Muscles that work opposite each other are called an **antagonistic pair**.

There are over 600 muscles attached to the human skeleton. They make up almost half of your total body weight.

Key words
- ✓ **joint**
- ✓ **ligament**
- ✓ **synovial fluid**
- ✓ **tendon**
- ✓ **antagonistic pair**

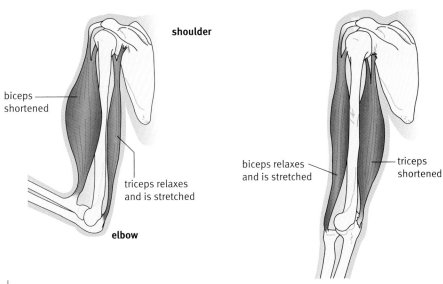

The biceps and triceps muscles contract to move the elbow joint.

Questions

1. Describe the difference between a tendon and a ligament.

2. Explain why this difference is important.

3. Name the parts of a synovial joint and explain how they are suited to their function.

4. Name the muscle that:
   a. bends the arm
   b. straightens the arm.

5. Explain what is meant by an antagonistic pair of muscles.

6. Professional dancers and gymnasts often develop osteoarthritis in their knee joints in later life. The surface of their cartilage becomes rough and wears away. Suggest what symptoms this will cause.

Find out about

Find out about

- ✔ **what you need to consider before starting an exercise programme**
- ✔ **measuring how your body changes when you exercise**

Circuit training is a good way to build up your strength and fitness level at a pace to suit you. The instructor can vary the difficulty of the exercises or the number of times that they have to be performed.

Scuba divers need to have a particularly thorough medical examination before they can train to dive with their club. They will need to have a chest X-ray and a doctor's signature in their diving log book.

Starting out

When you join a new sports club your instructor should find out some key facts about you. You will be asked to fill out a questionnaire about your **medical** and **lifestyle history**. This will help your instructor to plan an exercise regime that suits you.

If you start a new activity you should tell your instructor about your medical history and lifestyle. What adjustments might you need to make to these people's exercise regimes?

Medical history

Before starting a new exercise regime, your instructor might enquire if you, or anyone in your family, suffers from certain medical conditions. Your regime will be adjusted to take into account any circulatory and respiratory problems. Your instructor needs to know about any treatment you have had for injuries – especially to your joints or back. Let your instructor know of any **medication** you take. You might need to have medication, such as an inhaler, close at hand.

Lifestyle history

The coach might also ask questions about your lifestyle. If you have a healthy and active lifestyle you will progress quicker than someone who is new to the activity or who has been resting while recovering from an injury. The duration and difficulty of exercise will be adapted to suit your needs.

Getting fitter
Baseline data

When you begin a new activity you might take some initial measurements. This is your **baseline data**. The next time that you monitor yourself you will be able to see how much you have improved by.

Heart rate: As you exercise your heart rate increases. Your heart beats faster to deliver more food and nutrients to your muscles. It is recommended that you train at about 60% of your maximum heart rate.

Blood pressure: When you do strenuous exercise your heart beats more forcefully and your **blood pressure** increases. 120/80 mmHg is a typical value for a healthy person.

Recovery period: The fitter you get the faster your **recovery period** after physical activities.

Proportion of body fat: Too much body fat puts a strain on your heart and your arteries may become dangerously narrowed.

Body mass index (BMI): This measures your body mass based on your height. Use this formula to work out your **body mass index**.

$$\text{BMI} = \frac{\text{body mass (kg)}}{[\text{height (m)}]^2}$$

BMI tables indicate if your body mass is healthy for your size. For adults, a BMI between 18.5 and 24.9 is considered healthy.

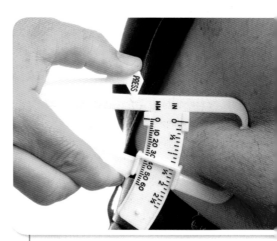

Callipers measure how much fat lies under your skin.

Key words
- ✓ **medical history**
- ✓ **lifestyle history**
- ✓ **medication**
- ✓ **blood pressure**
- ✓ **recovery period**
- ✓ **body mass index (BMI)**

Questions

1 If you worked in a fitness club, what health questions might you ask new clients when they joined?

2 Outline three different fitness tests that could be carried out. For each one, describe how the measurements would change as the person got fitter.

3 The table shows the heart rates of three people taken after five minutes of exercise. The measurements were repeated two months later.

Heart rate in beats per minute (bpm) after five minutes of exercise		
Person	**Baseline measurements (bpm)**	**Measurements two months later (bpm)**
A	148	122
B	161	158
C	132	152

i Who has been resting following a sports injury?

ii Who has not done much exercise?

Measurement	What happens after exercise as you get fitter
Heart rate	Your pulse will not beat so quickly.
Blood pressure	Your blood pressure will reduce.
Recovery period	The time for you to recover will get shorter.
Proportion of body fat	The proportion of body fat will get less.
Body mass index	Your BMI value will fall as your mass decreases.

How will your results change as you get fitter?

Find out about

- ✓ **the best way to gather accurate, reliable fitness measurements**

Try to take your fitness measurements as accurately as possible. Damaged or defective equipment will not provide the measurements you need.

Key words

- ✓ **accurate**
- ✓ **calibrated**
- ✓ **repeatable**

Questions

1 Explain the difference between accuracy and repeatability in your own words.

2 Describe three ways that you could mistakenly calculate that you are fitter than you actually are.

Accurate data

An **accurate** instrument or procedure gives a 'true' reading. Some of these measurements need equipment to take them, but the equipment could be faulty. Different instruments can give different readings – especially if they have been subjected to rough use. Double check your measurements with different equipment.

Equipment used by medical and sports professionals will be **calibrated** regularly. This means that the measurement from the equipment under test is compared to the measurement of equipment that is known to be of the correct standard.

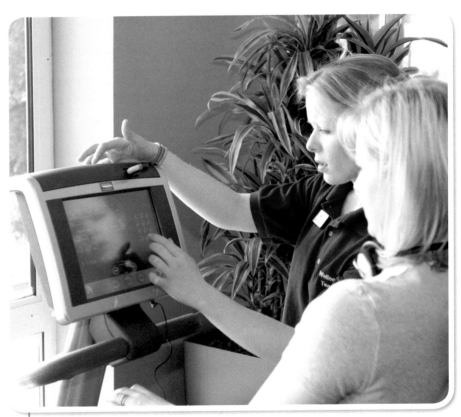

Measuring equipment should be checked and calibrated regularly to make sure that it is accurate.

Repeatable data

Scientists need data that can be trusted. If your data is **repeatable** you get similar results with each re-run of an experiment. Repeatable results suggest that you can have confidence in your techniques and methods. Take time and care when taking measurements; try to get a 'feel' for what the values should be, so that you can spot errors quickly.

Heart rate

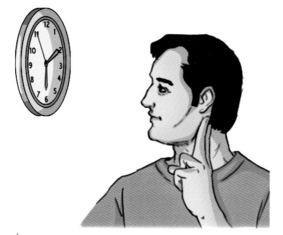

It is hard to measure your pulse rate when you have been exercising very hard. Work with a partner, but make sure they can find your pulse. Feel for the pulse with your fingers only – your thumb has its own pulse, which might confuse you.

Blood pressure

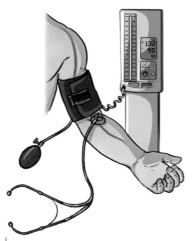

Make sure the measuring equipment is not damaged or has low battery power. Always measure your blood pressure while sitting down with your arm at chest height. Raising your arm will lower the pressure (which is why you should elevate a wound if it is bleeding). Your blood pressure can increase if you are feeling tense or angry. Recognise that the values will be higher if you are stressed.

Recovery period

Double check your calculations and use the average of several measurements. Don't be put off if it seems that your fitness measurements are only improving slowly.

Body fat

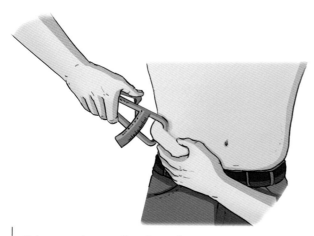

Take care when reading the scales on any measuring devices, particularly if they are worn. Look to see that you are reading the right units (some old-fashioned equipment may have imperial units). Take the reading at the right place on the scale.

Body mass index (BMI)

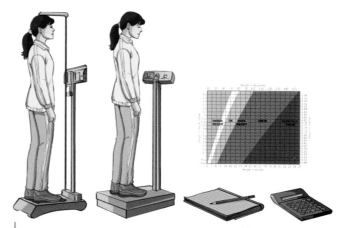

Your mass will often vary at different times of the day depending on whether you have just eaten and how dehydrated you are. Always measure your mass at the same time of day to compare like with like. When you refer to graphs or tables of data, make sure you are using a reputable source. Remember, different fitness graphs are prepared for men, women, and children.

Find out about

- ✓ injuries caused by excessive exercise

Joint injuries

If you follow a sports team, you will know how often players may get injured. It is an occupational hazard. Joints are tough and well-designed, but there is a limit to the force they can withstand. Common injuries include **sprains**, **dislocations**, **torn ligaments**, and **torn tendons**.

Football is particularly hazardous. There are lots of stops, starts, and changes of direction, and perhaps some bad tackles. It is not just professional footballers who suffer – 40% of knee injuries happen to under-15 footballers.

Sprains

The most common sporting injury is a sprain. This usually happens when you overstretch a ligament by twisting your ankle or knee. Often people will say that they have 'torn a muscle', when they have actually sprained a ligament. There are several symptoms:

- redness and swelling
- surface bruising
- difficulty walking
- dull, throbbing ache or sharp, cramping pain.

The usual treatment for sprains is **RICE** – rest, ice, compression, elevation.

Key words

- ✓ sprain
- ✓ dislocation
- ✓ torn ligament
- ✓ torn tendon
- ✓ RICE

REST means immobilising the injured part (e.g. keeping the weight off a torn muscle).

ICE acts as an anaesthetic, reduces swelling, and slows the flow of blood to the injured area. To avoid damaging the tissue, the ice is applied indirectly (e.g. in a tea towel or plastic bag) for up to 20 minutes at a time with 30 minutes between applications.

COMPRESSION usually involves wrapping a bandage round the injured part to reduce swelling. The bandage should be snug but not too tight.

AEROBIC EXERCISING of the injured part is not restarted until it has regained at least 75% of the previous level of strength, and then only moderately. This exercise helps build muscle and return the athlete to peak fitness.

SIMPLE STRETCHING ROUTINES help to regain mobility, but only when swelling stops.

ELEVATION means raising the injured limb. This reduces swelling by helping to keep excess fluid away from the damaged area.

Recovery from a sports injury often involves RICE followed by stretching and strengthening exercises. RICE stands for rest, ice, compression, and elevation.

After 72 hours of RICE treatment, heat and gentle massage can be used to loosen the surrounding muscles. If the injury keeps occurring, physiotherapy can be used to strengthen the surrounding muscles.

Torn ligaments and tendons

If a joint is twisted or overstretched then the ligaments and tendons attached to it may tear.

A ligament may tear with a popping sound, leaving the joint painfully bruised and very hard to bend. You might be able to see a dent where the ligament is torn. Tendons can stretch, become inflamed, and even snap like a worn-out elastic band. This might happen in sports involving a lot of jumping – like basketball.

If you tear a ligament, use the RICE treatment and see a physiotherapist. Don't do vigorous exercise for two to three months. In severe cases the joint might have to be immobilised with a brace or repaired by surgery. It is best to avoid injury in the first place by building up gradually to exercise and resisting over-exertion.

Dislocations

Gymnasts also suffer from joint injuries, often at the knee joint. Cartilage in the knee is an excellent shock absorber, but floor routines put a lot of force on the joints. If a gymnast lands off balance, their kneecap can become dislocated. This happens when the bone slips out of the joint. In contact sports such as rugby, dislocations of the shoulder are extremely common. Dislocations are very painful.

The Royal Navy Field Gun race claims many injuries.

Gymnasts land with great force. It can be equivalent to carrying ten times their body weight.

Joint injuries are common in football players.

Questions

1 Describe:
   a the symptoms and
   b RICE treatment for a sprain.

2 Describe two other types of common joint injury.

Mike's experience of physiotherapy

'I went running with my son Joe. He set a quick pace and the next day my knee really hurt. The pain didn't go away. When I went to the doctor, she prescribed me some strong anti-inflammatory tablets and referred me to the hospital physiotherapist. By the time I saw the physiotherapist my knee felt much better. After giving me a thorough examination, the physiotherapist explained everything carefully and gave me a list of exercises to do. These seemed a bit dull and repetitive, so I didn't bother much. Two weeks later I was back at the doctors with my knee as bad as ever – this time I'll follow the physiotherapist's advice!'

What the physiotherapist says

'That's quite a typical story for our middle-aged patients,' says Vicky Singleton. At 25 she is a senior physiotherapist – a professional who assesses how bad an injury is and treats it through physical exercises and manipulation. It takes a lot of training to qualify as a physiotherapist. Vicky had to get good A-level results (particularly biology) and then study for three years to get her degree. As part of her training she spent 1000 hours working with other physiotherapists and practising her skills on patients.

Vicky has seen lots of patients like Mike, with problems in their joints or muscles.

How can physiotherapy help?

Physiotherapy can be used immediately to treat sporting injuries, starting with RICE. From then on, physiotherapy is used to encourage healing and return a joint or muscle to full strength and movement.

Find out about

- ✔ **the role of a physiotherapist in the treatment of skeletal–muscular injury**
- ✔ **the need to comply with a physiotherapy treatment regime**

It's easy to damage your joints when you exercise.

'We use a series of gentle exercises to begin with,' Vicky explains. 'These make sure that the tissues heal well and don't shrink or tighten too much. Lots of rest is important too. Then we give more exercises, which strengthen the new tissues and make sure the joint moves as well as ever. It can take six to twelve weeks for the tissues to heal and then probably another six weeks before the joint is fully back to strength. Really bad injuries can take up to two years of physiotherapy to put them right!'

Speeding up recovery

Mike's injury wasn't very serious. The damage that footballers and other professional athletes do to their bodies can be much worse. They may try to get active again quickly by using injections to reduce the swelling, speed up healing, and kill the pain. They will also have physiotherapy several times a day. This often works well – but the problem with rushing a recovery is that the joint tissues may not be fully healed before they are used, so even more damage can result.

Keeping up the treatment

Physiotherapy involves repeating exercises many times to build up strength and movement.

Some sporting injuries are very severe and can take months to heal.

A good physiotherapist makes sure the patient understands what they need to do and why they need to do it. If patients don't comply with their treatment, like Mike, the tissues don't heal properly, and the joint may become stiff and painful permanently.

Physiotherapy doesn't just help skeletal and muscular injuries. It can be used to help children and adults with disabilities gain strength and control over their bodies.

Vicky is specially trained to do physiotherapy with disabled children on horseback. This helps their muscles and joints become stronger and more flexible, improving their balance and quality of life.

Questions

1 What are the advantages of physiotherapy when you have injured a joint?

2 Why is it important to comply with the treatment your physiotherapist gives you?

Find out about

- ✓ the circulation system
- ✓ what blood does and what it contains

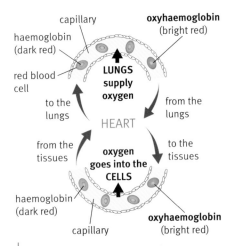

In the lungs oxygen is at high concentration and binds to **haemoglobin**. At low concentration in body tissues the oxygen is released. It diffuses into body cells, which use the oxygen for respiration.

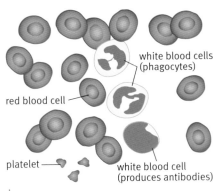

This diagram shows the cells in blood, but not in the correct proportions. Each 1 mm³ of blood contains approximately 5 million red blood cells, 250 000 platelets, and 7000 white blood cells.

Systems for moving molecules

Peak performance of your body relies on an efficient circulation system. It would take too long for oxygen and other molecules to diffuse from outside our bodies to the millions of cells inside. Active muscles need a good supply of glucose and oxygen. Carbon dioxide and other waste products need to be removed.

The circulatory system

When you are at rest, your heart beats about 60 to 80 times per minute, forcing blood through a network of blood vessels. Arteries carry the blood to your organs. In fine capillaries, useful molecules pass from the blood into the cells. Waste products are taken away. Veins return the blood to the heart.

Double circulatory system

Because the capillaries are so tiny, it was only a few hundred years ago that doctors first saw them. They proved that blood went round the body and back to the heart in a loop. In fact our blood is pumped around two separate loops: around the body and around the lungs. This is called double circulation.

A double pump

As we have a double circulatory system we need a heart that is two pumps in one. Blood needs to be at a high enough pressure to be carried all round our bodies. Lower pressure in the blood sent to the lungs stops fluid from being forced out into our airways.

Blood

Plasma

You have between five and seven litres of blood circulating around your body. A sample of blood looks completely red. A closer look shows that it consists of cells floating in pale yellow liquid called **plasma**. Plasma is mainly water. It transports a wide range of materials including nutrients such as glucose, antibodies, hormones, and waste such as carbon dioxide and urea. Plasma gives blood its bulk and also helps to distribute heat around the body.

There are three types of cells floating in plasma:

- **red blood cells** – to transport oxygen
- **white blood cells** – to fight infection
- **platelets** – which play an important part in blood clotting at an injury site.

Red blood cells

Red cells are the most obvious blood component because of their number and colour. The cells are adapted to their function of transport. They are packed with the protein haemoglobin. Haemoglobin binds oxygen as blood passes through lungs. The oxygen is released from haemoglobin as blood circulates through the tissues of the body.

Red blood cells have no nucleus, which allows more space for haemoglobin. If the haemoglobin circulated freely in the plasma instead, then the blood would be too thick to flow properly.

The biconcave shape gives the cells a large surface area, making diffusion of gases very efficient. This shape also gives cells flexibility to squeeze through tiny capillaries.

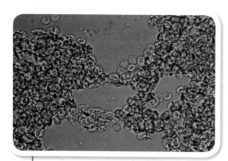
Clotted red blood cells.

White blood cells

White blood cells protect the body from infection by disease-causing microorganisms. They produce antibodies, and engulf and digest microorganisms by **phagocytosis**. You can read more about white blood cells and immunity in module B2.

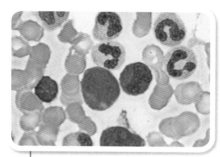
White blood cells.

Platelets

Platelets are fragments of cells that are made from the cytoplasm of large cells. When a blood vessel is damaged, for example, when you are cut, platelets stick to the cut edge. They send out chemicals that trigger a series of reactions that form a clot at the cut site. Clotting helps stop too much blood being lost from the body.

Key words

- ✔ **plasma**
- ✔ **red blood cells**
- ✔ **white blood cells**
- ✔ **platelets**
- ✔ **phagocytosis**

Questions

1 Simple single-celled pond organisms rely on diffusion for exchanging food, oxygen, and waste with the surrounding water. Explain why you need a circulation system whereas simple pond creatures do not.

2 Copy and complete the following table for the four main components of blood.

Blood component	Appearance	Function

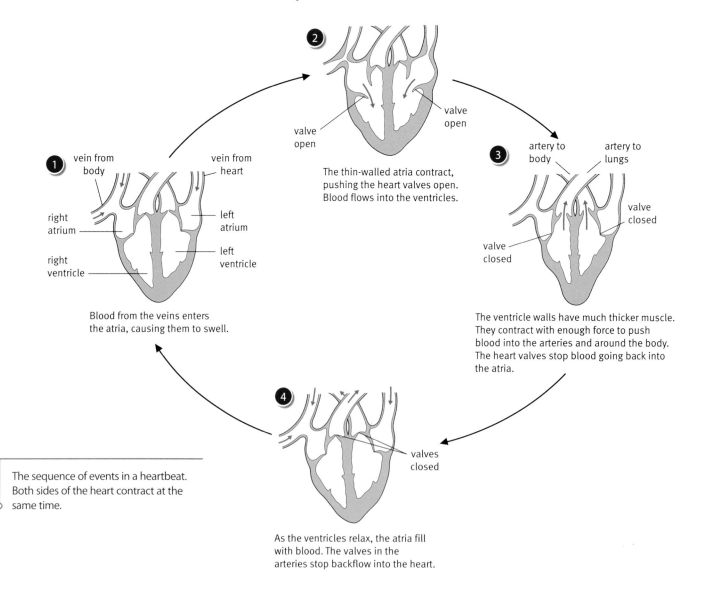

Find out about

✓ **the structure of the human heart**

A double circulation

Each side of the heart has two chambers – an **atrium** and a **ventricle**.

Blood from the body enters the right atrium of the heart. It is pumped out of the right ventricle towards the lungs to pick up oxygen. The blood becomes **oxygenated**. It returns to the left atrium and passes into the left ventricle. Here it gets another, harder pump, which carries it around the rest of the body. The left ventricle has a thicker wall of muscle than the right, because it has to pump blood to the whole of the body. The right ventricle only pumps blood as far as the lungs. As the blood passes around the body it gradually gives up its oxygen to the cells. It becomes **deoxygenated**. The blood then returns to the right atrium again. So blood passes through the heart twice on every circuit of the body. This is called a **double circulation**.

①
vein from body — vein from heart
right atrium — left atrium
right ventricle — left ventricle

Blood from the veins enters the atria, causing them to swell.

②
valve open — valve open

The thin-walled atria contract, pushing the heart valves open. Blood flows into the ventricles.

③
artery to body — artery to lungs
valve closed — valve closed

The ventricle walls have much thicker muscle. They contract with enough force to push blood into the arteries and around the body. The heart valves stop blood going back into the atria.

④
valves closed

As the ventricles relax, the atria fill with blood. The valves in the arteries stop backflow into the heart.

The sequence of events in a heartbeat. Both sides of the heart contract at the same time.

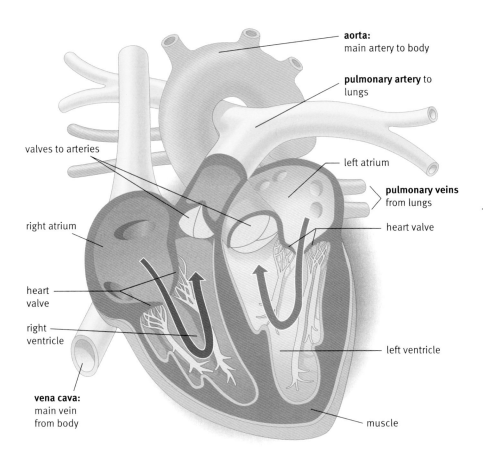

aorta:
main artery to body

pulmonary artery to
lungs

valves to arteries

left atrium

pulmonary veins
from lungs

heart valve

right atrium

heart
valve

right
ventricle

left ventricle

vena cava:
main vein
from body

muscle

Diagram of a human heart. 'Left' and 'right'
refer to the way your heart lies in your body.
The artery leaving the right-hand side of the
heart has been coloured blue to show that it
is carrying blood that is short of oxygen.

Key words

- ✓ **atrium**
- ✓ **ventricle**
- ✓ **oxygenated**
- ✓ **deoxygenated**
- ✓ **double circulation**
- ✓ **aorta**
- ✓ **vena cava**
- ✓ **pulmonary vein**
- ✓ **pulmonary artery**

Questions

1   Explain what is meant by a
    double circulatory system.

2   Explain the difference in
    wall thickness between:
    a   atria and ventricles
    b   the right and left
        ventricles.

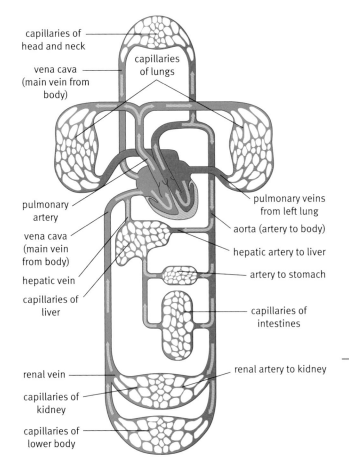

capillaries of
head and neck

capillaries
of lungs

vena cava
(main vein from
body)

pulmonary
artery

vena cava
(main vein
from body)

hepatic vein

capillaries of
liver

pulmonary veins
from left lung

aorta (artery to body)

hepatic artery to liver

artery to stomach

capillaries of
intestines

renal vein

capillaries of
kidney

capillaries of
lower body

renal artery to kidney

Blood is carried away from the heart by arteries,
and towards the heart in veins. Trace with your
finger the different routes that a red blood cell
might make around the body. You can read more
about the structure and function of blood vessels
in module B2.

Find out about

- ✔ **the function of valves in the heart and veins**
- ✔ **capillary beds, where nutrients and waste are exchanged**
- ✔ **why tissue fluid is important**

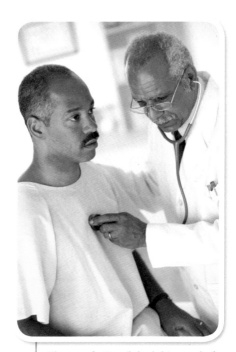

The comforting 'lub-dub' sound of a heartbeat is the sound of heart valves snapping shut. The 'lub' sound is caused by the valves between the atria and ventricles shutting. The 'dub' sound is made as the valves between the ventricles and the arteries close.

Key words

- ✔ **heart valves**
- ✔ **capillary**
- ✔ **tissue fluid**
- ✔ **capillary bed**

Valves – a one-way system

When the ventricles contract they push blood out of the heart. But what stops blood going backwards? This is the job of the **heart valves**. They act like one-way doors to keep the blood flowing in one direction. There are two sets of valves in the heart:

- between each atrium and ventricle — these valves stop blood flowing backwards from the ventricles into the atria
- between the ventricle and the arteries leaving the heart — these valves stop blood flowing backwards from the arteries into the ventricles.

Valves are also found in veins. Blood pressure is lower in veins than in arteries. Valves stop blood from flowing backwards in the veins in between each pump from the heart.

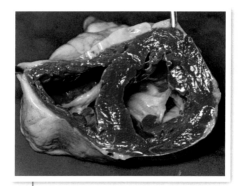

A valve between a ventricle and an artery. Strong tendons hold the valve flaps in place, preventing blood from flowing backwards.

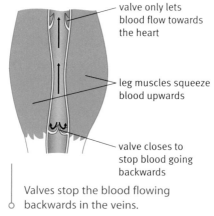

valve only lets blood flow towards the heart

leg muscles squeeze blood upwards

valve closes to stop blood going backwards

Valves stop the blood flowing backwards in the veins.

Capillary beds

The lungs and other body organs contain a bed or network of **capillaries**. As blood squeezes through these capillaries its pressure drops. It has less force moving it along. If blood went straight from the lungs to the rest of the body, it would move too slowly to provide enough oxygen for the body's cells. The double circulation gives the blood a pump to get through each bed of capillaries – the right ventricle pumps it through the lungs, and the left ventricle pumps it through the rest of the body.

Diffusion in the capillary beds

On average you have six litres of blood in your body. It is all pumped through the heart three times each minute. But the blood spends most of that time in capillary networks. Capillaries are where chemicals in the body's cells and in the blood are exchanged. The structure of capillaries makes them ideally suited for this function.

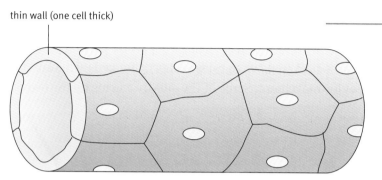

thin wall (one cell thick)

Capillary walls are very thin and porous.

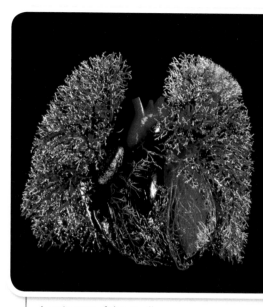

A resin cast of the capillary network of an adult human's lungs.

Tissue fluid

When blood enters a capillary bed from an artery it is at high pressure. Blood plasma is squeezed out of the capillary. It forms a liquid called **tissue fluid**, which bathes all of your cells.

Tissue fluid contains all the dissolved raw materials being carried by blood plasma, including glucose and oxygen. These chemicals diffuse from the tissue fluid into cells. Waste products from cells, including urea and carbon dioxide, diffuse out into the tissue fluid.

As blood passes through the capillary bed its pressure drops. Plasma stops being squeezed out, and tissue fluid with waste products from cells moves back into the capillaries.

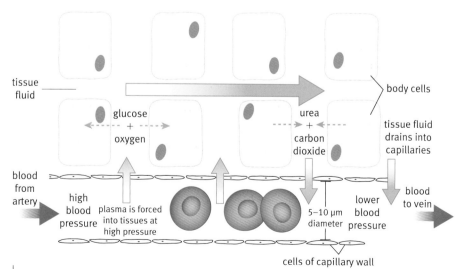

Tissue fluid helps nutrients and waste products to be exchanged by diffusion in the **capillary beds**.

Questions

1 Draw a flow chart to show the route blood takes on its journey around the body. Include the key words on pages 31–34 in your description. Start with: Blood leaves the left ventricle.

2 Describe the job of valves in the heart and veins.

3 What is tissue fluid made from?

4 Explain why tissue fluid leaks out at the start of capillaries, and moves back in towards the end of the capillary bed.

5 Explain how tissue fluid helps the exchange of chemicals between the capillaries and body tissues.

6 Name four chemicals that are exchanged between body cells and tissue fluid.

Find out about

- why you must balance heat gain and heat loss
- how your body detects and responds to temperature changes
- how sweating and being 'flushed' help to cool you down
- how shivering and turning pale may stop you getting too cold

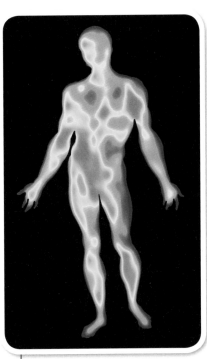

Our body radiates heat. On this thermal image, the hottest parts of the body are red and the coolest blue.

Key words

- respiration
- extremity
- core

For peak performance, your body needs to keep a constant internal environment. Enzymes are catalysts, speeding up chemical reactions in cells without taking part. Enzyme reactions need to work at their optimum temperature for maximum efficiency.

Gaining and losing heat

If your environment is hotter than you are, energy will be transferred to your body. Your body also gains heat from **respiration**. During respiration, glucose is broken down to release energy for cells. This energy is used by muscles for movement. Some of the energy warms up the body.

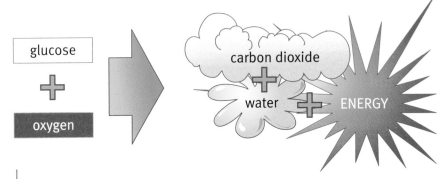

glucose + oxygen → carbon dioxide + water + ENERGY

Respiration releases energy from the breakdown of glucose.

If your environment is cooler than you are, energy will be transferred away from your body. The bigger the temperature difference, the greater the rate of cooling.

Getting the balance right

For your temperature to remain constant, energy gain must be balanced by energy loss. In other words, if heat gained = heat lost, your body temperature stays the same.

Not all of your body is at the same temperature. Your **extremities** (hands and feet) are cooler than your **core** (deeper parts). Extremities have a larger surface area compared with their size. So they lose energy to the environment faster than the main parts of your body.

The temperature of your hands, feet, and skin falls, but your core temperature hardly changes. It should be between 36 °C and 37.5 °C for your body to work properly. 'Normal' body temperature varies from one person to the next.

The amount of energy released in respiration and other reactions is greatest in your muscles and liver. The circulation of your blood transfers this energy to other parts.

Investigating temperature control

A physiologist called Sir Charles Blagden was Secretary of the Royal Society towards the end of the 18th century. Like many physiologists, he experimented on himself. He went into a very hot room to see how his body would react. The account below is adapted from Harry Houdini's book, *The Miracle Mongers: An Exposé*.

Another account describes Blagden taking a dog into the room with him, along with steak and eggs. The dog was unharmed but had to stay in its basket so it did not burn its feet on the hot floor.

Blagden's experiment

Sir Charles Blagden went into a room where the temperature was 1 degree or 2 degrees above 127 °C, and remained eight minutes in this situation, frequently walking about to all the different parts of the room, but standing still most of the time in the coolest spot, where the temperature was above 116 °C. The air, though very hot, gave no pain, and Sir Charles and all the other gentlemen were of the opinion that they could support a much greater heat.

During seven minutes Sir Charles's breathing continued perfectly good, but after that time he felt an oppression in his lungs, with a sense of anxiety, which induced him to leave the room. His pulse was then 144 [beats per minute], double its ordinary rate. In order to prove that the thermometer was not faulty, they placed some eggs and a beef-steak upon a tin frame near the thermometer, but more distant from the furnace than from the wall of the room. In twenty minutes the eggs were roasted quite hard, and in forty-seven minutes the steak was not only cooked, but almost dry.

Blagden's dog takes part in the experiment.

Questions

1 What two things must be balanced to keep your body temperature steady?

2 What part of your body is warmest?

3 At what temperature does this warmest part need to be maintained?

4 Why is your blood important in keeping extremities warm?

5 What effects did the very high temperatures have on Sir Charles Blagden?

6 What happened to the proteins in the steak and eggs as they cooked?

7 Why did the same thing not happen to Sir Charles's proteins?

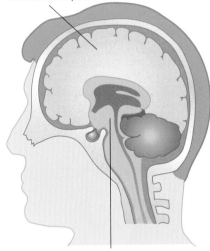

cerebral hemispheres

hypothalamus

The **hypothalamus** is the **processing centre** in the brain for sleep, water balance, body temperature, appetite, and other basic functions. The cerebral hemispheres are where you make conscious decisions to warm or cool yourself.

The fans in this Sikh temple provide a welcome breeze to help to keep the people cool.

Key words

- ✓ **hypothalamus**
- ✓ **processing centre**
- ✓ **shivering**
- ✓ **sweat glands**
- ✓ **evaporate**

Changes in your body temperature can have serious effects on health. Your brain is particularly sensitive to temperature changes. Temperature receptors in your skin can detect a change in air temperature of as little as 0.5 °C. There are temperature receptors in the area of the brain called the **hypothalamus** that detect blood temperature. The hypothalamus is also the **processing centre** for temperature control. When the temperature in your brain is above or below 37 °C, the hypothalamus triggers effectors to bring your body temperature back to normal.

Warming up

Shivering is one way your body keeps warm. When you shiver, muscle cells contract quickly. They respire faster to release the energy for this movement.

Shivering is an automatic response. You may also take a conscious decision to do something that will warm you up, for example, drinking a warm drink, putting on more clothes, or going inside.

Cooling down

When you are too hot, nerve impulses from the brain stimulate your **sweat glands**. Sweat passes out of small pores onto the skin surface. Water molecules in sweat gain energy from your skin. Soon they move quickly enough to **evaporate**. This cools you down. Even when it is cool and you are not very active, you can lose nearly a litre of water a day in sweat. When you are hot and active, you can lose up to three litres of water an hour. If you don't replace this water you could become dehydrated. Dehydration then reduces sweating, raising the body temperature further. This is what happens when you get 'heat stroke.'

How does sweat cool you down?

Sweating only works to cool you down if the sweat can evaporate quickly. In a hot, humid climate sweat drips off you and you feel uncomfortably hot. Air currents increase the rate of evaporation and so increase the cooling effect.

Is your body temperature the same all day?

All these responses keep your body temperature within a narrow range. Average core body temperature is about 36.9 °C, but this varies from person to person and it varies throughout the day. For example, when you are sleeping, you move around less and respire more slowly. So your body temperature drops to its lowest point at night.

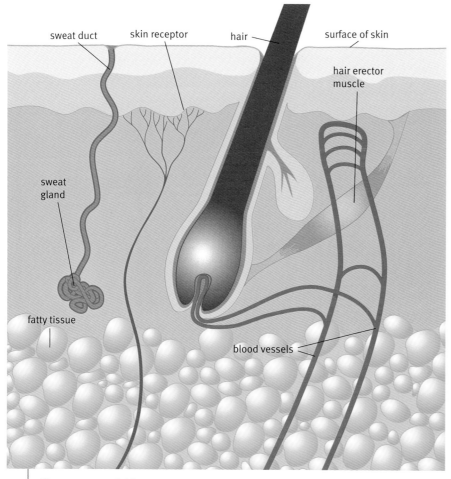

The structure of skin.

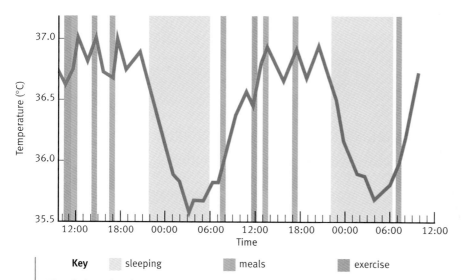

Key ▨ sleeping ▨ meals ▨ exercise

The daily cycle of variation in body temperature. You can see that eating, sleeping, and activity affect body temperature. These fluctuations happen even when you are at rest – they are controlled by our 'biological clocks'.

In hot, humid conditions, sweat cannot evaporate easily. Your clothes may become soaked in sweat.

Questions

1. Where in your body would you find:
   a. temperature receptors?
   b. the temperature processing centre?

2. Name two effectors for controlling body temperature.

3. Explain how shivering warms you up.

4. Explain how sweating cools you down.

Too hot or too cold?

The table below lists ways of controlling body temperature. Some of the effectors warm you up and some cool you down – they are **antagonistic**.

Too cold?	Too hot?
Muscles shiver Energy warms the body tissues as muscles contract when you shiver.	**Muscles don't shiver**
No sweat made	**Sweat produced** Energy is lost from the skin, when the water molecules in sweat evaporate.
Hair raising Erector muscles make your hair stand on end, trapping a layer of warm air.	**Hair lies flat**
Skin goes paler Blood is diverted away from the skin surface to the core to retain warmth (**vasoconstriction**).	**Skin becomes flushed** Blood vessels near the skin surface widen, helping heat to be lost to the surroundings (**vasodilation**).
Warming behaviours You could do exercises to warm up. Putting on more clothes will reduce heat loss. Moving to a warm place or having a hot drink will warm you up.	**Cooling behaviours** Taking a break from exercise or moving to the shade will let your body temperature recover. Removing clothes increases the rate of heat loss. If you wet your skin or fan yourself, evaporation will provide a cooling effect.

Question

1 For each picture on this page, say how the action cools the body.

Vasoconstriction and vasodilation

The boy on the right is flushed as a result of vasodilation. 'Vaso' is from the Latin for vessel, so vasodilation means widening of the blood vessels. More blood flows into the capillaries in the skin, so there is more energy transfer to the environment. The opposite is vasoconstriction. Less blood reaches the capillaries in the skin, so energy loss is reduced.

This boy has a fever. He is sweating and looking flushed.

Vasodilation
The blood vessels near the surface of the skin are filled with blood. Energy from the warm blood is transferred down the temperature gradient to the environment.

Vasoconstriction
The muscles in the walls of blood vessels near the surface of the skin contract. Less blood flows near the surface of the skin, so less energy is lost to the environment.

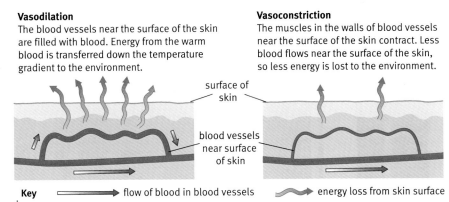

Key 〰▶ flow of blood in blood vessels 〰 energy loss from skin surface

Vasodilation and vasoconstriction are a good example of the effects of control by antagonistic effectors.

Key words

- ✔ **antagonistic**
- ✔ **vasodilation**
- ✔ **vasoconstriction**

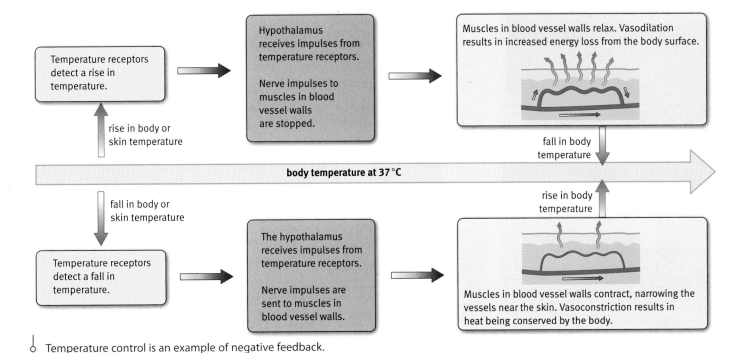

Temperature control is an example of negative feedback.

Questions

2 What are the effectors that cause vasodilation and vasoconstriction?

3 Explain why vasodilation and vasoconstriction are said to be controlled by antagonistic effectors.

4 Why does vasodilation not cool you when the temperature of the environment is higher than your body temperature?

Find out about

- ✔ **how you maintain a steady level of sugar in your blood**
- ✔ **the causes and symptoms of type 1 and type 2 diabetes**

Some diabetics wear a wrist band indicating that they have diabetes. Why do you think they do this?

Sugar for energy

Your cells need sugar to give them the energy to function.

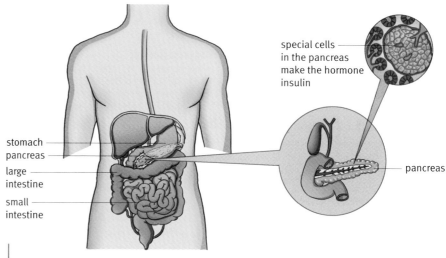

special cells in the pancreas make the hormone insulin

stomach
pancreas
large intestine
small intestine

pancreas

Blood sugar level is controlled by special cells in the **pancreas**.

Steady sugar release

Many processed foods have extra sugar added to them to improve their taste. A lot of sugar in one go causes a surge of the **hormone insulin** that removes it from the blood. The energy boost quickly turns into a sugar low, causing lack of energy, concentration, and mood swings. Foods that are high in fibre and complex carbohydrates like pasta, rice, and bread keep your blood sugar level balanced. These foods are digested slowly. Their sugars are released gradually into your blood stream, which is better for you.

People with diabetes cannot control their blood sugar level. There are two main types of **diabetes: type 1 and type 2**.

Type 1 diabetes

Some people develop type 1 diabetes when they are young. Their pancreas suddenly stops making enough insulin. Blood sugar levels could rise dangerously high, particularly after a sugary meal. Symptoms include thirst and the production of large volumes of urine containing sugar. Too high a level of blood sugar makes you drowsy, too low, and you may go into a coma.

People with type 1 diabetes need several daily injections of insulin to control their blood sugar level. They have to be careful about what they eat, to match their sugar intake to their lifestyle. They may have to prick their finger each day and measure their blood sugar level using a special test strip.

Type 2 diabetes

People with a poor diet, inactive lifestyle, or who are **obese** may develop type 2 (or 'late onset') diabetes in middle age. The number of young people with type 2 diabetes is rising. In type 2 diabetes the body gradually stops making enough insulin for your needs or the cells can't use the insulin properly. Symptoms include thirst, frequent urination, tiredness, and weight loss. Over time 'hardening of the arteries' takes place, which can lead to heart attacks, kidney damage, or sight problems – where blood vessels in the retina are involved.

People with type 2 diabetes need to take regular, moderate exercise to control their blood sugar levels. They have to eat carefully and plan their diet, so that sugar is released steadily.

All diabetics should keep a sweet snack or sugary sports drink at hand when they exercise in case their blood sugar level falls too low.

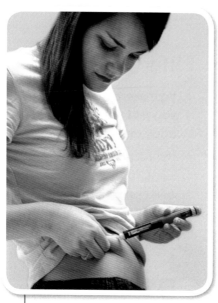

Type 1 diabetes can be treated with daily insulin injections and careful diet.

Which of these items contain sugars that are quickly absorbed? Which contain complex carbohydrates that release sugars slowly when digested?

In the 1920s scientist Frederick Banting tested different pancreas extracts on diabetic dogs. The purified active ingredient – insulin – was remarkably effective on patients, some of whom were close to death.

Questions

1 Suggest why insulin has to be injected – why can't it be swallowed like other medicines?

2 Make a table to compare the causes, symptoms, and treatments for type 1 and type 2 diabetes.

3 Outline how someone could reduce their risk of developing type 2 diabetes.

4 Your classmate feels faint after PE. You notice that she is wearing a wrist band showing that she is diabetic. You rush to tell your teacher. What do you think might have happened? What would you suggest that they do to help?

Key words

- ✓ **pancreas**
- ✓ **hormone**
- ✓ **insulin**
- ✓ **diabetes type 1**
- ✓ **diabetes type 2**
- ✓ **obese**

Find out about

✓ **how exercise can help you maintain a healthy body mass**

Why is exercise part of a healthy lifestyle?

Everyone knows that exercise is important for staying healthy. When you exercise you strengthen your muscles, improve your co-ordination, and develop your self-discipline. You also use up energy that you have taken in as food. If the energy that you use up matches the energy that you take in, then your body mass will stay fairly constant.

We all know that we need to exercise to stay in shape.

There are lots of ways to enjoy keeping fit.

How much energy does exercise use up?

Doing different activities will use different amounts of energy. The longer the time in a day that you are active, the more energy you will expend. You should always think carefully before starting a strenuous new exercise regime and ask your doctor if you are unsure.

Builders' breakfasts are highly calorific. Their intake matches the strenuous physical work that they do so their mass remains constant.

Activity	Energy (kJ/kg/h)
Sitting quietly	1.7
Writing	1.7
Standing relaxed	2.1
Vacuuming	11.3
Walking rapidly	14.2
Running	29.3
Swimming (4km/hour)	33

Energy used in different activities.

Sir Ranulph Fiennes pulled his own sledge unaided across the Antarctic continent. Although he consumed about 12,000 calories a day he still lost body mass.

What is a healthy body mass?

Doctors have studied the links between body mass and illness. If your mass is too great for your height then you may be at an increased risk of illness. It can also be dangerous to have a mass that is too low.

Exercise will not only help you to maintain a healthy body mass but can also bring you a lot of enjoyment and rewards. You might build up a circle of friends around your activities and be better placed to cope with the stresses of everyday life. You will get into good habits that will help to keep you healthy for your whole life.

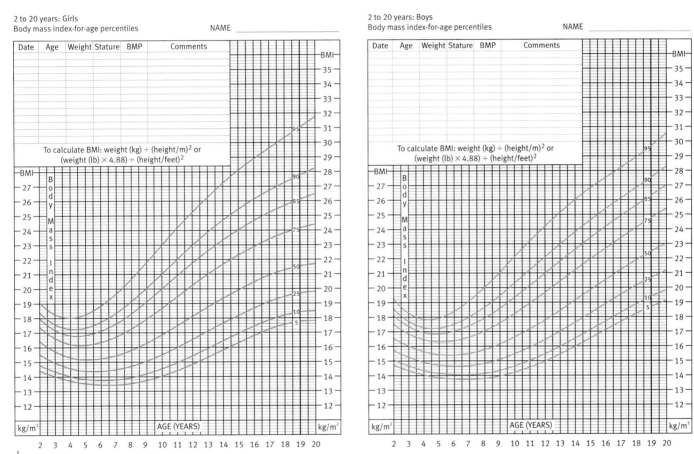

Graphs showing healthy height and body mass for young people in the UK. The numbers on the lines show the percentage of people with each BMI.

Questions

1 Find out how much energy (kilojoules) your favourite snack contains. Describe how much exercise you would need to do to 'work off' this energy.

2 Exercise can help to keep your body in shape. Describe the other benefits that doing exercise might bring.

Find out about

- ✔ how a poor diet could increase your chances of illness

These starving refugees have not had enough food.

During the Second World War food was in short supply in the UK. Food was rationed: there were strict controls on how much food everyone received. Despite this many people's diet was healthier than it is now – can you think why?

You are what you eat

In 2008 the United Nations reported that nearly one billion of the six and a half billion people on earth are starving. For economic, political, and environmental reasons (such as wars and natural disasters), they do not get enough to eat. But for most people in the UK food is abundant. Food can be flown in so we can eat fruit and vegetables that are out of season here. Modern farming methods and commercial food production have driven down prices and increased choice. It is still important to pay attention to the amount and type of food you eat to stay healthy.

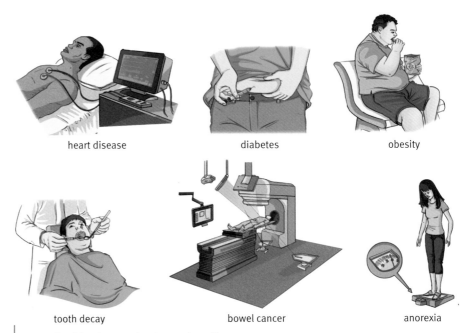

heart disease   diabetes   obesity

tooth decay   bowel cancer   anorexia

An unhealthy diet can lead to serious illness.

Risk factors

Things that increase our chance of becoming ill are called 'risk factors'. There are many lifestyle choices that we can take that have an impact on how healthy we are. Having an unhealthy diet increases the risk of you becoming ill – even if it takes several years before the symptoms appear. Scientists examine very large samples of the population to find links between diet and health as the patterns can be complex.

Looking for patterns

Scientists know that people in different countries have different rates of illness. Some of this can be explained by differences in the foods that people eat. For example, people in Japan eat less red meat and more fish than people tend to in the UK. As a result, Japanese rates of **heart disease** are lower than in the UK.

People in developed countries have a higher rate of bowel **cancer** than people in developing countries. Diets in developing countries are usually high in fibre from vegetables so food passes quickly through the digestive system. Refined, processed foods travel more slowly through our intestines so any toxins are in contact for longer.

Look at the following information about diet and cancer – will it change what you choose to eat?

Factor	Increased risk of cancer	Decreased risk of cancer
Alcohol	Breast, larynx, oesophagus, pharynx, oral cavity, liver and bowel	
Fruit and vegetables		Larynx, oesophagus, pharynx, oral cavity, stomach and lung
Processed and red meat	Bowel	
Fibre		Bowel
Salt	Stomach	
Dairy products		Bowel

Some foods increase the risk of cancer but some reduce it.

The Cancer Research UK EPIC programme is part of a project to monitor the health of 100,000 people across ten European countries. This large data sample, gathered over many years, will help scientists to find links between diet and illness.

Key words

- ✓ **heart disease**
- ✓ **cancer**

We can get cheap, 'tasty' food whenever we want – is this a good thing?

Questions

1 Describe what you understand as an 'unhealthy diet'.

2 Which foods should you eat only in moderation to stay healthy? Explain why.

3 Which foods should you try to include in your diet to stay healthy? Explain why.

4 Your friend suggests you should both get chips and a burger at the 'Greasy Spoon Cafe'. Make a list of replies that would lead to a healthier option for you both. Remember, your answers need to be practical!

Topic B7.4: Learning from nature

Stone statues (Moai) of Easter Island in an empty landscape.

Why study natural ecosystems?

Are we destroying our environment? Can the planet continue to support its growing human population? We are part of nature, but we are using natural resources too quickly. By studying nature we can learn to live in a sustainable way.

The Science

In nature, nutrients, gases, and food pass from species to species in a cycle. Very little is wasted so there is no pollution. Humans have changed this closed loop. We use natural resources to manufacture products such as paper, computers, and cars. We alter ecosystems, destroy wildlife, and produce a lot of waste. We are damaging the life support systems we depend on.

Ideas about Science

Science has provided new technologies that help us to grow more food and harvest more fish and timber. These have enhanced the quality of life for many people but have also had harmful effects on the environment. We must find alternative, sustainable methods before too much damage is done. Decisions about the exploitation of wildlife should be guided by ethics and international regulation.

A variety of organisms in their ecosystems.

Find out about

- ✔ linear and closed-loop systems
- ✔ natural ecosystems as closed-loop systems

Key words

- ✔ **linear system**
- ✔ **sustainable**
- ✔ **closed-loop system**
- ✔ **microorganisms**
- ✔ **ecosystem**

Questions

1 Explain in your own words what you understand by the term 'sustainable'.

2 Explain why linear systems for making products end up with toxic waste and depletion of natural resources.

3 Suggest how a manufacturing system can become more sustainable by copying natural closed-loop systems.

4 Give two reasons why our present way of life is not sustainable.

5 Explain why oxygen is taken up by some organisms and lost by others, in a natural ecosystem.

Linear systems

Easter Island was fertile and full of trees, but the people who lived there cut down the forest without ensuring that new trees grew. Look at the photo on page 48 to see what it is like now.

How can we avoid the fate of the people of Easter Island? Most of us live in a 'take–make–dump' society. We *take* natural resources from our environment, *make* them into products, and then *dump* the waste. This **linear system** is not **sustainable**. It can only continue for a short time before things go wrong because:

- fossil fuels, such as oil, are running out
- natural resources such as timber, clean air, fresh water, fertile soil, and fish stocks are being used more quickly than they are being replaced
- making products uses a lot of energy from fossil fuels, and creates a lot of waste
- waste also comes from broken and worn-out products that we throw away
- waste can be harmful to people and wildlife, and can stay in the environment for a long time
- waste means rare resources such as metals are spread thinly around the environment, so they can't be reused easily.

Natural closed-loop systems

Nature works in **closed-loop systems**. A closed-loop system has no waste. Output from one part of the system becomes the input for another part, so X's waste becomes Y's food. For example, plant waste, such as dead leaves, is eaten by snails. Faeces from snails is broken down by **microorganisms** (bacteria and fungi). Microorganisms release nitrogen and phosphorus from the faeces. Nitrogen and phosphorus are taken up again by plants. Chemicals go around in a cycle and nothing is wasted.

Natural closed-loop systems are called **ecosystems**. Examples of ecosystems include lakes, woodlands, grasslands, beaches, and coral reefs. In all of these ecosystems there is a community of organisms interacting with the non-living elements of their habitat.

Each species has its own job in the ecosystem. It could be a plant, herbivore, carnivore, decomposer, or parasite. Every species uses different foods and produces different products. All depend on each other.

Organisms in an ecosystem exchange materials with their surroundings. Plants take up carbon dioxide for photosynthesis, and animals take in food for growth and reproduction. At the same time organisms return substances, such as oxygen from photosynthesis, carbon dioxide from respiration, and faeces from digestion. The ecosystem is a closed loop for materials.

You can't recycle energy, so energy is always part of a linear system. This is why closed-loop systems need a constant supply of energy from a sustainable source.

What can we learn from natural ecosystems?

Can we change the way we live, from a linear 'take–make–dump' system, to a closed-loop system? A closed-loop lifestyle can be described as 'take–reuse–recycle'. Can copying nature provide us with all the answers we need for sustainable living?

Linear system

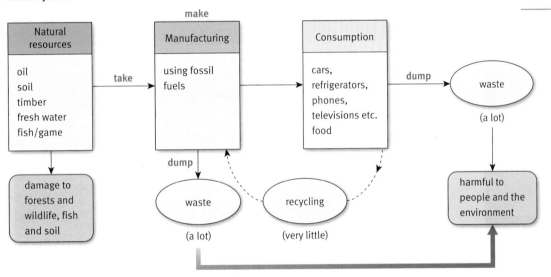

In a linear system, waste products can build up to levels where they become toxic to humans and wildlife. Closed loops reuse and recycle, minimising waste.

Closed–loop system

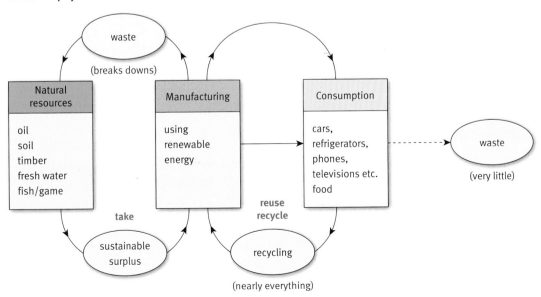

Find out about

- ✔ **how waste materials are reused in ecosystems**
- ✔ **human societies that live in a closed-loop system**

Burying beetles on a dead animal's body.

Barn owls in their nest.

Key word

- ✔ **reactants**

In natural ecosystems, waste materials from one species are often used as food by another species. Waste materials can also be used in chemical reactions as **reactants** by another species. Reactants include nitrate and phosphate waste from microorganisms. These reactants are taken up as plant nutrients.

Closed-loop lifestyles

Barn owls

Barn owls live all over the world. You may have seen one, hunting along the roadside for voles. All the inputs required by a barn owl come from its habitat, and all its waste is used by other organisms in its habitat – it lives in a closed-loop system.

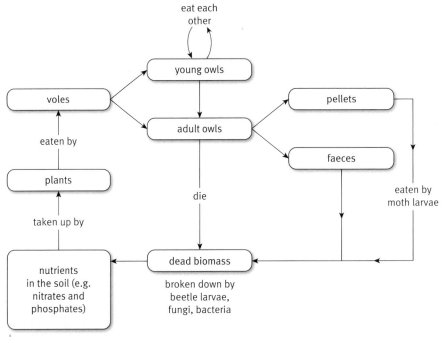

A barn owl lives in a closed-loop system. There is nothing left over and no pollution.

- **Droppings:** These are broken down by microorganisms. This releases nitrates and phosphates. Plants take up these minerals for growth.
- **Pellets:** These are indigestible parts of prey, swallowed whole. Bones from pellets slowly dissolve in the rain. Clothes moth larvae eat the fur.
- **Dead owls:** Burying beetles lay eggs in the bodies of dead owls and the larvae eat the dead flesh. After a few weeks very little is left. If a baby owl gets weak in the nest it is eaten by one of its brothers or sisters.

Maasai people

A few human communities, such as the Maasai, still live in a closed-loop, sustainable way.

Maasai live on the grasslands of Kenya and Tanzania in East Africa. They move from place to place, finding fresh grass for their herds of cattle, sheep, and goats. They make temporary villages. Their round huts are made from sticks, grass, mud, ash, and dung. The village is surrounded with a fence made of thorny branches. At night-time the domestic animals are brought inside for safety.

Maasai do not hunt game or birds, and they do not eat much meat. They drink milk and also take blood from the jugular vein of cattle as a ritual or as medicine. They use some wild plants as food. When they die, their bodies are left out for scavengers.

A Maasai temporary hut is fully biodegradable when the community moves on.

Questions

1 Explain why the Maasai diet causes little damage to their environment.

2 Traditionally Maasai used to wear clothes made of animal skins. More recently they have bought cotton clothes. Explain which of these two types of clothing is more sustainable.

3 Should the governments of Kenya and Tanzania encourage Maasai people to live in permanent villages? Suggest two reasons for and two against.

4 Explain whether you think it would it be possible for all of us to live like the Maasai.

Find out about

- ✔ **types of waste product in natural ecosystems**
- ✔ **the way waste products become food or reactants for other organisms**
- ✔ **storage and movement of chemicals through ecosystems**

Fallen cherry blossom is not waste in a natural system.

Dung beetle on rabbit droppings.

Cycling of materials

You have probably shuffled through piles of leaves and fallen acorns or apples on the pavement or on a woodland path in autumn. In spring the leaves may be replaced by carpets of cherry blossom. Most of this fallen material disappears quite quickly.

Fallen branches, leaves, petals, and fruits are called **dead organic matter** (though seeds inside the fruits can still be alive). Dead organic matter (DOM) is any material that was once part of a living organism. It also includes waste material from animals, such as faeces and bodies.

When DOM falls to the ground there are many different organisms waiting for it.

- Worms nibble leaves and grind them up in their gut with soil. The leaves are then digested by enzymes.
- Threads of fungi in the soil release **digestive enzymes** that break down DOM.
- Dung beetles roll up faeces into pellets, then bury the pellets and lay eggs in them. There are many different dung beetle species, using different types of dung.
- Hundreds of different kinds of bacteria live in the soil. They make a great variety of enzymes. Without bacteria there would be no recycling of reactants such as carbon and nitrogen in ecosystems.

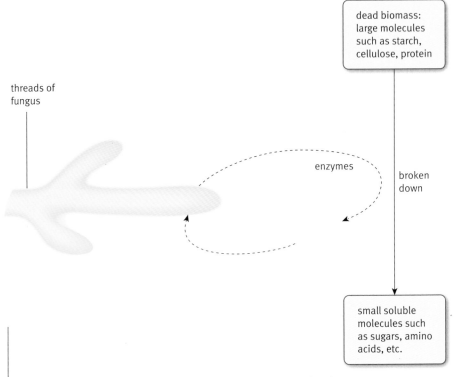

threads of fungus

dead biomass: large molecules such as starch, cellulose, protein

enzymes

broken down

small soluble molecules such as sugars, amino acids, etc.

Dead organic matter is broken down into small, soluble molecules, which are absorbed by fungal threads and used for growth.

Bacteria and nitrogen

Nitrogen gas is all around us in the atmosphere. Nitrogen is also a component of protein and DNA, so all organisms – including humans – contain nitrogen. Several different types of bacteria are essential in the nitrogen cycle.

- Nitrogen-fixing bacteria take nitrogen from the air and make it into nitrates. These bacteria live freely in the soil or inside the roots of some plants, such as beans and clover. Plants then use the nitrates to make protein and DNA.
- One type of decomposing bacteria in the soil breaks down proteins and amino acids into ammonium ions.
- Other bacteria in the soil convert ammonium ions into nitrates. Plants then take up the nitrates through their roots.
- In **anaerobic** soil, bacteria change nitrates into nitrogen gas. Anaerobic soils have no oxygen and include soils that are waterlogged or compacted.

Key words

- ✔ **dead organic matter**
- ✔ **digestive enzyme**
- ✔ **anaerobic**

Questions

1 Describe how a carbon atom in the carbon dioxide in the air can become a carbon atom in an animal.

2 Describe how a nitrogen atom in an animal can become a nitrogen atom in the air.

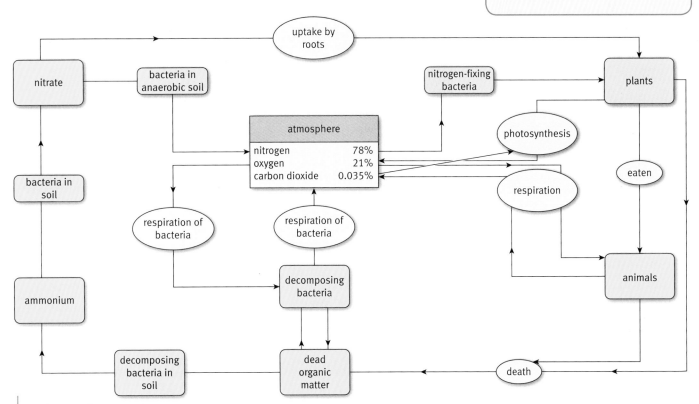

Exchange of reactants in an ecosystem.

Bacteria and carbon

Bacteria in the soil also break down carbohydrates in DOM, such as cellulose and starch. The carbohydrates provide the bacteria with glucose for respiration. Respiration releases carbon dioxide into the atmosphere. The carbon was originally taken from the atmosphere by photosynthesis. Carbon is a reactant that is recycled.

For an oak forest to survive, each tree must produce just one acorn that grows into a mature tree in its lifetime. Most acorns do not survive, but their materials are recycled into the ecosystem.

Laying hundreds of eggs is a strategy for successful reproduction in some species such as this squid.

Abundance without waste

If you suffer from hayfever you will know that plants, especially grasses, make a lot of **pollen**. The pollen grains blow in the wind to other grass flowers. This transfer of pollen is called **pollination**. Pollen contains the male sex cells of flowering plants. Pollination is needed for **flowers** to fertilise the female sex cells and produce seeds.

Producing lots of pollen increases the chance that some will reach other flowers and pollinate them. This is a natural insurance policy.

Colourful flowers are pollinated by insects, such as bumblebees. Bees carry pollen on their furry bodies and in pollen sacs attached to their legs.

Plants also make very large quantities of petals and **fruit**. They are maximising their chances of reproducing successfully. Plants compete with each other to attract **pollinators**. Lots of big bright petals will attract many bees and other insects. When the flower is pollinated the petals have no more use, and fall to the ground.

Animals produce lots of eggs and very large quantities of sperm. Eggs contain a lot of protein, so many are eaten by predators before the eggs hatch. Young hatchlings are also eaten in large quantities. Birds' eggs are fertilised within the body and mammals' eggs develop inside the body as well. This strategy is safer, so an insurance policy is not so important. For this reason, birds and mammals make fewer eggs than fish or insects.

A male producing many sperm cells increases his chances of fathering offspring. Many sperm cells die or do not find the egg. This is a male's strategy for successful reproduction.

Many eggs are taken by predators such as this monitor lizard.

Is nature wasteful?

Branches and leaves fall off trees. Large quantities of petals, fruits, eggs, and sperm are produced but not used. Fungi make millions of spores, but most spores do not grow into new fungi. In a **stable ecosystem** all this DOM decomposes, and the materials are recycled. It is very close to being a closed-loop system, so very little is wasted. Water, nitrogen, carbon, and oxygen simply circulate around the ecosystem.

Natural systems do not need to worry about wasting energy because they have a constant source – the Sun.

Are ecosystems perfect closed loops?

The organisms in an ecosystem constantly recycle food and reactants in a closed-loop system. But many ecosystems have inputs and outputs – they are not perfect closed loops.

- When birds migrate in the winter, not all of the birds will return in the spring. So some material (their bodies) is permanently removed from their summer homes.
- Rivers carry branches, leaves, nutrients, and silt away and deposit them further downstream.
- Coral reefs grow larger as they take minerals from the water.

A stable ecosystem has no overall gains or losses: the inputs and outputs are balanced.

This ecosystem is not a perfect closed loop because some migrating birds do not return.

Key words
- ✓ pollen
- ✓ pollination
- ✓ flowers
- ✓ fruit
- ✓ pollinators
- ✓ stable ecosystem

Questions

1 Explain why very few seeds result in new plants.

2 Suggest why mice and robins produce fewer eggs than frogs or fish.

3 Give two ways (other than those mentioned here) that materials can move into or out of an ecosystem.

4 Draw a flow diagram to show how natural systems can produce more material than is needed and still be sustainable.

5 Explain how most human manufacturing systems are different to natural systems, making them unsustainable.

Most of us take it for granted that the Earth will continue to provide us with fresh water to drink, clean air to breathe, a fertile soil for growing crops, and a supply of food such as fish and game. **Ecosystem services** include the different ways that living systems provide for human needs.

The growing human population is putting increasing pressure on ecosystem services worldwide. Understanding how ecosystem services work helps us to get the best out of them. This should help to avoid disasters similar to Easter Island, where ecosystem services broke down.

Clean water

Mexico City has a population of around 20 million people. Rainfall comes between June and September and mostly falls on the surrounding mountains. There is a danger of flooding during the rains, but severe water shortages occur in the dry season. Mexico City has damaged the natural closed-loop water cycle by **deforestation** (cutting down the forest) and cattle grazing. Each year more water is used in the city than is replaced by rainfall.

Mexico City.

The forests above Mexico City provide a natural ecosystem service.
- The soil is rich in DOM from rotting leaves, and holds water like a sponge. The water gradually drains into the rivers supplying the city, so that there are reserves for the dry period.
- Tree roots reduce **soil erosion** by holding the soil together and leafy branches prevent rain falling directly onto the soil. Rain drips

slowly off the trees and is absorbed rather than running off the soil surface. Soil is not washed away. Eroded soil would silt up rivers and block drains.

- Water evaporation from the forest canopy generates clouds and rain, and cools the air.

Now the forests above Mexico City are being protected and restored. The people of Mexico City have recognised that breaking a natural closed-loop system destroys a vital ecosystem service. The city's water policy includes:

- protecting forests on the slopes of Mount Popocatepetl above the city
- diverting flood water into wells to restore underground water levels.

Fertile soil

The Aran Islands off the west coast of Ireland are mostly covered in bare rock. People fled there from Cromwell in the 17th century. There was hardly any soil for growing crops. They made their own soil by using layers of sand and seaweed mixed with animal dung.

Bare rock only occurs where there is extreme wind, wave action, drought or ice. Everywhere else, rock is usually covered by a thick layer of fertile soil. Soil is formed from broken down rocks and DOM.

Earthworms play an important role in breaking down DOM, and mixing and aerating the soil. Ploughing damages earthworms. Soil then becomes compacted and crops do not grow so well. **Direct drilling** is now being tested. For example, rape seed can be planted directly into wheat stubble (stalks of newly cut wheat) with no ploughing. The worms are not damaged and the soil is more fertile. A good crop of oilseed rape is produced. This shows how we can grow crops without destroying the ecosystem services we depend on.

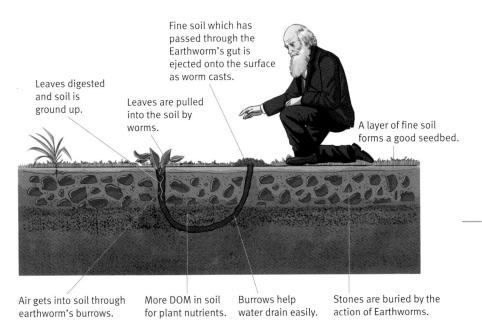

Fine soil which has passed through the Earthworm's gut is ejected onto the surface as worm casts.

Leaves digested and soil is ground up.

Leaves are pulled into the soil by worms.

A layer of fine soil forms a good seedbed.

Air gets into soil through earthworm's burrows.

More DOM in soil for plant nutrients.

Burrows help water drain easily.

Stones are buried by the action of Earthworms.

Direct drilling protects worms and keeps the soil healthy.

Key words

- ✓ ecosystem services
- ✓ deforestation
- ✓ soil erosion
- ✓ direct drilling

Questions

1 Describe how soil is formed.

2 Explain how forests help to keep rivers flowing during the dry season and suggest how they prevent flooding.

Much of the hard work of making soil is done by earthworms. They provide an essential ecosystem service. This was first described by Charles Darwin.

Our take–make–dump linear lifestyle produces a lot of waste that we need to get rid of. Waste comes from households, industry, and burning fossil fuels.

Most of our waste can be decomposed by microorganisms – but not all of it. Microorganisms are unable to produce the right enzymes to break down some waste materials. These substances are called **non-biodegradable**. For example, glass, synthetic fabrics, some pesticides, and many plastics are non-biodegradable. This means that they stay around in the environment for a very long time.

Plastics in the sea

Plastic floats down rivers and enters the sea. It can be eaten by sea birds, fish, and turtles. They cannot digest the plastic, so their guts get blocked. Wave action breaks some plastics down into fine granules. Small animals filter plastic granules from the water instead of their normal food. These small animals are the food supply of fish.

Bioaccumulation of toxic chemicals

Shiny coloured paper from magazines and printed cardboard contains heavy metals. Bleached paper, cardboard products, and certain plastics contain chlorine. Chemicals called **dioxins** are made when these bleached products are burned with other waste. Dioxins, heavy metals, and other chemicals from human waste accumulate in ecosystems. **Heavy metals** have been linked to birth defects and cancer in humans. Exposure to dioxins is associated with cancer, birth defects, and problems with the immune system.

Bioaccumulation

Chemicals that are released in small quantities can build up to toxic concentrations through food chains. This is called **bioaccumulation**. For example, a vole might take in a small amount of pesticide in its food (grass). The pesticide is stored in the vole's body as it cannot be broken down. When an owl eats a vole, all the pesticide goes into the owl. Each vole adds a bit more pesticide to the owl, as the owl also can't break down pesticides. Eventually enough pesticide accumulates in the owl to make it infertile, or even to kill it.

The end result of our take–make–dump lifestyle.

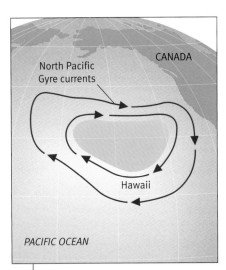

The Great Pacific gyre currents swirl around in the north Pacific, carrying plastic and other debris that harms marine life.

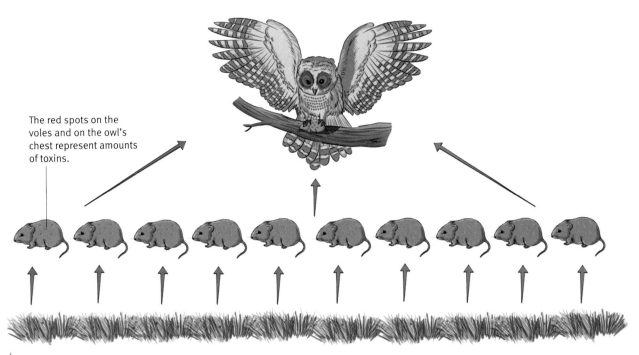

The red spots on the voles and on the owl's chest represent amounts of toxins.

Chemicals that are not broken down in living organisms can **bioaccumulate**. Toxic levels of heavy metals, pesticides, and other chemicals build up in birds, fish, and potentially humans. These chemicals are by-products of unsustainable human systems that produce waste.

Heavy metals and dioxins that are washed into rivers and the sea are concentrated in plankton, then fish and sea birds. If humans eat fish that have accumulated metals such as mercury, the levels can be high enough to cause concern.

What can we learn from natural waste disposal?

In natural ecosystems all waste is broken down by microorganisms, using enzymes. The substances released are then used by other organisms. Waste does not build up to toxic levels in natural systems.

We should try to imitate this process by making waste **biodegradable**. We can use cardboard instead of polystyrene for drink and food containers. Starch pellets can be used for packaging instead of plastic bubble wrap. Products and materials should be designed with a view to what will happen to them at the end of their useful life.

Questions

1 Turtles mistake plastic bags for jellyfish. Explain why turtles cannot digest plastic bags.

2 Explain how granules of plastic in the sea might affect fish stocks.

3 Explain why starch pellets are better than plastic for packaging.

Key words
- ✔ non-biodegradable
- ✔ dioxins
- ✔ heavy metals
- ✔ bioaccumulation
- ✔ biodegradable

Cow dung goes some way towards replacing the nutrients lost through the cows eating the grass.

Biological waste as part of a closed loop

When humans remove **biomass** from an ecosystem, it can cause irreversible changes. Biomass is any biological substance we harvest, such as grass, crops, wood, fish, and game. Agriculture involves removing biomass from fields. Soil nutrients need to be replaced using fertilisers.

Natural systems use waste as food for other organisms. To make agriculture into a closed-loop system, human faeces and urine would need to be returned to the fields as fertiliser. By collecting and removing human biological waste from the system, the system becomes linear, take–make–dump.

Fertiliser	500 litres of urine	500 litres of faeces	Total	Fertiliser needs of 250 kilograms of cereal
Nitrogen	5.6 kg	0.09 kg	5.7 kg	5.6 kg
Phosphorus	0.4 kg	0.19 kg	0.6 kg	0.7 kg
Potassium	1.0 kg	0.17 kg	1.2 kg	1.2 kg

The typical amount of nitrogen, phosphorus, and potassium in human waste. This can be compared with the fertiliser needs of a cereal crop.

Some societies process human waste to use as fertiliser. But this risks introducing high levels of toxins into food crops by **bioaccumulation**. It could also transmit infectious diseases. Other biodegradable organic wastes such as animal manure, unwanted food, and plant waste can be used to help make agriculture a closed-loop system.

Key word

- ✔ biomass

Eutrophication

Using organic fertiliser may reduce harm to the local environment. Nutrients from non-organic fertilisers often wash off fields and into rivers and lakes. Faeces and uneaten food from fish farms also add nutrients to water. These nutrients cause **algae** (simple green water plants) to grow rapidly. The water goes green in an **algal bloom**. The algae soon die and decay in the water. Bacteria causing the decay take dissolved oxygen from the water for respiration. The oxygen levels in the water go down quickly. This can kill animals in the water, such as fish. It also kills aquatic plants that would normally add oxygen to the water as they photosynthesise. This is called **eutrophication**.

The River Thames is now clean. It has been restocked with salmon from hatcheries to allow sustainable harvesting.

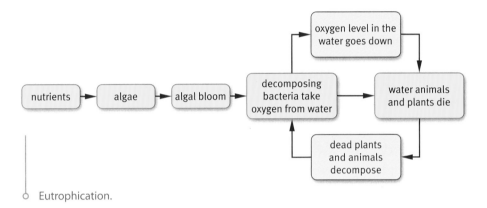

Eutrophication.

To make the agriculture system more 'closed' and so more sustainable, farmers can use manure and other organic fertilisers. These break down more slowly. Nutrients are released at the rate the crop can absorb them, so they do not get washed away in the rain. **Crop rotation** uses plants, such as clover, with **nitrogen-fixing bacteria** in their roots. Leaving a field with a **fallow crop** of clover once every few years replenishes the soil with nitrogen compounds.

Questions

1 Discuss whether agriculture to produce human food can be fully sustainable.

2 Suggest why, in some parts of China, visitors would traditionally be invited to leave behind their faeces before departing from the area.

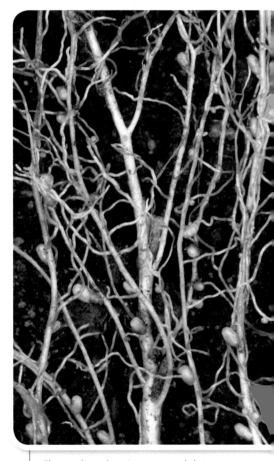

Clover plant showing root nodules. Root nodules of clover plants contain nitrogen-fixing bacteria. The bacteria and clover plant make nitrogen compounds by fixing nitrogen in the air. Clover is then ploughed into the soil to act as a green fertiliser.

California's almonds

Brazil nuts come from wild trees in the rainforest. The trees make a surplus of nuts, so there are plenty to spare. Many nuts are eaten by wild animals. The natural closed-loop system is not greatly changed.

California produces 80% of the world's almonds. Tonnes of almonds are taken away, creating a linear system. Not enough nutrients return to the ground. Fertilisers have to be added. The crop is low in **biodiversity** because there are no other crop species or weeds to support wildlife.

Pest insects and fungi have few natural enemies in an almond crop. They spread quickly and do a lot of damage. The pesticides used on California's almond crops kill pollinating insects, such as bees, in addition to the insect pests.

Over a million bee hives are transported to the Californian orchards every year. The honeybees do their work on the almond blossom in about three weeks. The hives are then moved to orange and apple crops. The bees are kept very busy.

California's almonds are an example of **intensive agriculture**. Intensive agriculture is linear, as it uses a lot of inputs, such as fertilisers and pesticides. Intensive methods can grow a lot of food, but crop failures are more likely. In the long term they are unsustainable.

Question

3 Suggest two ways California's almond industry could become more sustainable, using the idea of closed-loop systems.

Just almond trees are grown in over an area of around 243,000 hectares in California.

Unsustainable fishing

When you buy fish and chips, do you ask where the fish came from? North Sea cod stocks have crashed, but Icelandic cod is well managed. Consumers have a choice and can have a powerful influence.

Many of the world's fish stocks are overfished. Not enough fish are left to breed and replace the fish caught. But why should a fishing boat reduce its catch for everyone else's benefit? Other boats will simply take the fish instead.

Solutions to overfishing

The European Community sets **quotas** for North Sea cod. Countries agree the total fish catch that a boat can make each year. This does not solve all the problems.

- Politicians want to protect jobs and please electors. They often set higher quotas than scientists recommend.
- Fishing has to be monitored and policed.
- If a boat catches too many fish or the wrong species, they are often dumped.
- Fishing fleets move to unprotected areas, such as the African coast. Then the local people may resort to piracy or eating bush-meat because their fish stocks are reduced.
- There is more fishing for deep-sea fish, which grow very slowly. Deep trawling also damages the sea bed.

Fishing bans

The Mediterranean bluefin tuna fishery is close to collapse due to unsustainable modern fishing methods being used. In February 2010, the European Union proposed a fishing ban for bluefin tuna.

The collapse of predatory tuna fish may allow other **predators**, such as squid, to move in. If a ban is imposed too late, tuna populations may not recover. Their position on the food web will have been taken. Newfoundland's cod fishery collapsed in 1992 and is still unfishable. Protection came too late.

Fish farming (aquaculture)

Salmon farms produce cheap salmon, but are not sustainable. Food must be added and dirty water taken away. This linear system can cause environmental damage. Overfishing anchovies to provide food for salmon and polluting the local environment are just two of the problems.

Tuna fishing.

Questions

4 Suggest why politicians often set fish quotas higher than scientists would like.

5 The orange roughy is a deep-sea fish that grows very slowly. Suggest why it is not sold by some supermarkets.

6 Explain why some fish stocks do not recover after they have been overfished.

Find out about

- ✓ **the effects of replacing natural vegetation with farmland**
- ✓ **how farmland can turn to desert**
- ✓ **ways to reduce the effects of farming on biodiversity and soil**

One fifth of the world's population lives where the rainfall is less than 400 millilitres a year. These dry-land ecosystems are easily damaged and can turn to **desert**. A desert is a place where no crops can grow. What can we learn about sustainable agriculture from people who live in dry lands?

Desertification in the Sahel

The Sahel dry-land zone lies south of the Sahara. Local people have developed many techniques to prevent the land turning to desert, a process called **desertification**.

- Herds are moved from place to place to prevent overgrazing.
- Trees are not cut down in fragile areas. Acacia trees are planted as windbreaks.
- Thorny branches and rocks are used to reduce erosion in stream beds.
- Hundreds of small pits are dug in fields in the dry season. Compost (decaying plant material) is placed in the pits and covered with soil. Termites and fungi live in the compost and make the soil fertile. When the rains arrive, water drains into the pits, making a seedbed for food crops such as sorghum and millet.

In the 1970s and 1980s there were severe droughts in the Sahel. More than 100 000 people starved to death. International aid saved a lot of lives, but now a long-term solution is needed.

Today more Sahel people live in settled communities. The population has risen, though the area is much less crowded than western Europe. The rains have been better and people have been tempted to use intensive, linear-system farming methods, using fertiliser and pesticides. Some of the traditional skills have been lost. Much of the natural vegetation has been cleared, and there is **overgrazing**. Goats and other animals have eaten nearly all the plant cover. Wind and rain erode the soils.

Natural vegetation has been lost. The desert advances. Soil is lost and rivers silt up, increasing the risk of flooding when the rains do come.

Collection of native seeds for Kew Millennium Seed Bank in Burkina Faso.

The United Nations has a 'Desert Margins Programme for Africa'. Their aim is to encourage the best farming methods, and to conserve the unique native desert plants and animals. **Native species** are adapted to the dry conditions. They grow much better than imported species. Kew Royal Botanic Gardens is collecting seeds of native plants in Burkina Faso, with the help of local people. The seeds are being used for desert restoration.

Locust bean tree *Parkia biglobosa* provides protein-rich seeds, fuel, and medicine. It also fixes nitrogen.

Climate change and population pressures continue to threaten the survival of the Sahel's people. A return to traditional closed-loop systems, using native species and crop varieties, could bring sustainable solutions.

Solutions based on natural systems are also needed in developed countries. Often trees and shrubs are removed to plant crops in large fields. This is convenient for large farm machinery. Removal of hedges and trees has led to soil erosion, reduction of pollinating insects, and reduction of the natural predators of crop pests.

Shea tree *Vitellaria paradoxa* provides nuts and oil.

Questions

1 Explain the word 'desertification'.

2 Look back to Section E. Use the information to explain why planting and looking after trees helps to prevent soil erosion and desertification.

3 Explain why it is better to grow native desert plants than introduced ones.

4 Suggest why farmers should be encouraged to plant hedges to divide up their fields of crops.

Gamba grass *Andropogon gayanus* can survive fire, restores grassland, and is used for thatch.

Find out about

- ✓ **the benefits of conserving natural ecosystems**
- ✓ **the value of wild animals to human welfare**
- ✓ **ethical reasons for conserving wildlife**
- ✓ **tensions between conservation and local people**

Year	Tiger numbers in India
1800s	45 000
1972	1827
1990s	3500
2010	1500

Biodiversity is rapidly declining. 'Biodiversity' means the variety of life – the number of species and variation within each species. There are often tensions between conserving natural ecosystems and the needs of local people. In India, rapid economic development and a growing population are putting pressure on tiger reserves. Conserving ecosystems is beneficial to humans, as it protects the ecosystem services they provide.

The price of a tiger

Is a tiger worth more dead or alive? Sadly, living tigers are undervalued, but there is a huge market for dead tiger parts for traditional medicines. India is losing its tigers very rapidly. They may soon be extinct in the wild.

In 1972 the Indian Government established 28 tiger reserves spread across India. People were moved away and the vegetation was allowed to recover. Game increased rapidly and tiger numbers rose to 3500 by the 1990s.

In 1993, China banned the sale of farmed tiger products. More wild tigers were poached for traditional medicines. By 2008 tiger numbers in India declined to just 1400.

The greatest good

Should people be forced to move away from tiger reserves? The buffer zones around the reserves make good grazing land for cattle and a source of wild game. There is little other good land for people to go to. But moving people away could benefit more people than it harms.

Bengal tiger.

What are tigers good for?

Tigers are at the top of the food chain. A good tiger population means that the whole ecosystem is healthy. Tigers cannot survive without samba deer and chital prey. The deer will not survive without the right plants to eat.

Preserving India's ecosystems ensures that native plants and animals will survive. Wild plants provide medicines and food. Wild game can be harvested by humans for protein. Forests control climate and water resources.

The domestic chicken came from India. What other potential food sources do India's ecosystems hold?

Can we live without tigers? Tigers bring inspiration to many people. Tourists come to see them. Tiger reserves offer jobs to rangers and scientists. Without tigers fewer tourists would come, and the whole ecosystem would change.

There are **ethical** reasons (non-scientific reasons to do with right and wrong) for conserving tigers and other wildlife. Many people believe that wildlife has a right to exist, for its own sake, without human interference. Some people think it is wrong to use tiger parts for medicines or to keep tigers in captivity.

Should we value tigers for themselves and not just as a commodity?

Questions

1 Banning farmed tiger products sounds like a good idea. What have been the unintended impacts of this on the environment?

2 Explain whether you think people should be moved away from tiger reserves. Give two reasons for and two against.

3 List four ecosystem services provided by India's forests.

Tigers bring economic and environmental benefits to India.

Key words
✓ **biodiversity**
✓ **ethical**

Find out about

- ✓ **how forests maintain a healthy environment**
- ✓ **the importance of primary forests for wildlife conservation**
- ✓ **sustainable timber harvesting**
- ✓ **involving local people in conservation**

How many different uses of wood can you see around you? Did the wood come from your local area or from overseas? To use our forests sustainably we must know where wood comes from, and how the forests are managed. Most of the world's forests are being used unsustainably. They are being cut down more quickly than they are growing.

Old growth or new growth?

Some forests have never been cut down. They are called **primary forests** or old growth forests. They are very rich in biodiversity. They have taken millions of years to evolve and are irreplaceable. These forests are being destroyed rapidly for the needs of local people. They cut down forest for timber, to provide grassland for cattle, and to grow palm oil, soya, and **biofuels**. Loss of forests causes soil erosion, mud slides, **silting of rivers**, flash floods, loss of cloud cover, and drought. It also takes away a sustainable source of timber.

Biomass

Taking timber from a forest removes biomass. When biomass is removed it changes the natural closed-loop to a linear system. Nutrients are taken away in the biomass. If a crop is harvested, inputs of fertiliser are needed to replace the nutrients removed. Sustainable use of timber means replacing the trees and nutrients as quickly as they are taken away.

This diagram shows an island divided between sustainable forest and deforested land. Compare the ecosystem services on either side.

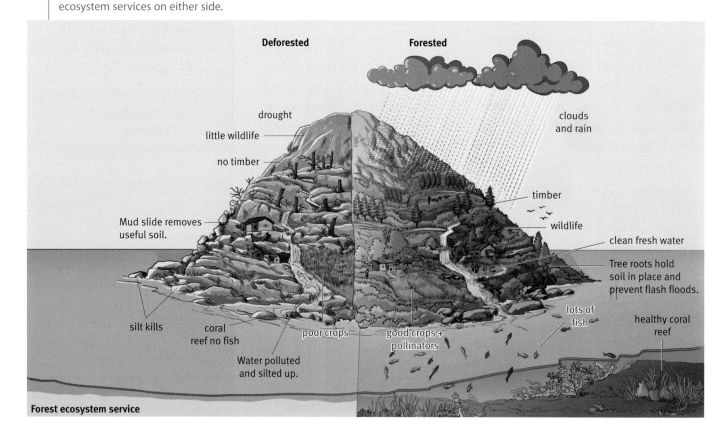

Deforested | Forested

drought
little wildlife
no timber
clouds and rain
timber
wildlife
clean fresh water
Mud slide removes useful soil.
Tree roots hold soil in place and prevent flash floods.
lots of fish
healthy coral reef
silt kills
coral reef no fish
poor crops
good crops + pollinators
Water polluted and silted up.

Forest ecosystem service

Where should we buy wood?

Many rich countries want to protect their remaining forests. They import a lot of their timber. This can damage forests in poorer countries.

One solution is to use **eco-labelling**. An eco-label shows that the timber was harvested from a sustainably managed forest. When we buy wood we can check the label to see where and how it was produced. Eco-labelling is still under development.

Restocking damaged forests

The National Forest in the East Midlands covers 518 000 hectares over three counties. The area was badly damaged in the past by coal mining and clay pits. Since the 1990s, forest cover has increased from 6% to 18% and more trees are being planted.

The growing forest removes carbon dioxide from the atmosphere by photosynthesis. Forest is a **carbon sink** as it stores carbon in the wood. It also helps to restore soils and cleans water supplies. The forest creates jobs through leisure and tourism. Wildlife spreads from areas of old woodland, increasing biodiversity. Local seed sources are used for the trees. This means the trees are adapted to local conditions. They will come into leaf and fruit at the right time for local birds and insects.

Conservation charities lease the Harapan Rainforest in Sumatra, to prevent it being used for logging. The forest contains tigers, elephants, hornbills, and the world's largest flower. As the tree canopy recovers, the humidity of the forest is increasing. The temperature varies less and fires do not spread so easily. The roots of the trees take up water, and this evaporates from the leaves. The water cycle of **cloud formation**, rainfall, and uptake by plants maintains the rainforest ecosystem.

Local people can harvest rattan, wild honey, and medicines sustainably from the recovered forest. This reduces tensions between local people and the conservationists. Local people get involved in the conservation effort. For example, young Sumatran volunteers visit the area and plant trees grown from local seed.

Key words

- ✓ **primary forests**
- ✓ **biofuels**
- ✓ **silting of rivers**
- ✓ **eco-labelling**
- ✓ **carbon sink**
- ✓ **cloud formation**

Questions

1 Many trees are imported from Eastern Europe for planting in Britain. Explain why this is not a good idea.

2 Explain why involving local people is important for conservation.

3 Explain how eco-labelling could help to protect forests.

What would happen if there were no elephants in the forest?

Find out about

- ✓ **the way oil forms**
- ✓ **why using oil is unsustainable**
- ✓ **oil as 'buried sunshine'**
- ✓ **the effects of burning fossil fuel on carbon dioxide levels**

We are living in the age of oil, but we must quickly move to a post-oil economy because:

- fossil fuels are running out
- burning fossil fuels is increasing carbon dioxide levels in the atmosphere.

Where does oil come from?

Oil comes from the dead bodies of minute plants and animals. They lived in the sea millions of years ago. They fell to the sea bed and were slowly covered by layers of sand and silt. This is why oil is called a **fossil fuel**. Heat and pressure changed the dead biomass into oil. The sand and silt became rock, so the oil was trapped underground. Drilling into the rock allows the oil to flow up to the surface.

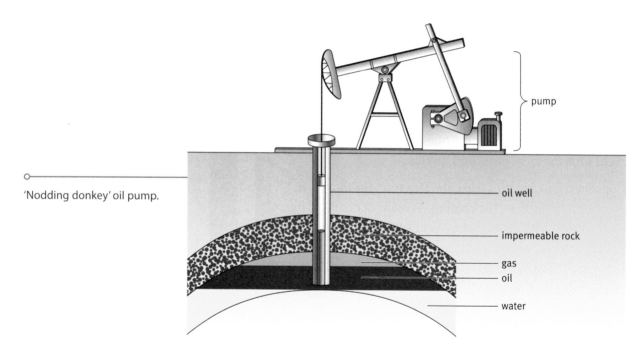

'Nodding donkey' oil pump.

Oil is made of **hydrocarbons** – chemicals made by photosynthesis long ago, containing hydrogen and carbon atoms. So when we burn fossil fuel we are releasing energy from fossil sunlight. The energy was stored as buried **fossil sunlight energy** for millions of years.

When will oil run out?

Oil takes millions of years to form. It is being used far more quickly than it can be replaced.

Some **crude oil** is easy to extract. We have already taken most of this. Oil is rapidly becoming more difficult and expensive to extract. We will stop extracting oil only when other energy sources become cheaper. But alternatives to oil are still some way off.

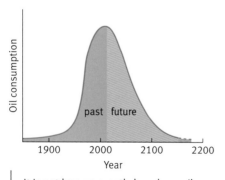

It is not known exactly how long oil will last. Production has passed its peak and may soon start to decline.

Linear systems and oil

The oil economy is a take–make–dump linear system. We take crude oil, refine it to make fuel, and dump carbon dioxide into the atmosphere. We also dump other products made from oil, such as plastics and synthetic fabrics. These products are not reused and they are not biodegradable. Oil is not renewable within our lifetime. Use of oil is not part of a closed-loop system. Waste from oil products accumulates in ecosystems, and is harmful to humans and wildlife.

Carbon dioxide

Carbon dioxide is taken up by plants in photosynthesis. If the concentration of carbon dioxide goes up slightly, plants grow more quickly and bring it down again. This natural **negative feedback** system regulates itself, rather like our body temperature. But, like our body temperature, the system can break down.

As oil is burnt for fuel, carbon dioxide is released. We are now releasing too much carbon dioxide for plants to mop up. Carbon dioxide levels are rising. This is beginning to cause atmospheric temperatures to rise. When carbon dioxide dissolves in water, it produces a weak acid. This makes the seas more acidic, harming marine life such as corals. Corals use carbon dioxide in sea water to make their coral reefs, so removing them adds to the problem.

Climate change threatens ecosystems worldwide. Wildlife may not be able to move or adapt. Melting ice causes sea levels to rise, threatening cities. Climate change does happen naturally. Only 10 000 years ago there was an ice age. But the changes we are causing are more rapid than any recent natural events.

Questions

1 Explain what is meant by a 'fossil fuel'.

2 Oil is made constantly from minute plants and animals, which were built from carbon that was fixed in photosynthesis. When we burn oil, this returns the carbon in these organisms into the atmosphere. Explain why this system cannot be regarded as a closed loop.

The Greenland ice sheet is likely to melt because of climate change, causing sea levels to rise.

Find out about

- ✔ **dependence on oil energy for food production**
- ✔ **biofuels**
- ✔ **models for sustainable living, using recently captured energy from the Sun**

How can the world's people be fed sustainably? To survive without fossil fuels, energy has to come from recent sunlight, not fossil sunlight.

Energy for producing food

Food for today's large human population is produced using energy from oil. Energy is needed for:

- ploughing and planting crops
- making fertilisers and pesticides
- food processing
- transport and distribution of food.

Intensive farming causes pollution, soil erosion, loss of biodiversity, and climate change. It is a take–make–dump, linear system.

Traditional methods

Many parts of the world still use pre-oil farming methods. Fields are cultivated using horses or oxen. The animals' energy comes from biomass (recent sunlight energy) and not from oil. The animals' faeces enrich the soil. Crops are harvested and separated using hand tools. Food is produced and consumed locally. This is a closed-loop sustainable system.

But traditional methods cannot produce enough food for the millions of people living in cities. Traditional methods also leave little time for other activities.

Are biofuels the answer?

Why not harness energy from the Sun by growing oil on farmland? Many plants make oil in their seeds. These can be harvested and turned into biofuel. Biofuel is fuel made from crops and is carbon neutral. The same amount of carbon dioxide fixed in photosynthesis is released when the biofuel is burnt.

Biofuel is now added to petrol. There are targets to increase its use in order to fight climate change. But there are some unwanted effects of growing biofuels:

- biofuels take land needed to produce food
- forests, grasslands, and other wild places are being lost to biofuel crops.

There is no simple pathway to sustainable food production, but biofuels can play a part.

Rice winnowing by hand in India.

It would take the whole of the cultivated land of the USA to grow enough biofuel to meet the country's needs.

Closed-loop systems in industry

There is a drive to change industry from take–make–dump to take–reuse–recycle as in natural ecosystems. Waste from industry can be reused, so that it is a 'technical nutrient', which goes back into the system. Some companies already produce goods sustainably in this way. This is called 'cradle-to-cradle' manufacturing. Goods, such as furniture, computers, and refrigerators are made of reusable materials. Toxic materials are avoided. After their useful life goods are broken down into technical nutrients for re-making.

We don't always need to own all our goods. Leasing cars, bicycles, washing machines, and furniture could make the manufacturer responsible for reusing and remaking. Production–recovery–remanufacture is a closed-loop system, similar to natural systems. Leasing the goods to people helps to control this cycle.

In a sustainable model for living, only biodegradable waste would be returned to the soil. Food made within biological closed-loop systems would feed the population. Energy for manufacturing would come from recent sunlight or other sustainable energy sources, not fossil fuels. Resources would be conserved in technical, closed-loop systems.

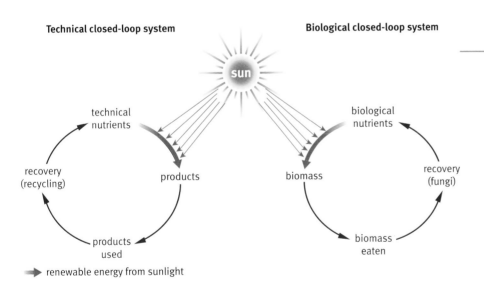

Biological and technical closed-loop systems.

To change to sustainable living, the next generation of scientists, politicians, economists, and businesses will have to apply the model of closed-loop systems in nature to human systems. However, this will need to take into account the needs of local human communities too. This will require research, imagination, determination, and education.

Questions

1 What is biofuel?

2 Explain the term 'carbon neutral' with reference to biofuels.

3 Explain why resources last longer using closed-loop technical systems rather than linear systems.

Topic B7.5: New technologies

The bacteria growing in this tank have been genetically modified to make a protein for use in drug manufacture.

Our scientific understanding of the world changes all the time as scientists make new discoveries and find new solutions to problems. New technologies are based on scientific ideas, but new processes, tools, and machinery take years to develop.

Understanding the science behind the technology that affects your life helps you to evaluate the claims that others make. It also helps you to choose, when faced with an ethical decision.

The Science

To make many of the chemicals we use daily, we grow bacteria and fungi on an industrial scale. We can change the genetic information in microorganisms and plants to make them even more useful to us.

DNA technology helps us to identify individuals, track diseases, and gives evidence that could solve crimes.

Some scientific ideas are regularly in the news. This topic introduces nanotechnology and stem cell technology that could have a great impact in your future.

Ideas about Science

We develop new technologies to improve our lives, but some applications of science can have impacts that we did not predict. Making decisions means balancing benefits against cost. In some areas of science, decisions about what we can do are made by official regulatory groups.

Nothing is completely free of risk. To make a good assessment of risk we need to know what damage might happen and how likely it is to happen.

Find out about

✓ how microorganisms can be grown to produce useful chemicals

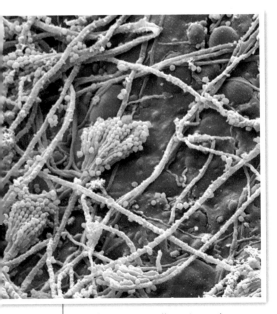

The fungus *Penicillium*. It produces penicillin and secretes it outside its cell.

Early stages of cheese production – churn milk.

There is an amazing variety of microorganisms. Each species produces different **enzymes** and other proteins. Some produce **antibiotics**. Many of these molecules are difficult to make by conventional chemistry. Scientists select species and strains of microorganisms that are able to produce useful chemicals. They then grow the microorganisms in conditions where they will produce chemicals in large quantities. The chemicals are then extracted for use.

Microorganisms are usually grown in batches using huge industrial tanks called **fermenters**. It is difficult to keep the conditions for **fermentation** right for the microorganism. Fast-growing microorganisms use up a lot of oxygen and nutrients. They produce toxic waste products and heat. The conditions inside the fermenter must be carefully monitored and controlled.

Feature	Benefit
Rapid reproduction	Large quantities of products can be made rapidly in a fermenter.
Presence of plasmids	New genes can be introduced into the plasmids in the lab so the bacteria make what we want.
Simple biochemistry	The way that bacteria work is well understood, so the nutrients and growth conditions in a bioreactor can be controlled for optimum production.
Lack of ethical concerns in their culture	There are no animal welfare issues; many processes are similar to age-old brewing and any bacteria are usually removed from the final products.
Ability to make complex molecules	Bacteria can make complex antibiotics, food additives, and hormones that can't be easily synthesised in the lab.

Antibiotics

Antibiotics can treat certain infections. The **fungus** *Penicillium* secretes the antibiotic penicillin. This kills bacteria in its immediate environment. In optimum conditions *Penicillium* can double its mass every six hours. When the fungus grows in a tank of nutrient solution, the antibiotic is secreted into the solution. It is then easy to extract the antibiotic for use as a human medicine.

Harnessing enzymes

Enzymes from microorganisms are very important in food production. They are used to control the flavour, aroma, texture, or rate of production for many food products.

All young mammals make enzymes that help them digest their mother's milk. These enzymes cause milk to form solid lumps so it moves more slowly through the gut. This gives more time for other enzymes to digest the food and for useful molecules to be absorbed.

An extract of enzymes from calves' stomachs is called **rennet**. Rennet is used to make some kinds of cheese. One of the enzymes in rennet is called **chymosin**. Scientists have developed strains of fungus that make chymosin. Some 'vegetarian' cheese is made with fungal chymosin.

Microbial enzymes are added to detergents to make 'bio' laundry liquids and powders. These enzymes digest the fats, carbohydrates, and proteins in the stains on our clothes. 'Bio' detergents often give good results at lower temperatures.

Enzymes to make biofuels

Many scientists are working to produce alternative fuels to fossil fuels. One of these is ethanol, which is an alcohol. We can make ethanol by fermenting the sugars in plant crops such as sugar cane. But crops like this might be needed to feed animals or humans.

Wood is made up of plant cells with cellulose cell walls. Tough fibres called lignin fill the spaces in the cell walls and make the cellulose hard to digest. Scientists have developed a commercial way of making an enzyme, called lignocellulase that breaks down lignin and cellulose. This enzyme can be used to turn woody stalks and leaves into sugars. This means **biofuel** can be made from waste plant material instead of useful crops.

Growing microorganisms for food

Microbial cells contain the same building blocks as cells from other organisms – carbohydrates, fats, and proteins. Some microorganisms produce proteins that are similar to the proteins in fish or soya beans. Microorganisms can be grown on simple nutrients, and they can reproduce rapidly in the right conditions. This means they could be used as food for people or farmed animals.

Quorn is made from a fungus that grows as a cluster of interwoven fungal threads. The threads are extracted from a fermenter, pressed together, and processed to match the taste and texture of meat. Quorn, and some other **single-celled proteins,** have been cleared for human consumption. You can buy Quorn as mince, burgers, and sausages.

Rennet causes the milk to form into solid lumps – the start of cheese.

Quorn is an example of a **single-celled protein** – it is made by fungi. Quorn is nutritionally similar to meat but lower in fat.

Key words
- ✔ **enzymes**
- ✔ **antibiotics**
- ✔ **fermentation**
- ✔ **fungus**
- ✔ **rennet**
- ✔ **chymosin**
- ✔ **biofuel**
- ✔ **single cell protein (SCP)**

Questions

1 Produce a flow chart to explain the main steps in the fermentation of microorganisms to produce antibiotics.

2 Why is it important to control the conditions inside a fermenter?

3 Name three categories of useful product that can be produced by fermentation using microorganisms. Give one example of each.

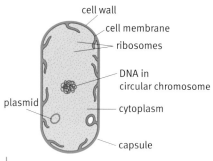

cell wall
cell membrane
ribosomes
DNA in circular chromosome
plasmid
cytoplasm
capsule

Typical bacterial cell.

Plants are sprayed with chemicals to reduce disease and pest damage. The chemicals are expensive to make and can cause pollution.

PRIVATE LAND
GMO TRIAL
KEER OFF

GM varieties of crops could transform farming by cutting the use of chemical sprays.

Bacterial cells make proteins

Bacterial cells are about one-tenth the length of typical animal cells. They have no nucleus, but their DNA forms one large circular chromosome in their cytoplasm. Most bacteria also have small rings of DNA that contain extra genes. These DNA rings are called **plasmids**.

Bacteria produce some proteins that do similar jobs to human proteins, for example, proteins in cell membranes. But bacteria don't make many proteins that are identical to those in human cells. Any cell can make a protein but only if it has the gene that codes for it. Scientists can add a human gene to bacterial cells so that they make a human protein.

Genetic modification

Changing the genes of an organism is called **genetic modification (GM)**. Bacterial cells can be modified by adding genes from other microorganisms, plants, or animals. People do not have the same ethical concerns about modifying bacteria as they do animals or plants.

Many drugs used to treat diseases are proteins. An example of such a drug is **insulin**. Before genetic modification, insulin to treat diabetes was extracted from animals such as pigs. This worked, but pig insulin could produce harmful side effects. GM bacteria can be made that produce insulin identical to human insulin, and that does not cause these side effects.

Genetic modification of plants

Despite producing new varieties of crops by selective breeding over thousands of years, pests, diseases, and weeds still reduce crop yields by about one-third. Genetic modification means developers can add new genes to plants. These genes code for new proteins to give the plant desired properties. Some genetically modified plants are **resistant** to some **herbicides**. Farmers can use these herbicides to kill weeds without harming the crop. However, this may mean that farmers use more herbicides.

Putting new genes into cells

A **vector** is needed to carry the gene into the cell. To modify bacteria, scientists use bacterial plasmids as vectors. Plasmids are easier to manipulate than a bacterial cell's main chromosome. They are small and they move easily in and out of cells.

Not all the cells in a population of bacteria will take in the added plasmid. Scientists put a second gene into the plasmid to make the genetically modified cells easy to select. For example, there is a gene in jellyfish that codes for a green fluorescent protein and several genes make bacteria resistant to particular antibiotics.

To produce human insulin from bacteria, scientists carry out the following steps:

- Isolate the gene for human insulin and make copies of it.
- Make a modified plasmid that contains the human insulin gene and another gene that gives resistance to an antibiotic.
- Add the modified plasmid to a population of bacteria.
- Treat the population with the particular antibiotic.
- The bacteria that survive must contain the plasmid, so they will also make insulin.
- Grow these modified bacteria and harvest the insulin.

Bacteriophages are **viruses** that can infect bacteria. Scientists use them as vectors to carry larger genes into bacterial cells.

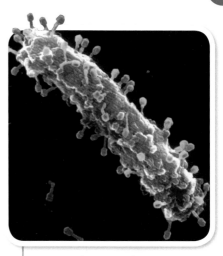

Bacteriophage attacking a bacterium (x15 000).

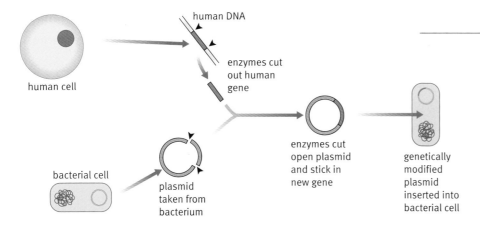

human DNA

enzymes cut out human gene

human cell

bacterial cell

plasmid taken from bacterium

enzymes cut open plasmid and stick in new gene

genetically modified plasmid inserted into bacterial cell

Plasmids are used as vectors in genetic modification of bacteria.

Questions

1 Draw a labelled diagram of a bacterial cell. Highlight the parts of the cell that contain genetic information.

2 Give one example of genetic modification in:
   a bacteria
   b plants.

3 Write a flow chart to show the main stages in the genetic modification of bacteria. Highlight the vector in the process.

4 Which features of bacteria make them ideal for industrial applications such as producing insulin?

5 When genes are inserted into plasmids, marker genes are also added. Explain how the markers are used.

6 Which, if any, ethical issues can you see in genetically modifying bacteria to make useful products?

Key words
- ✔ **plasmid**
- ✔ **genetic modification (GM)**
- ✔ **insulin**
- ✔ **resistant**
- ✔ **herbicide**
- ✔ **vector**
- ✔ **virus**

Philippe Vain.

Philippe Vain is a plant biotechnologist at the John Innes Centre in Norwich. His team, along with researchers at the University of Leeds, has been designing genetically modified crops aimed at helping many of the world's poorest farmers. 'Our goal is to improve the pest resistance of key crops – rice, bananas, and potatoes – for developing countries', says Philippe. 'In 10 years there will still be more than half a billion people in the world without a reliable source of food. It is a much better strategy to give these people the means of food production instead of supplying food aid all the time.'

Nematode worms reduce crop yields

The target of Philippe's research is nematodes – microscopic worms that live in the soil. These worms attack the roots of crops, taking nutrients from the plant and laying their eggs inside the tissues. 'If you have a small infestation, you're going to get a reduced yield, a large infestation, and you'll lose most of the crop.' For a poor farmer this can be a matter of life and death.

Farmers could kill the worms by spraying the crops using chemicals called nematicides, but these are expensive and highly toxic to humans and the environment. Instead, it was decided to develop a crop that was resistant to the pests.

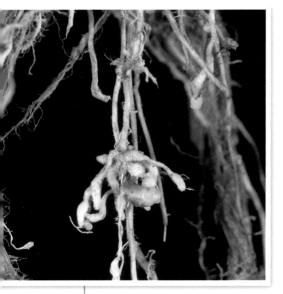

Philippe works on a species of root-knot nematode worm called *Meloidogyne*.

Adding an extra gene

The plants already have genes for natural substances called cystatins. The cystatin genes are active in certain parts of the plant, such as their seeds. Cystatins affect insect digestion, so insects cannot eat parts of the plant that contain them. Cystatins have no effect on humans. In fact we eat them all the time, in seeds from crops such as rice and maize.

When a particular gene is active in a cell we say that it is being expressed. This means that the protein for which it codes is being made in the cells. Philippe's team added another copy of the cystatin gene to the plants, which is expressed in the root cells.

Agrobacterium species cause cancer in plants. This plant is infected with *Agrobacterium tumifaciens*, which causes crown-gall disease.

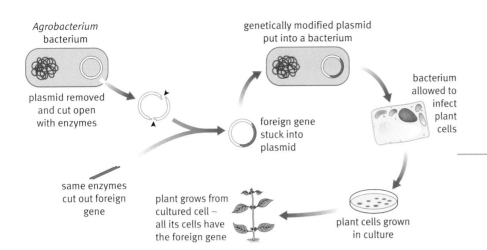

Agrobacterium bacterium

plasmid removed and cut open with enzymes

genetically modified plasmid put into a bacterium

bacterium allowed to infect plant cells

foreign gene stuck into plasmid

same enzymes cut out foreign gene

plant grows from cultured cell – all its cells have the foreign gene

plant cells grown in culture

Agrobacterium is used to transfer a gene into a plant's DNA. The bacterium's plasmid acts as the vector in this example of genetic modification.

The cystatin gene makes the roots indigestible to the nematodes. The researchers used the bacteria *Agrobacterium* as a vector to carry the extra gene into the plant's genetic material.

The only difference between the final genetically modified plant and the original is an extra copy of the cystatin gene. Nevertheless, by law, any genetically modified plant has to go through extensive testing and safety trials before it can be released into the environment.

The resulting plants show a high level of resistance to the nematode and are ready to be offered to farmers as part of a government aid project. Phillipe Vain: 'You want to make a contribution. It's very rare to have a crop improvement strategy that really works, so it's very exciting to see the outcome.'

'For us, the best result will be people trying the crop and it making a difference to their lives.'

Much of Philippe's work is on banana plants and rice.

Question

1 What is the vector for the foreign gene in this case?

Find out about

- ✔ **how the use of GM crops in the UK is controlled**
- ✔ **some of the risks and benefits of GM crops**

Genetically modified soya.

Making decisions about GM

To introduce a genetically modified organism (GMO) into the UK environment an application must be made to a government department. Each application is looked at by an outside agency. This agency advises the government on every GMO application. At the beginning of 2010, there had been some field trials of GM crops in the UK, but none were grown commercially.

In the USA there is also a series of committees that manage what can be done with GM crops. GM soya, cotton, corn, and canola (a variety of oilseed rape) are grown commercially there. Genetic modifications to crops have improved their resistance to pests and diseases, to reduce spraying and crop losses. Some crops have been genetically modified so that they are resistant to herbicides. Herbicides kill weeds, so the crop has less competition and grows better. When the GM crop is sprayed with the recommended herbicide the only plants left alive are those with the matching herbicide-resistance gene.

Why are some people concerned about GMOs?

GMOs are living things. They reproduce between themselves and interbreed with non-GMOs. It is impossible to predict how GMOs will interact with other species. The potential risks and benefits of introducing GMOs into an ecosystem need to be balanced.

This table outlines some of the arguments about GMOs.

Arguments against introducing herbicide resistance gene into a plant	Counter arguments
Added genes could make 'safe' plants produce toxins or allergens.	Food-safety organisations can check for these.
Marker genes for antibiotic resistance could be taken up by disease organisms.	The antibiotics are not used in medicine, so it wouldn't matter.
Pesticides could 'leak' out of the roots of GM plants and damage insects or microorganisms that they were not designed to kill.	Insect-resistant plants reduce pesticide application so they have an overall benefit to the environment.
GM crops may cause changes to ecosystems that cannot be reversed.	New crops produced by selective breeding have not caused huge changes to ecosystems so far.
It will cost farmers more to buy seeds of GM crops, so food costs will increase.	Farmers may benefit from healthier crops and lower costs of production.
Multinationals will increase their domination of world markets.	Some GM technology has already been shared with developing nations.
Many consumers in EU countries refuse to buy GM products so farmers may lose markets.	Consumers in most countries would buy GM crops.
Poor farmers will not be able to afford the GM seeds.	Gene technology could develop more nutritious, higher-yielding or drought-resistant crops that could benefit developing countries.

Evaluating evidence for and against GMOs

The arguments about GMOs are complicated. This is partly because it is a new technology and people cannot be certain about predicting the outcomes. Also, the technology involves living things in environments where many factors can affect the results.

Most of the information available about GMOs is produced by people who feel very strongly about the issue. They might focus on the benefits to promote the development of GMOs or the potential hazards to discourage the use of GMOs. When you find information about genetic modification, it is important to know who has produced it. This helps you to decide how much to trust their judgment.

On big issues like GM crops, the government makes decisions for us. They make **regulations** and laws allowing or forbidding new developments. Companies with an economic interest in making new products try to influence decision makers. Members of the public and action groups also have an influence. Outside agencies try to make sure they have independent, scientifically reliable information, so that the government can make an informed decision.

Genetically modified cotton.

Questions

1 A herbicide-resistance gene is added to a crop plant. What advantages could there be for the:
   a seed/herbicide seller?
   b farmer in the developed world?
   c farmer in the developing world?
   d environment?
   e consumer?

2 What possible disadvantages or risks could there be for each group in question 1?

3 How could potential risks of new technologies be reduced?

4 What evidence would convince *you* that the risks of GM organisms are worth taking, in order to have the benefits of this new technology?

Key word
✓ **regulations**

Find out about

✓ how genetic fingerprinting works – the technique from which genetic profiling has been developed

Sir Alec Jeffreys in the 1980s.

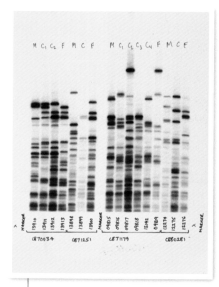

Each black line shows where pieces of DNA contain minisatellite sequences. They were separated out by gel electrophoresis.

'My life changed on Monday morning at 09:05 am 10 September 1984. In science it is unusual to have such a "Eureka moment". We were getting extraordinarily variable patterns of DNA, including the DNA of our technician and her mother and father. My first reaction to the results was "this is too complicated"; then the penny dropped and I realised we had genetic fingerprinting.'

Sir Alec Jeffreys is describing the discovery that made him one of the most famous scientists in the world. Firstly, his research group broke cells in the tissue sample and purified the DNA. They cut the DNA into fragments, using enzymes. Sir Alec Jeffreys and his research group developed a short length of DNA called a **probe**. Probes attach to complementary sections of DNA. The probe they used stuck to DNA in minisatellite sequences. These sequences repeat thousands of times throughout a person's DNA. The number and pattern of repeats varies between individuals.

CGCCTCGGCCTCCCAGAGTGCTGAGATTACAGGCGTGAACCACCATGCCTAGCCGTTAGCTCCCA
CTTATGAGTGAGAACAGGTGATGTTTGGTTTTCCATTCCTGAGTTACTTTACCCAGAATTGTTGT
CTCCAATCTCATCGAGGTCTCTGCGAATGCCAGTAATTCATTCCTTTTTATGGCTAAGTAGTATT
CCATCGTATATATACATATACATATATATGTATACACACATATACATATATATGTATACACACAT
ATACATATATATGTATACACACATATACATATATATGTATACACACATATACATATATATGTATA
CACACATATACATATATATGTATACACACATATACATATATATGTATACACACATATACATATAT
ATGTATACACACATATACATATATATGTATACACACATATACATATATATGTATACACACATATA
CATATATATGTATACACACATATACATATATATGTATACACACATATACATATATATGTATACAC
ACATATACATATATATGTATACACACATATACATATATATGTATACACACATATACATATATATG
TATACACACATATACATATATATGTATACACACATATACATATATAGTATACACACATATACATA
TATATGTATACACACATATACATATATATGTATACACACATATACATATATATGTATACACACAT
ATACATATATATGTATACACACATATACATATATATGTATACACACATATACATATATACATATA
TACACAAACACACATGCACCGCACTTTTTTTTTTTTTTTTTTTTGAGATGGGAGTCTCACTCTAT
CACCAGGCTGGAGTGCAGTGGTGTGATCTTGGCTCACTGCAACCTCTGTCTCCTGGGTTCAAGCT
ATTCTCCTGCTTCAGCCTCCTGAGTAGCTGGGATTACAGGTGCTCACCACCATGCCCAGCTAATT
TTTGTATTTTTTACCATGTTGGCCAGGATGATCTCCATCTCCTGACCTCCTGATCCTCCTGCCTTG

Part of the DNA sequence from chromosome 21, showing repeating minisatellite DNA sequences.

Fragments of DNA were placed on a gel with an electrical field across it. This is called **gel electrophoresis**. Fragments move through the gel at different rates, according to their size. Fragments of the same size move together, and form a band. Radioactive probes latched on to minisatellite sequences and showed the bands as dark lines on X-ray film. Each person's DNA gives a different pattern of bands. Closely related individuals have some bands in common.

Developing genetic profiling

The first DNA fingerprints were difficult to interpret and needed quite large samples of high-quality DNA for the technique to work. In some situations, for example, at crime scenes, there are only small samples of DNA. These may be in a few drops of blood or a hair follicle. If the sample is old, it may have decomposed.

Since 1985, techniques used to analyse DNA from different sources, have developed. **DNA profiling** is still done using electrophoresis, but now with gels in narrow capillary tubes. Profiling highlights around 20 different repeating sequences in a DNA sample. The differences between samples are shown as differences in the patterns of multiple repeats in these regions.

Bands of DNA in gels are made visible with marker chemicals. At first, radioactive markers were used that could be detected with X-ray film. Now, safer fluorescent markers are used, which glow (fluoresce) when stimulated by light. Computers interpret the patterns of bands in gels and produce a printout. Scientists no longer study and measure the gels directly.

Modern DNA profiling can be carried out with smaller samples of DNA than earlier methods. Even a very small spot of blood will contain DNA in the white blood cells. The DNA from samples can be copied many millions of times using a technique called a polymerase chain reaction (PCR).

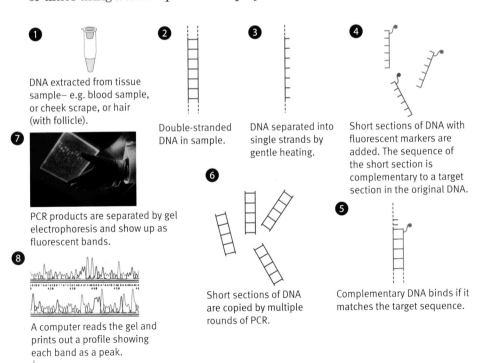

1 DNA extracted from tissue sample– e.g. blood sample, or cheek scrape, or hair (with follicle).

2 Double-stranded DNA in sample.

3 DNA separated into single strands by gentle heating.

4 Short sections of DNA with fluorescent markers are added. The sequence of the short section is complementary to a target section in the original DNA.

5 Complementary DNA binds if it matches the target sequence.

6 Short sections of DNA are copied by multiple rounds of PCR.

7 PCR products are separated by gel electrophoresis and show up as fluorescent bands.

8 A computer reads the gel and prints out a profile showing each band as a peak.

Flow diagram of genetic profiling methods.

Key words

- probe
- gel electrophoresis
- DNA profiling

Question

1 What are the main advantages of genetic profiling over the early DNA fingerprinting techniques?

Find out about

- ✓ **how genetic testing makes use of DNA technology**

What does a genetic test do?

Everybody's DNA is different. Genetic tests using DNA profiling identify sequences at particular places in a DNA sample. Genetic tests are used to identify an individual, for example, to match someone to the DNA found at a crime scene.

For each of us, any part of our DNA has come from either our mother or our father. A genetic test can show family relationships between people. For example, it can show that a particular man is the father of a child. Genetic testing is also used to identify human remains and can identify criminals.

DNA profiling was first used to prove a person's innocence. In 1985 a man confessed to the brutal murder of a young girl. However, DNA fingerprinting proved him innocent. The man responsible was caught when DNA samples were taken from the local male population and analysed by profiling.

Modern laboratory procedures make it much easier to find out the exact sequence of bases in a section of DNA. It is possible to find out if a gene in a DNA sample is a variant of the gene (allele) that is linked to the genetic disorder. This makes it possible to identify affected individuals or carriers of a disorder or disease with a genetic component.

DNA profiling works on DNA from other species too. It is used to study populations of endangered animals to find out how closely related the individuals are. This information is used to plan breeding programmes in zoos. It can also match individual animals to DNA from crime scenes or to identify ownership.

Developing DNA analysis

Probes for DNA analysis

Genetic testing using DNA technology can identify genes associated with diseases in a person's DNA. Some genetic tests use specially made pieces of DNA called **gene probes**. A gene probe is a short piece of single-stranded DNA, just like the probe used by Alec Jeffreys, but that has a sequence of bases complementary to the gene being tested for. As a result, the probe will bind to the DNA in the sample if the gene is present.

Archeologists at work. Genetic testing can provide information about people who died a long time ago.

The impact of DNA profiling

DNA profiling does not directly solve crimes. Just because a person's DNA is present at a crime scene does not mean that they committed the crime.

Government, lawyers, and civil-liberties action groups have been discussing the ethical position of the UK DNA database. In England and Wales in 2010, the law permits the police to take DNA samples from anyone arrested. Those samples and their DNA profiles can be kept in the database even if the person is not convicted of any crime. Some people argue that this means criminals can be quickly identified and innocent people eliminated. Others argue that keeping DNA, or DNA profiles, is not a good idea as the information could have other uses in future.

Individuals may find it interesting or useful to learn about their genetic profile and their likelihood of contracting particular diseases. However, it could also be possible for employers and insurance companies to use genetic test information to make decisions affecting people's lives.

How are genes copied?

PCR (the polymerase chain reaction) is now central to DNA analysis. Using PCR scientists can make millions of copies of a selected piece of DNA in a few minutes.

PCR is used:

* in forensic science when the amount of DNA found at a crime scene is very small
* to copy a gene for genetic modification
* to make gene probes
* to make many copies of a region of interest so that it can be studied further – for example, to look for changes related to disease.

Forensic scientists can identify individuals from tiny samples of hair, sweat, or blood at crime scenes.

Questions

1 List four uses of genetic tests.

2 Describe the structure of a DNA probe.

3 How does a DNA probe help you to carry out a genetic test?

4 How do scientists find out which DNA sequence has a gene probe stuck to it?

5 Suggest why blood is a good source for a DNA sample.

Key word
✓ **gene probe**

What is 'nanotechnology'?

Nanotechnology is a technology that makes use of very tiny particles. The particles used in nanotechnology are as small as 100 **nanometres** in at least one dimension. They are individual particles, not joined together into larger structures. A nanometre is extremely small. There are a million in a millimetre. A cell membrane, for example, is 6–10 nanometres thick.

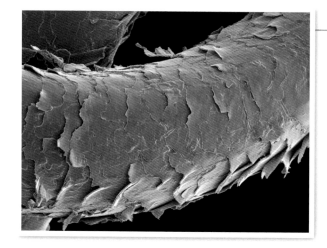

A human hair is one hundred thousand nanometres in diameter.

Some sunscreens have nanoparticles of zinc or titanium oxides.

Nanotechnology meets biology

A wide range of uses for nanotechnology are being developed by biologists.

People have known for centuries that silver can make food last longer. More recently, manufacturers have developed plastic with tiny particles of silver embedded in it. This can be used for making food storage boxes and film wraps for food. The silver particles reduce contamination of the food by microorganisms.

Several companies have developed plastic food wrapping films that change colour when:

- antibodies in the film react with bacteria in the food
- nanoparticles in the film react to changes in the amount of oxygen in the packet, which is a sign that the wrapping could be damaged
- fruit ripens and releases gases that react with nanoparticles in the film.

Plastic containing nanoparticles of silver has antibacterial properties.

How does nanotechnology work?

When materials are made with smaller and smaller particles their properties often change. For example, they may conduct electricity better, allow light through, or change from solid to liquid. When you divide a particle, you increase the exposed surface without increasing its volume. Some of the properties of nanoparticles may be the result of this increase in surface area.

Nanosilver

Nanometre-sized particles of silver can be absorbed into animal cells. Once inside the cells, nanosilver particles react with cell contents and release silver ions. Silver ions are similar in size to sodium ions and disrupt normal cell activities. Solutions of silver salts contain silver ions and can be used directly for their antibacterial effect. But ions in a silver salt solution react with other molecules before they can be absorbed. This means you would need to use higher concentrations of silver in a silver salt solution to get the same antibacterial effect as a nanosilver product.

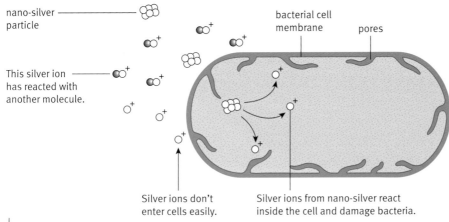

nano-silver particle

This silver ion has reacted with another molecule.

bacterial cell membrane

pores

Silver ions don't enter cells easily.

Silver ions from nano-silver react inside the cell and damage bacteria.

Cells absorb silver ions from nanosilver more easily than silver ions in silver salt solutions.

Risks and benefits

Technological developments are often made with the goal of improving lives. However, any new technology may bring with it an unpredicted hazard or **risk**. Nanometre-sized particles may behave in unexpected ways or be toxic to humans. For example, there have been some concerns that silver in food packaging could leak out into landfill or into waterways and cause environmental damage.

Current safety measurements and risk assessments are based on chemicals in their more usual form. We may need to revise our ideas of what is safe and what is not safe when working with nanometre-sized particles of any chemical. As with any new technology, it is important that systems are in place to test its safety before it is widely used.

Questions

1 What is nanotechnology?

2 What are some of the potential risks of nanotechnology?

3 What do you think are the chances of nanotechnology damaging the environment? How severe would the consequences be if unexpected problems happened?

Key words

✓ **nanotechnology**
✓ **nanometer**
✓ **risk**

Nanosilver film ends up in landfill sites like this one, but where does the nanosilver go?

Find out about

- ✔ how stem cell technology can be used to treat leukaemia and to culture tissues and organs
- ✔ the potential of stem cell technology for treatment of spinal-cord injuries

What are stem cells?

Most of the cells in our bodies are **differentiated**. This means they have become specialised to do a particular job in our body. For example, nerve cells (neurons) are long strands connecting two points in the body. They produce an electrical charge that carries a signal from one place to another.

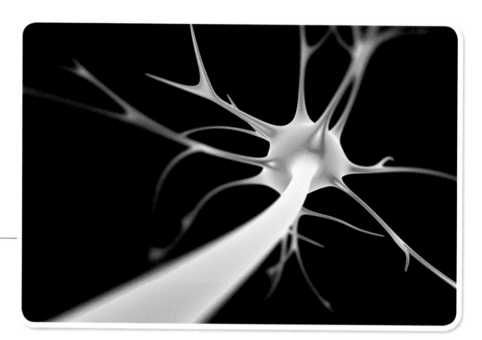

Neurons carry nerve impulses through your nerve network.

Differentiated cells cannot make copies of themselves to repair or replace damaged tissues. **Stem cells** in specialised tissues have the potential to develop into a range of different cells. For example, skin stem cells can multiply and differentiate to repair damaged skin **tissue**.

Medical treatments with stem cells

For over 30 years, blood disorders, such as **leukaemia,** have been treated with bone marrow transplants. Bone marrow contains stem cells that divide and differentiate to make eight different kinds of blood cell. Leukaemia is a kind of cancer where the body makes too many white blood cells. Treatment involves killing the patient's own bone marrow cells with radiation. New bone marrow introduced from a donor can make healthy blood.

More recently scientists have carried out **tissue culture** in the laboratory. Stem cells are grown in a special growth solution containing proteins and sugars to stimulate growth. Skin tissue culture produces a thin layer of skin cells that can be used as a skin graft to treat burned skin.

Scientists grew this skin from skin stem cells in sterile conditions. Doctors use it for skin grafts. A skin graft from a person's own stem cells reduces the risk of rejection.

Potential of stem cells

Researchers are working to see if stem cells can be used to repair damaged spinal tissue. Potentially this could restore movement to people paralysed by spinal cord injuries. Researchers inject stem cells into the damaged area in some of their patients or experimental animals and compare their recovery with patients who have different treatments.

It may be possible in the future to repair brain damage, such as that caused by Parkinson's disease or Alzheimer's. Stem cells could be used to treat some kinds of diabetes, particularly in young people, if the cells can develop in the pancreas to produce insulin.

It is difficult to develop a complete **organ** in the laboratory, as organs are such complicated structures. In our bodies, each organ works because it is connected to our circulatory system and includes a network of capillaries. Growing complete organs from stem cells will need a lot of research.

Where do stem cells come from?

All our bodies contain some stem cells, for example, in our skin, blood, and bone marrow. For some conditions, the patient might be the best donor. If a disease or condition is caused by a faulty gene in the patient's cells, another closely matching donor is needed.

Umbilical cord blood is one source of stem cells. Each baby born could provide some stem cells for research and future treatments. The many embryos left over from fertility treatments are another potential source of stem cells. There are regulations controlling how these embryos can be used. Only very early embryos, made up of a few cells, can be used for research. With special treatments in cell culture, ordinary differentiated body cells can sometimes be made to behave like stem cells. If stem cells can be reliably made in this way, it would solve many of the ethical problems surrounding the use of embryos.

Questions

1 What is the important difference between stem cells and differentiated cells?

2 Are stem cells a completely new technology?

3 What new treatments could stem cells be used for?

4 What do you think about using bone marrow, umbilical cord blood, or embryos as sources of stem cells?

Key words

✔ **differentiated**
✔ **stem cells**
✔ **tissue**
✔ **leukaemia**
✔ **tissue culture**
✔ **organ**

Very early human embryos, such as this, can provide embryonic stem cells.

Find out about

- ✔ how hearts can fail
- ✔ how we design and engineer replacements for faulty heart valves
- ✔ how pacemakers are used to restore normal heart function

How does the heart work?

Look back at page 34 in this book to remind you of how the heart works. **Heart valves** make sure the blood flows in one direction only. An area of the heart called the **pacemaker** controls the muscle contractions, using electrical signals. This makes sure the heart muscle contracts in the right sequence and pace. It keeps your heart beating at a slow and steady pace when you are resting and at a higher rate when you exercise.

What goes wrong with our hearts?

Blood vessels run into the heart muscle and provide the muscle with blood containing oxygen and food. These blood vessels can get blocked, for example, by fatty deposits on their lining. When this happens, parts of the heart muscle receive no blood and the muscle tissue quickly dies. This is what happens when you have a heart attack.

Other problems can be caused by the valves in our hearts not working properly. The tissue making up the valve flaps may get stiff or torn with wear, so the valve won't work properly.

Sometimes problems with the pacemaker result in an irregular heartbeat.

Valves in your heart keep the blood flowing in the right direction and electrical signals from the pacemaker keep your heart beat regular.

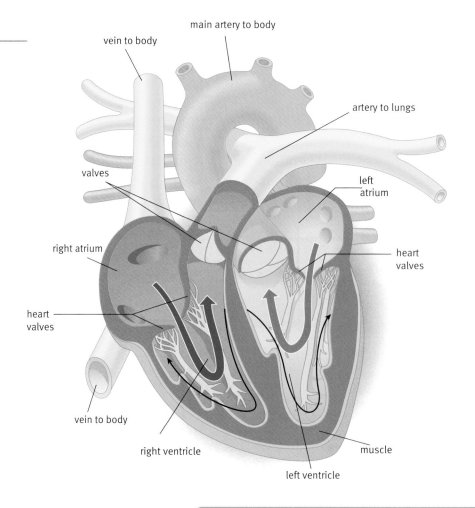

vein to body

main artery to body

artery to lungs

valves

left atrium

right atrium

heart valves

heart valves

vein to body

right ventricle

muscle

left ventricle

Replacing valves

To replace a heart valve, a surgeon connects the patient's blood supply to a heart–lung machine. Then the surgeon stops the heart, cuts it open, and replaces the damaged valve.

Replacement valves can come from a human or animal donor. The main disadvantage of a tissue transplant is that the immune system may cause **rejection** of the transplant. This happens because our immune system sees the new tissue as foreign, and attacks it as if it were an invading bacteria or virus. Another option is to use an artificial valve that has been engineered to do the job. Disadvantages of these products of **biomedical engineering** are that they cause damage to blood cells and make regular clicking noises as the valve closes.

The metals and plastics used to make replacement body parts such as heart valves have to be resistant to wear and tear. They must also be made from materials that do not corrode in the body, and do not stimulate the body's rejection systems. This avoids patients having regular operations to replace worn out valves. Developing new materials to replace body parts is an important application of chemistry.

Restoring rhythm

If the heart loses its natural rhythm, it might just feel strange or it might make any exercise difficult. An artificial pacemaker can monitor your heart rate and stimulate the muscle to contract in a regular rhythm.

Some scientists have used stem cells to develop muscle tissue in the laboratory. These muscle fibres contract and relax regularly, like a beating heart. If the cells can be encouraged to develop in the same way inside a heart, it might be possible to repair the damage caused by a heart attack. Clusters of these new cells could be used as a natural pacemaker.

Key words

- ✓ **biomedical engineering**
- ✓ **heart valves**
- ✓ **pacemaker**
- ✓ **reject ion**

Questions

1 What is the job of the heart?

2 What do the valves within the heart do?

3 Why might heart valves need to be replaced?

4 What are the main problems following heart-valve replacement surgery?

5 Why is a pacemaker important in your heart's function?

6 If you ever need surgery, would you prefer an artificial valve or a donated valve from another human or an animal? Give your reasons.

These photographs show examples of replacement heart valves.

LEARNING FROM NATURE

soil erosion

silting

Easter Island

deforestation

timber

fewer tigers

biodiversity loss

eutrophication

fertilisers

desertification

farming

climate change

oil reserves

running out

fossil fuels

linear

fishing

overfishing

job loss

collapse of
fish stocks

take–make–dump

non-biodegradable

sewage

pollution

bioaccumulation

raw materials
non-renewable

timber

clean air

ecosystem services

water

soil

fish + game

plants

ecosystems

closed loop

sustainable

lifestyle

soil conservation

dead organic
matter

animals

rural societies:
Maasai

post-oil world

well-managed
fish stocks

renewable energy

fungi + bacteria

faeces

dead animals

sustainably managed
forests

biofuels

stable human
population

new sustainable
lifestyles

extensive farming

cradle-to-cradle
manufacture

nutrients

carbon dioxide

no waste

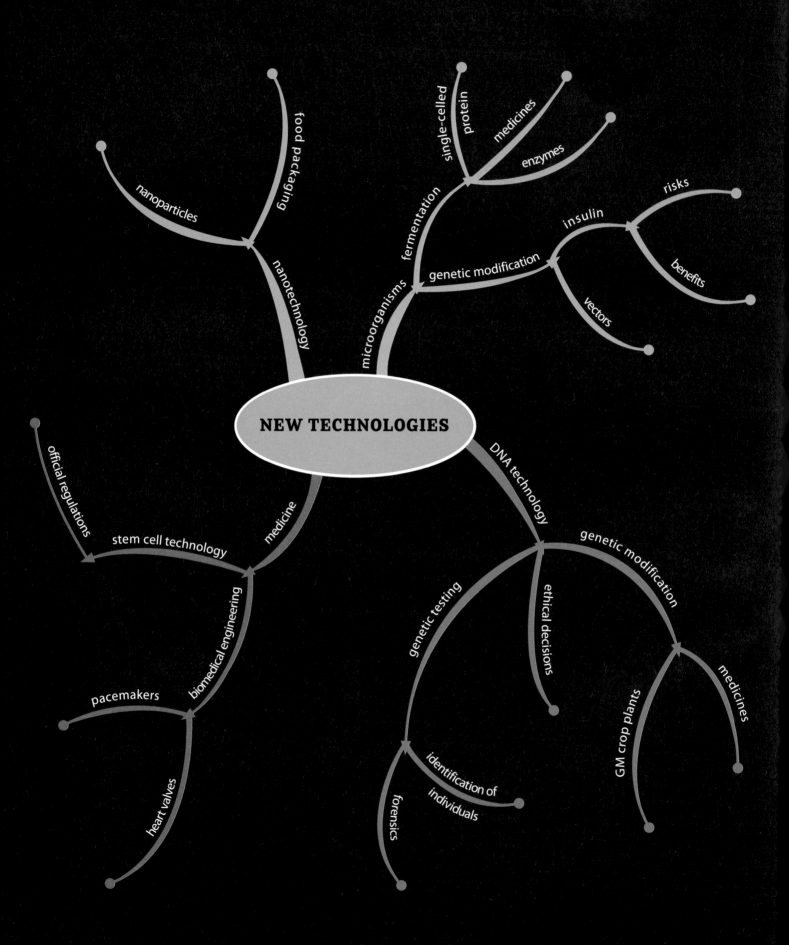

NEW TECHNOLOGIES

food packaging

nanoparticles

nanotechnology

single-celled

protein

medicines

enzymes

fermentation

microorganisms

genetic modification

insulin

risks

benefits

vectors

official regulations

stem cell technology

medicine

biomedical engineering

pacemakers

heart valves

DNA technology

genetic testing

ethical decisions

genetic modification

GM crop plants

medicines

forensics

identification of individuals

Science Explanations

The human body is capable of remarkable things – climbing mountains, swimming and diving, running, and weight lifting – as well as tasks needing dexterity such as crafts and typing. To get the best from our bodies and to avoid injury it is helpful to know how the body works.

You should know:

- that vertebrates have an internal skeleton, supporting the body and allowing movement
- that muscles can pull but not push, so are arranged in opposing pairs to move joints
- the properties of tendons, ligaments, cartilage, and synovial fluid and how they are arranged in a joint
- why a person's medical history should be considered before an exercise plan is set up
- how to interpret data about heart rate, blood pressure, and recovery period during and after exercise
- how to calculate body mass index (BMI) as a measure of fitness
- that recorded changes in fitness may be affected by monitoring errors and need to be repeated for reliability
- the types, symptoms, and treatments of injuries that can be caused by excessive exercise, and the role of a physiotherapist for sports injuries
- what is meant by a double circulatory system
- the components of blood and their role in transport, fighting infection, and blood clotting
- how red blood cells are adapted to their function of carrying oxygen
- the names and functions of the chambers and main blood vessels of the heart
- the function of valves in the heart and veins
- how materials are exchanged between capillaries and cells
- how humans maintain a constant body temperature
- that foods with high sugar content can lead to a rapid rise in blood sugar level but a high-fibre and high-starch diet causes less fluctuation
- about the differences between type 1 and type 2 diabetes in terms of their causes and treatment, including the role of insulin, diet, and exercise
- how to interpret data on the risks to health caused by an unhealthy lifestyle.

Learning from nature

We are running out of energy and food resources and damaging the planet's ability to sustain life. By studying natural ecosystems we can learn to live in a more sustainable way and leave a healthy environment for future generations.

You should know:
- how ecosystems behave as closed loops
- that ecosystems create no waste because the output from organisms is used as input for other organisms
- some examples of the outputs and inputs within ecosystems
- how fungi and other microorganisms use enzymes to feed on dead organic matter and release nutrients
- how to interpret data and diagrams showing the movement of nitrogen, carbon, and oxygen through ecosystems
- that stable ecosystems, such as rainforests, recycle most materials, with few gains or losses
- why flowers, pollen, seeds, and other reproductive structures are produced in large quantities
- the importance of ecosystem services provided by natural systems
- that humans rely on natural ecosystems for life support in the form of food, clean water, clean air, fish, game, soil, and pollination services
- the consequences of linear, unsustainable systems used in farming, timber production, fishing, and manufacturing industries
- how non-biodegradable waste can accumulate in food chains (bioaccumulation), harming wildlife and possibly human health
- that humans alter the balance of natural ecosystems by changing inputs and outputs, leading to problems such as eutrophication
- why oil production and use is not within a closed-loop system
- solutions to restore the balance in damaged ecosystems caused by fishing, agriculture, and timber production
- how conservation helps to preserve ecosystem services but can be against the short-term interests of local communities
- how human activity can be sustainable if it can harvest enough energy from current sunlight.

New technologies

To evaluate and make sense of new technologies, we need to understand the background science involved. Even with a good understanding of science, some decisions about the applications of new technologies are made for ethical reasons or because of the balance of risks and benefits.

You should know:
- how we manipulate bacteria and fungi to produce useful chemicals
- the process and uses of genetic modification of microorganisms and plants
- how gene probes are used to analyse DNA
- that detailed analysis of DNA allows us to track diseases and to identify individual people or animals
- about nanotechnology in the food industry
- about the ways in which stem cell technology could be used to treat disease
- some biomedical engineering solutions to problems in the heart.

Ideas about Science

Achieving 'peak performance' is not easy. We can try different diets and exercise regimes but we need to know how well they are working. People vary greatly in their health and physical makeup and scientists must take this into account when measuring fitness. We need to know how diet and lifestyle affect our health and fitness. This means finding a correlation between particular foods or exercise regimes and a person's physical condition.

You should be able to:
- explain why measurements of fitness vary, both within an individual and between people
- judge the reliability of a set of data based on the repeatability of the measurements
- interpret where the true value lies in a set of measurements, based on the mean
- suggest whether there is a real difference between two sets of measurements
- take account of outliers and explain reasons for including or discarding these
- understand that correlation means *either* that one factor increases *or* decreases the chance of the other factor occurring, or that the value of one factor increases/decreases in step with the value of the other factor
- recognise and interpret correlations in data
- discuss why a correlation does not always indicate cause.

Science has enabled us to grow more food and harvest more fish and timber. These have enhanced the quality of life for many people, but have also had harmful effects on the environment. We must find alternative, sustainable methods before too much damage is done. Decisions about the exploitation of wildlife should be guided by ethics and regulation.

You should be able to:
- give examples of non-sustainable farming methods, explaining their benefits and disadvantages
- explain why different groups of people might reach different decisions about using these technologies
- identify examples of unintended impacts of human activity and suggest sustainable alternatives
- interpret data to assess the sustainability of different methods of resource use and manufacturing
- discuss the regulation of wildlife, fish, and timber use, and its effectiveness
- distinguish between questions that can be answered using scientific methods and those that can not
- summarise different views about ethical issues
- identify and develop arguments based on different ethical standpoints.

Any new application of science brings with it some benefits and also some risks. Scientific work is officially regulated, and the regulators use their scientific knowledge to make assessments and decisions when the outcomes are uncertain. Some decisions are made using ethical arguments rather than scientific ones.

You should be able to:
- identify risks that might be involved in using new technologies and suggest ways to reduce them
- show awareness of, and discuss, how science and the applications of science are officially regulated
- identify the ethical issues involved in suggested new technologies
- identify who might be affected by a suggested new technology, and discuss the main benefits and disadvantages of that technology.

Review Questions

1. Muscles work in pairs to move a joint.
   a Give the name for this muscle arrangement.
   b State which muscle contracts and which relaxes to bend the elbow joint shown below.

   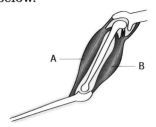

2. a Match functions i, ii, and iii to the blood components in the list below.

   Functions:
   i   transport oxygen
   ii   fight infection
   iii help the blood to clot when injured

   Blood components:
   white blood cells
   red blood cells
   platelets

   b Explain why white blood cells but not red blood cells can be used as a source of DNA.

3. a Explain why the body tends to get hotter during exercise.
   b Name the part of the brain that controls body temperature.
   c Explain two ways in which the body can lose heat when the body temperature rises.

4. A person's body mass index (BMI) is 30. Their height is 1.8 m.
   a How many kilograms should the person lose to bring their BMI down to 24?
   b Suggest three reasons why it would not be a good idea for the person to immediately join their local jogging group.

5. Which of the following involve linear systems and which involve closed-loop systems?
   a decaying leaves in a forest
   b disposal of domestic waste
   c traditional Maasai village
   d burning fossil fuels
   e commercial fishing
   f food chains in a natural lake

6. Briefly explain why starch is biodegradable and polythene is not.

7. Photosynthesis uses carbon dioxide and respiration releases it.
   a Explain why the concentration of carbon dioxide in the air in a mature forest remains roughly constant.
   b Explain why carbon dioxide in the atmosphere has increased over the past 100 years.

8. A scientist measured the levels of mercury in fish and birds living in a polluted bay. Small herbivorous fish had a concentration of 1 unit in their livers. Larger predatory fish had a concentration of 100 units and herons that fed on the predatory fish had a concentration of 1000 units.
   a Give the term used to describe this change in concentration of pollutant in food chains.
   b Explain how the differences in mercury concentration happened.

9 A farmer decided to plough a hillside to plant corn and applied fertiliser to the crop in the spring. In summer there was a bloom of green algae in the lake below the hillside. By autumn fishermen complained that many of the fish had died.

   a Explain the link between applying fertiliser and the bloom of algae.

   b Suggest a reason why many of the fish died.

   c Give the appropriate term for these effects of nutrients in water.

   d Explain how farming breaks the rules of a closed-loop system, and how this makes it unsustainable.

10 Crop plants can be genetically modified to improve their qualities. For each statement below, explain if it is a risk or a benefit of GM crops.

- Less of a GM crop is lost to pests and competition with weeds.
- Added genes could produce unexpected toxins or allergens.
- Added herbicide resistance means farmers can control weeds with special herbicides.
- Added pest resistance means farmers don't need to use chemicals.
- New crops could change ecosystems.

Explain your view of GM crops.

11 Bacteria and fungi can be used to make useful products by fermentation.

   a Describe a fermenter.

   b Explain what is needed for bacteria or fungi to grow well in a fermenter.

   c Name three different types of chemical made using bacteria and fungi.

12 This diagram shows genetic modification of a bacterium to produce human insulin.

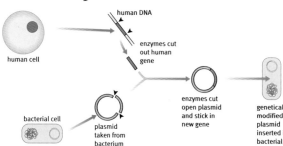

human cell · human DNA · enzymes cut out human gene · bacterial cell · plasmid taken from bacterium · enzymes cut open plasmid and stick in new gene · geneticall modified plasmid inserted i bacterial

   a What is genetic modification?

   b In this diagram, what is the vector?

   c What does the vector do in this process?

   d How would you select modified bacteria?

   e What are the benefits of producing human insulin?

13 Chymosin is an enzyme produced commercially using genetically modified bacteria. It is used to make cheese from milk as an alternative to extracts from calves' stomachs.

   a What are the advantages of bacterial chymosin over calf chymosin?

   b Do you think it is right for manufacturers to use genetically modified bacteria in this way?

14 Stem cell technology could provide treatments for many medical conditions. Human embryos could provide a source of stem cells for treatments.

   a What is special about stem cells in the body?

   b How do healthy bone marrow stem cells help to treat leukaemia?

   c What are the concerns that some people have about how human embryos could be used?

C7 Chemistry for a sustainable world

Why study chemistry?

Chemistry is the science that helps us to understand matter on an atomic scale. It is the central science. Knowledge of chemistry informs materials science and engineering as well as biochemistry, genetics, and environmental sciences.

What you already know

- The chemical industry produces bulk and fine chemicals.
- Manufactured chemicals bring both benefits and risks to society and the environment.
- New materials are made through chemical synthesis.
- Crude oil is a mixture of hydrocarbons.
- Hydrocarbons are the feedstock for many synthetic materials.
- Exothermic and endothermic reactions involve energy changes.
- Paper chromatography is used to separate mixtures.
- How to write chemical formulae.
- How to write word equations and balanced equations.

Find out about

- the 'greening' of the chemical industry
- the chemistry of carbon compounds (organic chemistry)
- energy changes in chemistry
- catalysts and the rates of reactions
- reversible reactions and equilibria
- chemical analysis by chromatography and titrations.

The Science

There are so many carbon compounds that chemists study them in families such as the alcohols, carboxylic acids, and esters. When chemists synthesise new chemicals they use ideas about energy changes and equilibrium to control reactions and maximise yield. Analytical techniques are used to protect us by checking that food and water are safe, diagnosing disease, and solving crimes.

Ideas about Science

Chemists have theories to explain observed data and answer key questions about chemical reactions – how much? how fast? how far? Science-based technologies often improve our quality of life, but may also harm the environment. Benefits must be weighed against costs. The chemical industry is changing to become more sustainable.

Topic 1: Green chemistry

The chemical industry takes crude oil, air, seawater, and other raw materials and converts them to pure chemicals such as acids, salts, solvents, compressed gases, and carbon compounds.

The chemical industry

The chemical industry converts raw materials into useful products. The products include chemicals for use as drugs, fertilisers, detergents, paints, and dyes.

The industry makes **bulk chemicals** on a scale of thousands or even millions of tonnes per year. Examples are ammonia, sulfuric acid, sodium hydroxide, and phosphoric acid.

On a much smaller scale the industry makes **fine chemicals** such as drugs, food additives, and fragrances. It also makes small quantities of speciality chemicals needed by other manufacturers for particular purposes. These include such things as flame retardants, and the liquid crystals for flat-screen televisions and computer displays.

Greener industry

The chemical industry is reinventing many of the processes it uses. The industry seeks to become 'greener' by:

- turning to renewable resources
- devising new processes that convert a high proportion of the atoms in the reactants into the product molecules
- cutting down on the use of hazardous chemicals
- making efficient use of energy
- reducing waste
- preventing pollution of the environment.

Key words
- **bulk chemicals**
- **fine chemicals**

Harvesting a natural resource. Lavender is distilled to extract chemicals for the perfume industry.

Find out about

- ✔ **feedstocks for the chemical industry**
- ✔ **products from the chemical industry**
- ✔ **people who work in the chemical industry**

Key words

- ✔ **feedstocks**
- ✔ **synthesis**
- ✔ **by-products**

Transport workers bring materials in and out of the chemical plant.

Raw materials

The basic raw materials of the chemical industry are:

- crude oil
- air
- water
- vegetable materials
- rocks and minerals such as metal ores, salt, limestone, and gypsum.

The first step in any process is to take the raw materials and convert them into a chemical, or mixture of chemicals, that can be fed into a process. Crude oil, for example, is a complex mixture of chemicals. An oil refinery distills the oil and then processes chemicals from the distillation column to produce purified **feedstocks** for chemical synthesis.

Chemical plants

At the centre of the plant is the reactor. This is where **synthesis** takes place and reactants are converted into products. The feedstock may have to be heated or compressed before it is fed to the reactor. The reactor often contains a catalyst.

Generally, a mixture of chemicals leaves the reactor. The mixture includes the desired product, but there may also be **by-products** and unchanged starting materials. So the chemical plant has to include equipment to separate the main product and by-products and to recycle unchanged reactants.

After separation, samples of the product are analysed to monitor the purity. By-products and waste are either fed back into production processes, sold on for other uses, or disposed of carefully.

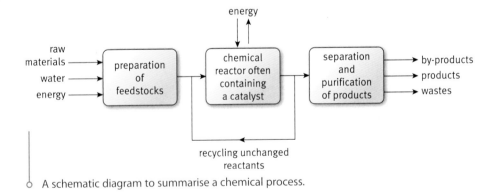

A schematic diagram to summarise a chemical process.

Chemical plants need energy. Some chemical reactions occur at high temperature, so energy is often needed for heating. Also, a lot of electric power is needed for pumps to move reactants and products from one part of the plant to another.

Sensors monitor the conditions at all the key points in the plant. The data is fed to computers in the control centre where the technical team controls the plant.

Products from the chemical industry

The chemical industry produces five main types of product. Some of these are made in huge quantities. Other chemicals have high value but are made in much smaller amounts.

Basic inorganics including fertilisers

The industry makes large amounts of these chemicals. Chlorine, sodium hydroxide, sulfuric acid, and fertilisers are all bulk chemicals.

Petrochemicals and polymers

Petrochemical plants use hydrocarbons from crude oil to make a great variety of products, including polymers.

Dyes, paints, and pigments

Modern dyes are made from petrochemicals, but in the past coal-tar was the main source of carbon compounds for chemicals such as dyes.

Pharmaceuticals

The pharmaceutical industry grew from the dyestuffs industry. The industry produces drugs and medicines.

Speciality chemicals

Speciality chemicals are used to make other products. They include food flavourings and the liquid-crystal chemicals in flat-screen displays.

People who work in the chemical industry

The chemical industry employs a wide range of people. Research chemists carry out investigations to find the best methods for making new products. Production chemists scale up these methods to see if they will work on a large scale. Members of the technical team monitor the data collected from computer sensors to make sure everything is working correctly. In quality assurance, analytical chemists test the purity of samples to make sure they are up to standard.

Research chemists play an important role in developing new materials.

A maintenance worker inside a large chemical reactor, checking to make sure the pipes are not leaking and that the rotating paddles can move freely.

Questions

1 Why do you think it is important for the chemical industry to employ
   a a technical team?
   b maintenance workers?
   c analytical chemists?

2 When the tank in the picture above is in use, it is filled with a reaction mixture. Suggest the purpose of
   a the rotating paddle in the centre of the tank
   b the network of pipes round the edge of the tank.

Find out about

- new sources of chemicals
- measures of efficiency
- safer ways to make chemicals
- energy efficiency
- reducing waste and recycling

In the second half of the 20th century, the chemical industry found that its reputation with the public was falling. Many people were worried about synthetic chemicals and their impact on health and the environment. Politicians responded by passing laws to regulate the industry. This included controls on the storage and transport of chemicals. At first, these laws were aimed at dealing with the industry as it was then by treating pollution and minimising its effects.

Controlling the flow of oil at a refinery. Crude oil is the main source of organic chemicals today.

Crops can be grown to supply feedstocks for the chemical industry rather than for their food value. In Europe this includes growing wheat, maize, sugar beet, and potatoes as sources of sugars or starch.

More recently, legislation has set out to prevent pollution by changing the industry. New laws encourage companies to reduce the formation of pollutants through changes in production methods, and using raw materials that are cost effective and renewable.

In the early stages the aim was to cut risks by controlling people's exposure to hazardous chemicals. Now green chemistry attempts to eliminate the hazard altogether. If the industry can avoid using or producing hazardous chemicals, then the risk is avoided.

Green chemistry has the potential to bring both social and economic benefits. Innovative green chemistry can benefit industry by increasing efficiency and cutting costs, and benefit society by helping to avoid the dangers of hazardous chemicals.

Renewable feedstocks

One of the aims of green chemistry is to use renewable raw materials. At the moment, crude oil is the main source of chemical feedstocks. Less than 3% of crude oil is used to make chemicals. All the rest is burnt as fuel or used to make lubricants. Even so, reducing our reliance on petrochemicals would help to make the industry more **sustainable**.

Currently, most polymers are made from petrochemicals. This includes the polyester fibres that are widely used in clothing.

DuPont has developed a way of making a new type of polyester by fermenting renewable plant materials. The company calls this polymer Sorona. Manufacturers convert Sorona into fibres for clothing, upholstery, and carpets.

The chemical starting point for the synthesis of Sorona is malonic acid. DuPont has found that it can produce this acid by fermenting corn starch with bacteria. Other feedstocks include soybeans, sugar cane, and wheat.

Plants can be grown year after year. They are a **renewable resource**. However, growing plants for chemicals takes up land that could be used to grow food. Energy is needed to make fertilisers and for harvesting crops, but the production of Sorona uses 40% less energy than that required to make the same amount of nylon. This reduces emissions of greenhouse gases and saves crude oil.

Manufacturers have to weigh up both sides of the argument and decide which is the most sustainable process.

Key words

✓ **sustainable**
✓ **renewable resource**

Fabrics made from Sorona are used for clothing. It is made using renewable resources, reducing the use of raw materials based on crude oil. Sorona can be recycled. This helps reduce waste.

Questions

1 Classify these raw materials as 'renewable' or 'non-renewable':
   a salt (sodium chloride)
   b crude oil
   c wood chippings
   d limestone
   e sugar beet.

2 Which of the ways of making industry 'greener' are illustrated by the development of Sorona?

Thermal decomposition of calcium carbonate.

RULES FOR WORKING OUT REACTING MASSES

STEP 1   Write down the balanced symbol equation.

STEP 2   Work out the relative formula mass of each reactant and product.

STEP 3   Write the relative reacting masses under the balanced equation, taking into account the numbers used to balance the equation.

STEP 4   Convert to reacting masses by adding the units (g, kg, or tonnes).

STEP 5   Scale the quantities to amounts actually used in the synthesis or experiment.

Spreading lime on a field. Lime contains calcium hydroxide, which is formed by reacting calcium oxide with water. Lime is used to reduce soil acidity.

Converting more of the reactants to products

Yields

Chemists calculate the **percentage yield** from a production process to measure its efficiency. This compares the quantity of product with the amount predicted by the balanced chemical equation.

A high yield is a good thing, but it is not necessarily an indicator that the process is 'green'. This is illustrated on a small scale by the thermal decomposition of calcium carbonate to produce calcium oxide.

Suppose that 10 g of calcium carbonate is heated strongly for 20 minutes and the product is 4.8 g of calcium oxide.

To work out the percentage yield, you must first find the theoretical yield. This is found from the reacting masses.

Step 1: $CaCO_3(s) \longrightarrow CaO(s) + CO_2(g)$

Step 2:   relative formula mass of $CaCO_3 = 40 + 12 + (16 \times 3) = 100$

relative formula mass of $CaO = 40 + 16 = 56$

Steps 3 & 4: $CaCO_3(s) \longrightarrow CaO(s) + CO_2(g)$

$\quad\quad\quad\quad 100\,g \quad\quad\quad 56\,g$

So, 100 g of calcium carbonate could theoretically produce 56 g of calcium oxide.

Step 5:   If the theoretical yield of calcium oxide = x g, then

$$\frac{\text{mass of calcium oxide}}{\text{mass of calcium carbonate}} = \frac{56\,g}{100\,g} = \frac{x\,g}{10\,g}$$

So the theoretical yield from 10 g of calcium carbonate

$$= 10\,g \times \frac{56\,g}{100\,g} = 5.6\,g \text{ calcium oxide}$$

The percentage yield from the laboratory process is

$$\frac{\text{actual yield}}{\text{theoretical yield}} \times 100$$

$$= \frac{4.8\,g}{5.6\,g} \times 100 = 85.7\%$$

This would be a good yield. However, the actual result is that only 4.8 g of product is made from 10 g of reactant.

Even with 100% yield, only 5.6 g of calcium oxide could be produced from 10 g of calcium carbonate.

Atom economy

In 1998, Barry Trost of Stanford University, USA, was awarded a prize for his work in green chemistry. He introduced the term **atom economy** as a measure of the efficiency with which a reaction uses its reactant atoms.

$$\text{atom economy} = \left(\frac{\text{mass of atoms in the product}}{\text{mass of atoms in the reactants}}\right) \times 100\%$$

In an ideal chemical reaction, all the atoms in the reactants would end up in the products, and no atoms would be wasted. If this was the case the atom economy for the reaction would be 100%.

$CaCO_3(s) \longrightarrow CaO(s) + CO_2(g)$

Total of atoms in the reactants: 1Ca, 1C, 3O
(total relative atomic mass = 100)

Total of green atoms ending in the product: 1Ca, 1O
(total relative atomic mass = 56)

Total of brown atoms ending up as waste: 1C, 2O
(total relative atomic mass = 44)

$$\text{Atom economy} = \frac{56\,g}{100\,g} \times 100 = 56\%$$

Calculating the atom economy for the thermal decomposition of calcium carbonate. The atoms in the reactants that end up in the product are described as 'green'. The atoms that end up as waste are described as 'brown'.

At the very best for this thermal decomposition reaction, just over half of the mass of starting materials can end up as product. So this is not a green process.

This approach does not take yield into account and does not allow for the fact that many real-world processes use a deliberate excess of reactants.

For example, in many neutralisation reactions, such as the reaction between magnesium carbonate and sulfuric acid, the carbonate is in excess. Reactants are also used in excess in the preparation of many carbon-based compounds, such as the preparation of bromoethane from ethanol. This preparation needs an excess of sulfuric acid and sodium bromide. You will learn more about reactions like these later in this module.

Key words

- ✔ **percentage yield**
- ✔ **atom economy**

Questions

3   16 g of methane (CH_4) was burned in the air. 32 g of carbon dioxide was collected during the reaction. During the reaction, some sooty deposits were noticed. The equation for the combustion of methane is:

$CH_4 + 2O_2 \longrightarrow CO_2 + 2H_2O$

   a   What was the percentage yield of carbon dioxide?
   b   Why do you think the percentage yield was so low?
   c   Calculate the atom economy for the reaction.

4   Heating with a catalyst converts cyclohexanol, $C_6H_{11}OH$, to cyclohexene, C_6H_{10}.
   a   What is the percentage yield if 20 g of cyclohexanol gives 14.5 g of cyclohexene?
   b   What is the atom economy, assuming that the catalyst is recovered and reused?

This weedkiller can now be made by a method that does not involve the use of toxic cyanide compounds.

Avoiding chemicals that are hazardous to health

The chemical industry produces a large number of synthetic chemicals. Some of these are reactive intermediates that are only used in manufacturing processes.

One aim of green chemistry is to replace reactants that are highly toxic with alternative chemicals that are not a threat to human health or the environment.

The aim is to protect the health of people working in the industry and also people who live near industrial plants. It is important to avoid chemical accidents, including accidental release of chemicals through explosions and fires.

Originally the company Monsanto used hydrogen cyanide in the process to produce the weedkiller that the company markets as 'Roundup'. Hydrogen cyanide is extremely toxic. The company has now developed a new route for making the herbicide. The new method has a different starting material and runs under milder conditions because of a copper catalyst.

Similarly, a new process for making polycarbonate plastics has replaced the gas phosgene with safer starting materials: methanol and carbon monoxide. Carbon monoxide is poisonous but it is not as dangerous as phosgene, which is so nasty that it has been used as a poison gas in warfare.

Energy efficiency

All manufacturing processes need energy to convert raw materials into useful products. In the chemical industry, energy is used in several ways, such as:

- to raise the temperature of reactants so a reaction begins or continues
- to heat mixtures of liquids to separate and purify products by distillation
- to dry product material
- to process waste.

The energy used in separation, drying, and waste management may be more than that used in the reaction stages.

Burning natural gas or other fossil fuels is the usual source of energy. Often the energy from burning is used to produce super-heated steam, which can then be used for heating around the chemical plant.

The most direct way of reducing the use of energy is to prevent losses of steam from leaking valves on steam pipes and by installing efficient insulation on reaction vessels or pipes.

Some of the reactions in the chemical process may be so **exothermic** that they provide the energy to raise steam and generate electricity. The energy is transferred using a heat exchanger. The first step in the manufacture of sulfuric acid is to burn sulfur. This is so exothermic that a sulfuric acid plant has no fuel bills and can raise enough steam to generate sufficient electric power to contribute significantly to the income of the operation.

Chemical production in general has become much more energy efficient than in the past. The average energy required per tonne of chemical product is less than half that needed 50 years ago.

The development of efficient **catalysts** has made a significant contribution. With a suitable catalyst, it is possible to speed up the reaction that gives the desired products, without speeding up other reactions that give unwanted by-products. This reduces waste, and reactions work at lower temperatures, saving energy.

One aim of green chemistry is not only to make processes more energy efficient but also to lower their energy demand. New processes are being developed that run at much lower temperatures. One way of doing this is to use biocatalysts – the **enzymes** produced by microorganisms. Enzymes operate within a limited temperature range, above which they are **denatured** and no longer work. Each enzyme also works within a limited pH range. This limits the conditions that can be used for enzyme-catalysed processes.

A large heat exchanger works like a laboratory condenser. One liquid or gas flows through pipes surrounded by another liquid flowing in the opposite direction. The hotter liquid or gas heats the cooler fluid.

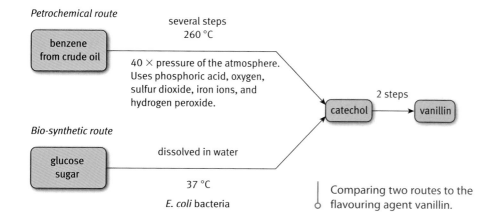

Petrochemical route

benzene from crude oil

several steps
260 °C

40 × pressure of the atmosphere. Uses phosphoric acid, oxygen, sulfur dioxide, iron ions, and hydrogen peroxide.

Bio-synthetic route

glucose sugar

dissolved in water

37 °C

E. coli bacteria

catechol

2 steps

vanillin

Comparing two routes to the flavouring agent vanillin.

Questions

5 The reaction involving cyanide in the older process for making the active ingredient for Roundup was exothermic. The replacement reaction in the newer process is endothermic. Suggest why this difference contributes to safety.

6 a Write a short paragraph to explain why the biosynthetic route to vanillin is 'greener' than the petrochemical route.

b Explain why it may not be a good idea to try and speed up the biosynthetic route by heating the reaction mixture.

A plant for recycling chemicals on a large scale.

Reducing waste and recycling

One of the principles of green chemistry is that it is better to prevent waste than to treat or clean up waste after it is formed.

One way of cutting down on waste is to develop processes with higher atom economies. Another way is to increase **recycling** at every possible stage of the life cycle of a chemical product. A third way is to find uses for by-products that were previously dumped as waste.

Recycling

Industries have always tried to recycle waste produced during manufacturing processes. Recycling is easier when the composition of the waste material is known.

A major manufacturer of polypropylene, Basell Polyolefins, used to burn unreacted propene. Much was burnt in an open flame so that not even the energy was recovered. This changed when the company installed a distillation unit to separate chemicals from the waste gases. The recovery unit cut the amount of waste. It collected over 3000 tonnes of propene per year.

Closed-loop recycling

Recycling is at its best when the waste material that is collected can be used to manufacture the same product with no loss in quality. With plastic waste this can be done by breaking down the waste into the monomers originally used to make the polymer. Several companies have developed processes for depolymerising the polyester (PET) in soft-drinks bottles. The result is fresh feedstock for making new polymer.

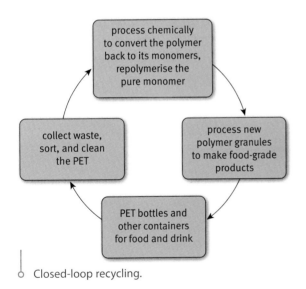

Closed-loop recycling.

(Diagram labels: process chemically to convert the polymer back to its monomers, repolymerise the pure monomer → process new polymer granules to make food-grade products → PET bottles and other containers for food and drink → collect waste, sort, and clean the PET)

Open-loop recycling

In some cases, waste from one product is recovered and used in the manufacture of another, lower-quality product. This is open-loop recycling. It cuts down the amount of fresh feedstock needed, and the amount of waste going to landfill. But it is not as good value as closed-loop recycling.

Discarded PET soft-drinks bottles can be collected and fed through grinders that reduce them to flake form. The flake then proceeds through a separation and cleaning process that removes all foreign particles such as paper, metal, and other plastic materials.

The recovered PET is sold to manufacturers, who convert it into a variety of useful products such as carpet fibre, moulding compounds, and non-food containers. Carpet companies can often use 100% recycled polymer to make polyester carpets. PET is also spun to make fibre filling for pillows, quilts, and jackets.

New uses for by-products

All chemical processes give a mixture of products: the one that the chemists want to make and others – the by-products. The process is more sustainable if the by-products can be used to make another product, so that less waste has to be dumped.

Titanium dioxide is an important pigment used in paint, plastics, paper, cosmetics, and toothpaste. By-products of the process for producing titanium dioxide include iron sulfate, which is sold to water companies to treat water, and gypsum, which is used to make plasterboard.

Cutting pollution by waste

It is usually impossible to eliminate waste completely. This means that it is important to remove or destroy any harmful chemicals before waste is released into air, water, or landfills. On many sites, ground water must also be collected and processed, as it may contain traces of the chemicals made and used on the site.

Many manufacturing sites have a single processing plant for dealing with waste. A wide range of separation techniques may be used, including filtering, centrifuging, and distillation.

Waste may also be treated chemically to neutralise acids or alkalis, to precipitate toxic metal ions, or to convert chemicals to less harmful materials. Microorganisms or reed beds may be used to break down some chemicals.

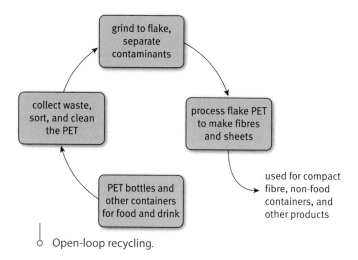

Open-loop recycling.

Titanium dioxide is the white pigment in the paint protecting a railway bridge in Newcastle-upon-Tyne.

Questions

7 a Explain in a short paragraph the difference between open-loop and closed-loop recycling.

 b Suggest one possible advantage and one possible disadvantage of each of these approaches to recycling.

8 Why is it important to carefully control waste from industrial processes?

Chemistry in action

Designing new catalysts

Matthew Davidson in his laboratory.

Matthew Davidson works at the University of Bath, where he designs new catalysts for the synthesis of polymers. His main strategy is to wrap an organic structure around a metal ion. He has helped a manufacturer to devise a catalyst for making a type of polyester by wrapping citrate ions around titanium ions. This catalyst produces a clear, rather than a yellowish, polymer and replaces a catalyst made of antimony, which is a toxic metal.

'The main thing about a catalyst is that it has to be highly reactive towards the starting materials but not to the products.'

Matthew enjoys making new complex molecules and then analysing their structure to see what makes them active. 'I have to think about two main things – firstly the size and shape of the catalyst molecules and secondly how they interact with the electrons of other molecules.'

The need for new catalysts

But why do we need new catalysts? Matthew says there are several reasons: 'First, many older catalysts were toxic or contained harmful metals. That is why we wanted to replace the antimony used to make polyesters.'

'Second, old catalysts may not be as efficient as possible. Our new titanium citrate catalyst is up to 15% more efficient than the traditional antimony catalyst. This allows more polymer to be made with less catalyst – good for both commercial and environmental reasons.'

'Third, there are many useful chemical transformations for which there are no suitable catalysts yet. New ones can help our lives by making new medicines or new polymers.'

Matthew Davidson uses physical models and computer models in his work.

Green chemistry and sustainable development

Many people think that green chemistry and sustainable development are the same thing, but there are differences. **Sustainable development** has a much wider brief.

Sustainable development is about how we organise our lives and work so that we don't destroy our planet, our most valued natural resource. It is about meeting the needs of the present without compromising the ability of future generations to meet their own needs.

Green chemistry is about the long-term sustainability of the planet and the short-term impacts of the chemical industry on our health and the environment. It is a way of thinking that can help chemists in research and production to make more eco-friendly and efficient products.

A green pain reliever

When Boots patented ibuprofen in the 1960s, there were six stages in the process of making the drug. The process had a low atom economy. It needed 75 atoms for each ibuprofen molecule formed. So, 42 of these atoms ended up as waste.

20 years later, the patent ran out. The Celanese Corporation used ideas about green chemistry to develop a new process with a more efficient atom economy, fewer harmful by-products, less waste, and catalysts that could be recovered and recycled.

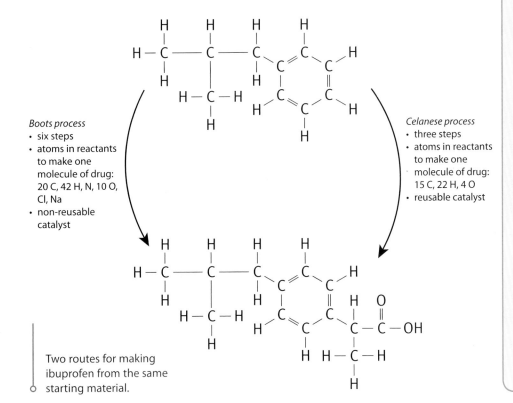

Boots process
• six steps
• atoms in reactants to make one molecule of drug:
  20 C, 42 H, N, 10 O, Cl, Na
• non-reusable catalyst

Celanese process
• three steps
• atoms in reactants to make one molecule of drug:
  15 C, 22 H, 4 O
• reusable catalyst

Two routes for making ibuprofen from the same starting material.

Questions

9 Compare sustainable development and green chemistry. What is the difference?

10 What is the molecular formula for ibuprofen?

11 a What is the atom economy for making ibuprofen:
   • by the Boots process?
   • by the Celanese Corporation process?

   b Calculate a new value of the atom economy for the Celanese process, if the ethanoic acid (CH_3COOH) formed as a by-product in one step is recycled and does not go to waste.

Topic 2: The chemistry of carbon compounds

Synthetic polymers make good nets to catch fish for food.

Spiders spin webs with a natural organic polymer to catch food.

There are more carbon compounds than there are compounds of all the other elements put together. The chemistry of carbon is so important that it forms a separate branch of the subject called **organic chemistry**.

Organic chemistry

The word 'organic' means 'living'. At first, organic chemistry was the study of compounds from plants and animals. Now that we know a wide variety of compounds can be made artificially, the definition of organic chemistry has been broadened. It now includes the study of synthetic compounds, such as polymers, drugs, and dyes.

Key word
✓ **organic chemistry**

Chains and rings

It helps to think of organic compounds being made up of a skeleton of carbon atoms supporting other atoms. Some of these other atoms may be reactive, while others are less so. In organic compounds, carbon is often linked to hydrogen, oxygen, nitrogen, and halogen atoms.

Carbon forms so many compounds because carbon atoms can join up in many ways, forming chains, branched chains, and rings. The chains can be very long, as in the polymer polythene. A typical polythene molecule may have 10 000 or more carbon atoms linked together. A polythene molecule is still very tiny, but much bigger than a methane molecule.

To make sense of the huge variety of carbon compounds, chemists think in terms of families, or series, of organic compounds.

Bonding in carbon compounds

The bonding in organic compounds is covalent. The structures are molecular. The structures can be worked out from knowing how many covalent bonds each type of atom can form. Carbon atoms form four bonds, hydrogen atoms form one bond, while oxygen atoms form two bonds.

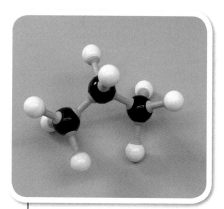

Propane: a hydrocarbon with three carbon atoms in a chain.

Methylbutane: a hydrocarbon with a branched chain.

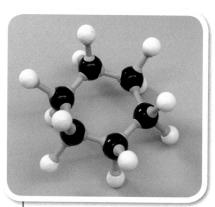

Cyclohexane: a hydrocarbon with a ring of carbon atoms.

Find out about

- ✔ the alkane series of hydrocarbons
- ✔ physical properties of alkanes
- ✔ chemical reactions of alkanes
- ✔ saturated and unsaturated hydrocarbons

CH_4 — the molecular formula

the structural formula showing the chemical bonds

the ball and stick representation showing the tetrahedral shape of the molecule

the space filled by the molecule

Ways of representing a molecule of methane.

Alkanes do not mix with water and are less dense than water. Here a dye colours the upper alkane layer.

The **alkanes** make up an important family of **hydrocarbons**. They are well known because they are the compounds in fuels such as natural gas, liquid petroleum gas (LPG), and petrol. The simplest alkane is methane. This is the main gas in natural gas.

The table below shows four alkanes.

Name	Molecular formula	Structural formula
methane	CH_4	
ethane	C_2H_6	
propane	C_3H_8	
butane	C_4H_{10}	

Physical properties of alkanes

The alkanes are oily. They do not dissolve in water or mix with it.

At room temperature, alkanes with small molecules (up to four carbon atoms) are gases, those with 4–17 carbon atoms are liquids, and those with more than 17 carbon atoms are solids.

Chemical properties of alkanes

Burning

All alkanes burn. Many common fuels consist mainly of alkanes. The hydrocarbons burn in air, forming carbon dioxide and water.

If the air is in short supply, the products may include particles of soot (carbon) and the toxic gas carbon monoxide.

Reactions with aqueous acids and alkalis

Alkanes do not react with common laboratory reagents such as acids or alkalis. The C—C and C—H bonds in the molecules are difficult to break and are therefore unreactive.

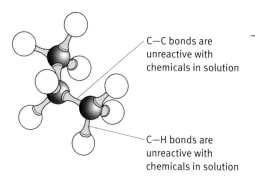

C—C bonds are unreactive with chemicals in solution

C—H bonds are unreactive with chemicals in solution

Alkanes are generally unreactive because the C—C and C—H bonds do not react with common aqueous reagents.

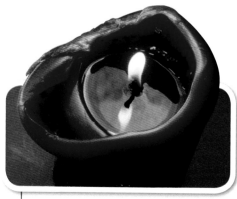

At room temperature the alkanes in candle wax are solid. The flame first melts them and then turns them to gas in the hot wick. The hot gases burn in air.

Saturated and unsaturated hydrocarbons

Alkenes are not very reactive. They are examples of **saturated** hydrocarbons because all the C—C bonds are single.

The **alkenes** are another important series of hydrocarbons. These are examples of **unsaturated** hydrocarbons. In unsaturated hydrocarbons there are C=C **double bonds** found between some carbon atoms. The presence of the double bond increases the reactivity of the hydrocarbon. Plastics such as polythene are made by polymerisation from the monomer **ethene**. It is the presence of the double bond that allows this to happen.

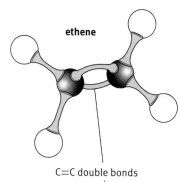

ethene

C=C double bonds

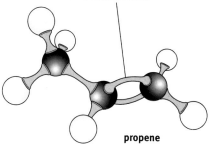

propene

Ethene and propene are examples of alkenes. These are unsaturated hydrocarbons. The double bonds in unsaturated hydrocarbons are more reactive than single bonds.

Questions

1 a In which group of the periodic table does carbon belong?
   b How many electrons are there in the outer shell of a carbon atom?
   c Which groups in the periodic table include elements that form simple ions?
   d Is carbon likely to form simple ions?

2 Petrol contains octane molecules with the formula C_8H_{18}. Draw the structural formula of octane.

3 Write a word equation for propane burning in plenty of air. Write a balanced equation with state symbols for the same reaction.

4 Write a word equation for methane burning in a limited supply of air to form carbon monoxide and steam. Write a balanced equation with state symbols for the same reaction.

5 Explain why the ethene molecule is more reactive than the ethane molecule.

Key words

- ✓ **alkane**
- ✓ **hydrocarbon**
- ✓ **saturated**
- ✓ **unsaturated**
- ✓ **ethene**

2B | The alcohols

Find out about

- ✔ physical properties of alcohols
- ✔ chemical reactions of alcohols

Ethanol (C_2H_5OH): a simple alcohol. Chemists name alcohols by changing the ending of the name of the corresponding alkane to '-ol'. Ethanol is the two-carbon alcohol related to ethane.

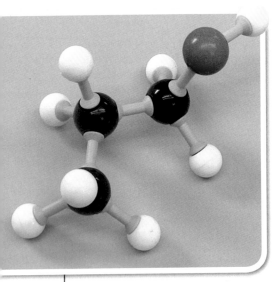

Propanol (C_3H_7OH): a three-carbon alcohol related to propane.

Uses of alcohols

Ethanol is the best-known member of the series of **alcohols**. It is the alcohol in beer, wine, and spirits. Ethanol is also a very useful solvent. It is a liquid that evaporates quickly, and for this reason it is used in cosmetic lotions and perfumes. Ethanol easily catches fire and burns with a clean flame, so it can be used as a fuel.

The simplest alcohol, methanol, can be made in two steps from methane (natural gas) and steam. This alcohol is important as a chemical feedstock. The chemical industry converts methanol to a wide range of chemicals needed to manufacture products such as adhesives, foams, solvents, and windscreen washer fluid.

Structures of alcohols

The first two members of the alcohol series are methanol and ethanol.

methanol   ethanol

There are two ways of looking at alcohol molecules that can help us to understand their properties. On the one hand, an alcohol can be seen as an alkane with one of its hydrogen atoms replaced by an —OH group. On the other hand, the same molecule can be regarded as a water molecule with one of its hydrogen atoms replaced by a hydrocarbon chain.

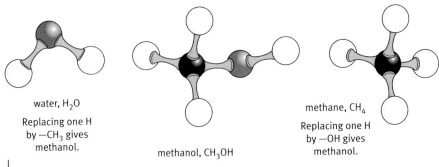

water, H_2O
Replacing one H by —CH_3 gives methanol.

methanol, CH_3OH

methane, CH_4
Replacing one H by —OH gives methanol.

Two ways of looking at an alcohol molecule.

Physical properties

Methanol and ethanol are liquids at room temperature. Alkanes with comparable relative molecular masses are gases. This shows that the attractive forces between molecules of alcohols are stronger than they are in alkanes. The presence of an —OH group of atoms gives the molecules this greater tendency to cling together, like water.

Even so, the boiling point of ethanol (78°C) is below that of water (100°C). Ethanol molecules have a greater mass than water molecules, but the attractions between the hydrocarbon parts are very weak, as in alkanes.

Overall, ethanol molecules have less tendency to stick together than water molecules.

Similarly methanol and ethanol mix with water, unlike alkanes. This is because of the —OH group in the molecules. However, alcohols with longer hydrocarbon chains, such as hexanol ($C_6H_{13}OH$), do not mix with water because the oiliness of the hydrocarbon part of the molecules dominates.

Chemical properties

The —OH group is the reactive part of an alcohol molecule. Chemists call it the **functional group** of alcohols.

Burning

All alcohols burn. Methanol and ethanol are highly flammable and are used as fuels. These compounds can burn in air, to produce carbon dioxide and water, because of the hydrocarbon parts of their molecules.

Reaction with sodium

Alcohols react with sodium in a similar way to water. This is because both water molecules and alcohol molecules include the —OH group of atoms. With water, the products are sodium hydroxide and hydrogen. With ethanol, the products are sodium ethoxide and hydrogen.

$$2 \text{ H}-\overset{\overset{\displaystyle H}{|}}{\underset{\underset{\displaystyle H}{|}}{C}}-\overset{\overset{\displaystyle H}{|}}{\underset{\underset{\displaystyle H}{|}}{C}}-O-H + 2Na \longrightarrow 2 \text{ H}-\overset{\overset{\displaystyle H}{|}}{\underset{\underset{\displaystyle H}{|}}{C}}-\overset{\overset{\displaystyle H}{|}}{\underset{\underset{\displaystyle H}{|}}{C}}-O^-Na^+ + H_2$$

sodium ethoxide

Only the hydrogen atom attached to the oxygen atom is involved in this reaction. The hydrogen atoms linked directly to carbon are inert, or unreactive.

The product has an ionic bond between the oxygen of the ethoxide ion and the sodium ion. Sodium ethoxide, like sodium hydroxide, is an ionic compound and a solid at room temperature.

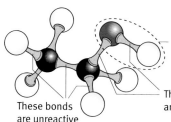

This active group is found in all alcohols

These bonds are unreactive

These bonds are reactive

The number of carbon and hydrogen atoms does not have much effect on the chemistry of alcohols.

Some bonds in ethanol are more reactive than others. Alcohols are more reactive than alkanes because C—O and O—H bonds are more reactive than C—C and C—H bonds. The alcohols share similar chemical properties because they all have the —OH group in their molecules.

Questions

1. Produce a table for three alcohols similar to the table of alkanes in Section 2A.

2. a. Use values of relative atomic masses from the periodic table in C4 Section A to show that propane and ethanol have a very similar relative mass.

   b. Propane boils at −42 °C, but ethanol boils at 78 °C. Suggest an explanation for the difference.

3. Write a balanced equation for propanol burning.

4. Write balanced equations for the reactions of sodium with:
   a. water
   b. methanol.
   c. ethane.

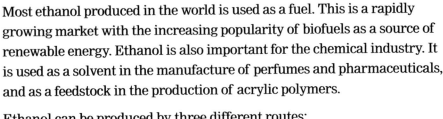

- ✔ **the production of ethanol**
- ✔ **the influence of green chemistry**

Bioethanol is the most widely used green car fuel in the world.

Most ethanol produced in the world is used as a fuel. This is a rapidly growing market with the increasing popularity of biofuels as a source of renewable energy. Ethanol is also important for the chemical industry. It is used as a solvent in the manufacture of perfumes and pharmaceuticals, and as a feedstock in the production of acrylic polymers.

Ethanol can be produced by three different routes:
- fermentation
- biotechnology
- chemical synthesis.

The method used usually depends on what the ethanol is to be used for and the availability of feedstocks.

As the principles of green chemistry are continuously applied to each method, suitable modifications are made.

Fermentation

Most of the world's alcohol, 93%, is produced by the traditional method of **fermentation** of sugar with yeast. Ethanol produced by this method is mainly used as a fuel, with smaller amounts used in alcoholic beverages and the chemical industry.

Feedstocks

Common feedstocks are sugar cane, sugar beet, corn, rice, and maize. Large areas of land are needed to grow the crops, and only some parts of the plants can be fermented. The parts that cannot be fermented are used to make animal feeds and corn oil. Recent developments mean that more plant material can be fermented, and agricultural waste, paper mill sludge, and even household rubbish can be used for fermentation.

The reaction

Cellulose polymers from the feedstock are heated with acid to break them down into simple sugars such as glucose. Glucose is then converted into ethanol and carbon dioxide. This reaction is catalysed by enzymes found in yeast:

$$\text{glucose} \longrightarrow \text{ethanol} + \text{carbon dioxide}$$
$$C_6H_{12}O_6 \longrightarrow 2C_2H_5OH + 2CO_2$$

The optimum temperature for the fermentation reaction with yeast is in the range 25–37 °C. At lower temperatures the rate of reaction is too slow, and at higher temperatures the enzymes are denatured. Enzymes are also affected by pH. This is because changes in pH can make and break bonds within and between the enzymes, changing their shape and therefore their effectiveness.

Sugar cane is a feedstock for the production of ethanol by fermentation.

The concentration of ethanol solution produced by the fermentation process is limited to between 14 and 15% ethanol. If the ethanol concentration rises higher than 15%, it becomes toxic to the yeast, which is killed, and the fermentation stops.

If higher concentrations of ethanol are required, the mixture must be distilled. Spirits such as brandy and whisky contain about 40–50% ethanol, and are produced by **distillation**.

Distillation is a technique for separating a mixture of liquids by their boiling points. The boiling point of ethanol is 78.5 °C, while the boiling point of water is 100 °C. By heating the mixture to a temperature above 78.5 °C and below 100 °C the ethanol turns into a vapour; this is then condensed and collected, leaving much of the water behind.

Energy balance

In order to produce bioethanol, energy needs to be used. This energy often comes from fossil fuels. The main stages that require energy are:
- producing fertilisers for the plants to grow
- transporting the feedstock to the factory
- processing the feedstock
- transporting the ethanol to its point of use.

When bioethanol is used as a fuel, energy is released. It is important that the amount of energy released from the fuel when it is burnt is greater than the amount of energy used in its production. This is the energy balance. The energy balance for fermentation is different for different feedstocks.

A row of whisky stills. The whisky is distilled to increase the concentration of alcohol.

Feedstock	Energy balance	Comments
sugar cane	8.3–10.2	Sugar cane can only be grown in tropical and subtropical climates. It is the feedstock used for most bioethanol produced in Brazil.
sugar beet	1.4–2.1	Sugar beet is commonly used to produce bioethanol in the UK.
corn	1.3–1.6	Corn is commonly used to produce bioethanol in the US.

The energy balance of ethanol production by fermentation from different feedstocks.

The energy balance number tells you how many times more energy is released than is used in production. For example, with a corn feedstock, one unit of fossil fuel energy is required to create enough ethanol to release 1.3–1.6 units of energy when it is burnt. The energy balance for sugar cane from Brazil is much more favourable. The higher the energy balance, the more 'green' the process.

Questions

1. Explain why the concentration of ethanol solution made by fermentation will never reach 16%.

2. A new process for producing ethanol by fermentation uses a wheat feedstock. 42 MJ of energy is used to produce a gallon of ethanol, which releases 80 MJ of energy when it is burnt.
   a. What is the energy balance for this process?
   b. Is the energy balance better or worse than for corn?

Biotechnology can convert this waste biomass into ethanol.

Key words
- ✔ fermentation
- ✔ distillation
- ✔ biomass

Grangemouth petrochemical plant in Scotland is a major producer of synthetic ethanol.

Biotechnology

Yeast is good at converting glucose to ethanol; however, many plant feedstocks also contain other sugars that cannot be broken down by yeast. To make use of these feedstocks an alternative method is needed.

In 1987 Professor Lonnie Ingram, a microbiologist from the University of Florida, used biotechnology to genetically modify *E. coli* bacteria. He was looking for a way to make biofuels suitable for cars. He found that ethanol could be produced from a wide range of feedstocks. This method can be used to produce fuels and feedstocks for the chemical industry. At present only a very small proportion of bioethanol is produced in this way.

Further developments

In the continuing search for more efficient ways of producing ethanol, scientists have been researching other genetically modified microorganisms including bacteria, fungi, and yeast.

They have been developing new processes using:
- bacteria that can break down a wide range of sugars into ethanol
- fungi that can break down biomass into glucose for use in traditional fermentation
- yeast that can turn sugars other than glucose into ethanol
- yeast that can withstand higher concentrations of ethanol.

Feedstocks

A wide range of **biomass** waste can be used as a feedstock, including forestry and wood waste, rice hulls, and corn stalks.

The reaction

The genetically modified *E. coli* bacteria convert all plant sugars, not just glucose, into ethanol. The bacteria would normally produce ethanoic or lactic acid, but the modification means ethanol is produced instead:

$$\text{sugar} \longrightarrow \text{ethanol} + \text{carbon dioxide}$$

The optimum conditions for the reaction to occur once again lie within the temperature range 25–37 °C and the pH range 6–7.

Chemical synthesis

The UK is the world's largest producer of synthetic ethanol. It is produced by the petrochemical industry. Ethanol for use in the chemical industry is often made by the method shown in the next diagram.

Feedstocks

The main feedstock for producing synthetic ethanol is ethene. Ethene is produced by the cracking of ethane from natural gas. Ethene is also

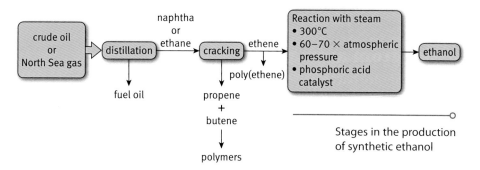

A cosmetics researcher smelling a prototype perfume. Perfume oils are usually diluted in a solvent. Synthetic ethanol can be used as a solvent in perfumes.

produced by cracking of naphtha from crude oil. The feedstock is not renewable. When oil and gas supplies eventually run out, an alternative feedstock will have to be found.

The reaction

Ethene reacts with steam in the presence of a phosphoric acid catalyst, at temperatures of about 300 °C and at 60–70 times atmospheric pressure:

$$\text{ethene} + \text{steam} \longrightarrow \text{ethanol}$$
$$C_2H_4 + H_2O \longrightarrow C_2H_5OH$$

The atom economy for the reaction is 100%, but some side reactions do occur, producing by-products such as polythene. Any unreacted molecules are recycled through the system again. The overall yield for the reaction is 95%.

Purifying the product

The end product is 96% ethanol, 4% water. It is really difficult to remove the last of the water and obtain 100% ethanol.

Older purification methods required a lot of energy to remove the water and sometimes introduced toxic chemicals into the system. New methods use special compounds called 'zeolites' that have tiny holes all over their surface. At room temperature, water molecules are absorbed onto the surface, leaving behind the larger ethanol molecules, which are too big to fit into the holes. The zeolites can then be dried and reused.

Questions

3 Suggest a reason why it is not safe to drink ethanol produced by the synthetic method.

4 Make a table listing the advantages and disadvantages of each method of producing ethanol.

5 Which method do you think has the largest impact on the environment? Give reasons for your answer.

6 Which method do you think is the 'greenest'? Use your answer to question 4 to explain your choice.

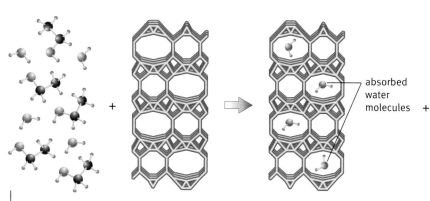

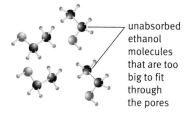

absorbed water molecules

unabsorbed ethanol molecules that are too big to fit through the pores

Zeolites can be used as a dehydrating agent as they only absorb the very small water molecules, leaving the ethanol molecules behind.

Find out about

- ✔ structures and properties of organic acids
- ✔ acids in vinegar and other foods
- ✔ carboxylic acids as weak acids

The sting of a red ant contains methanoic acid. The traditional name for this acid is formic acid, from the Latin word for ant, *formica*.

Do you like a dash of dilute solution of ethanoic acid on your chips?

Acids from animals and plants

Many acids are part of life itself. These are the organic acids, many of which appear in lists of ingredients on food labels. Ethanoic acid, traditionally known as acetic acid, is the main acid in **vinegar**. Citric acid gives oranges and lemons their sharp taste.

Some of the acids with more carbon atoms have unpleasant smells. The horrible odours of rancid butter, vomit, and sweaty socks are caused by the breakdown of fats to produce organic acids, including butyric, hexanoic, and octanoic acids. Butyric acid is the traditional name for butanoic acid. The word 'butyric' comes from its origins in butter.

Structures and names of organic acids

The functional group in the molecules of organic acids is:

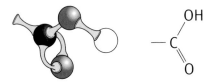

The series of compounds with this reactive group are the **carboxylic acids**. The chemical names of the compounds are related to the alkane with the same number of carbon atoms. The ending 'ane' becomes 'anoic acid'. So the systematic name for acetic acid, the two-carbon acid, is ethanoic acid.

Formation of vinegar

Oxidation of ethanol produces ethanoic acid. Vinegar is a dilute solution of ethanoic acid, and is manufactured by allowing solutions of alcohol to oxidise.

Oxidation converts beer to malt vinegar. Cider oxidises to cider vinegar and wine to wine vinegar.

Acidity of carboxylic acids

Some acids ionise completely to give hydrogen ions when they dissolve in water. Chemists call them **strong acids**. Hydrochloric, sulfuric, and nitric acids are strong acids.

Carboxylic acids ionise to produce hydrogen ions when dissolved in water to a lesser extent than the strong acids. Only a small proportion of the molecules ionise so not all the hydrogens are released as ions into the solution. They are **weak acids**. This helps to explain why vinegar is pH 3 but dilute hydrochloric acid is pH 1.

In a molecule of ethanoic acid, there are four hydrogen atoms. Three are attached to a carbon atom and one to an oxygen atom. Only the hydrogen atom attached to oxygen is reactive. This is the hydrogen atom that ionises in aqueous solution.

ethanoic acid → ethanoate ion + H⁺

Methanoic acid, HCOOH.

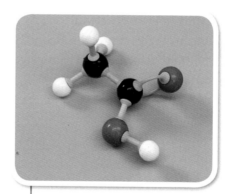

Ethanoic acid, CH₃COOH.

Ethanoic acid and the other carboxylic acids show the characteristic reactions of acids with metals, alkalis, and metal carbonates:

- acid + metal ⟶ salt + hydrogen
- acid + soluble hydroxide ⟶ salt + water
- acid + metal carbonate ⟶ salt + water + carbon dioxide

When ethanoic acid reacts with sodium hydroxide, the salt formed is sodium ethanoate.

There is an ionic bond between the sodium ion and the ethanoate ion:

Key words

- ✓ vinegar
- ✓ carboxylic acid
- ✓ strong acid
- ✓ weak acid

Questions

1 Write these formulae (the table of alkane names in Section 2A will help you):
   a the structural formula of methanoic acid
   b the molecular formula of ethanoic acid
   c the structural formula of propanoic acid
   d the molecular formula of butanoic acid

2 Write word equations and balanced symbol equations for the reactions of methanoic acid with:
   a magnesium
   b potassium hydroxide solution
   c copper carbonate ($CuCO_3$).

3 A good way of removing the disgusting smell of butanoic acid from vomit on a carpet or inside a car is to sprinkle it with sodium hydrogencarbonate ($NaHCO_3$) powder. Write a word equation for the reaction that takes place. Can you explain why the smell might disappear after this reaction?

Find out about

✓ esters from acids and alcohols
✓ synthesis of an ester

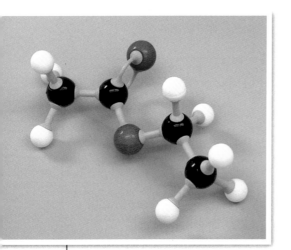

Ethyl ethanoate (ethyl acetate) is a colourless liquid at room temperature. It has many uses. As well as flavouring food, it is a good solvent, used for decaffeinating tea and coffee and removing coatings such as nail varnish. It is an ingredient of printing inks and perfumes.

Fruity-smelling molecules

When you eat a banana, strawberry, or peach, you taste and smell the powerful odour of a mixture of **esters**. A ripe pineapple contains about 120 mg of the ester ethyl ethanoate in every kilogram of its flesh. There are also smaller quantities of other esters together with around 60 mg of ethanol.

Esters are very common. Many sweet-smelling compounds in perfumes and food flavourings are esters. Some drugs used in medicines are esters, including aspirin and paracetamol. The plasticisers used to make polymers such as PVC soft and flexible are esters. Esters are also used as solvents, such as nail-varnish remover.

Compounds with more than one ester link include fats and vegetable oils such as butter and sunflower oil. The synthetic fibres in many clothes are made of a polyester. The long chains in laminated plastics and surface finishes in kitchen equipment are also held together by ester links.

Ester formation

An alcohol can react with a carboxylic acid to make esters. The reaction happens on warming the alcohol and the acid in the presence of a small amount of a strong acid catalyst such as sulfuric acid.

ethanoic acid + methanol ⟶ methyl ethanoate + water

Key words

✓ esters
✓ heat under reflux
✓ drying agent
✓ tap funnel

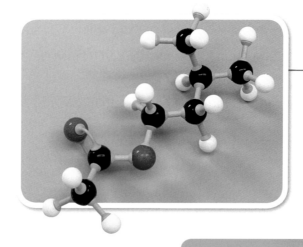

The ester with a very strong fruity smell, 3-methylbutyl ethanoate (3-methylbutyl acetate). It smells strongly of pear drops.

Making an ester

The synthesis of ethyl ethanoate on a laboratory scale illustrates techniques used for making a pure liquid product.

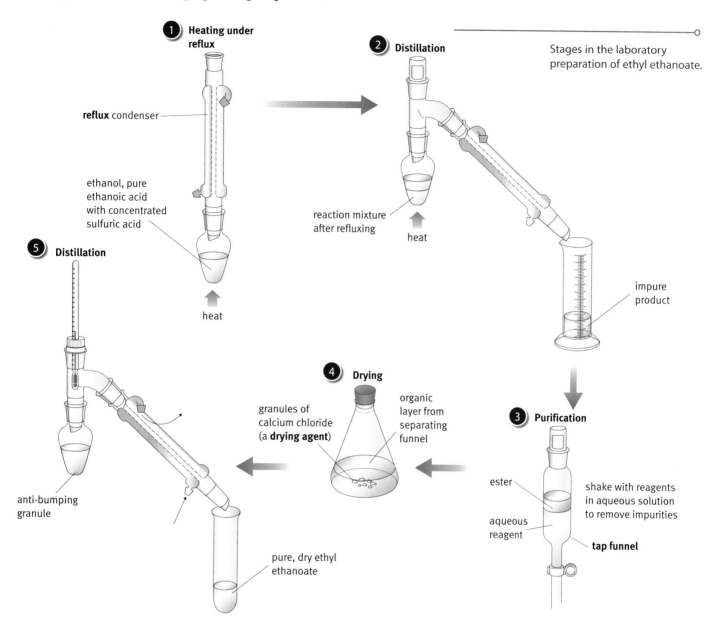

Stages in the laboratory preparation of ethyl ethanoate.

Questions

1 a To which atoms are the hydrogen atoms bonded in ethyl ethanoate?
   b Would you expect ethyl ethanoate to react with sodium?
   c Would you expect ethyl ethanoate to be an acid?

2 Explain what is happening at each step in the synthesis of ethyl ethanoate.

3 In step 1 of the synthesis of ethyl ethanoate:
   a what is the purpose of the condenser?
   b what is the purpose of the sulfuric acid?

4 Calculate the percentage yield if the yield of ethyl ethanoate is 50 g from a preparation starting from 42 g ethanol and 52 g ethanoic acid.

Looking and smelling good

Mimicking nature

Tony Moreton is a chemist working for The Body Shop. Fruit esters crop up all the time in his work: 'We use fruit esters in products that have a fruity smell. They have low molecular masses and low boiling points, which give them the volatility that makes them easy to smell. Their high volatility means they don't linger around for long, and they are referred to as "top notes" in a perfume.'

Fruit esters flavour these products.

'As with many organic chemicals, they are flammable, and with their high volatility as well, precautions have to be taken during manufacture.'

'The esters used in the industry are "nature identical", which means they are identical to materials found in nature but are made synthetically. Extracting the natural esters would cost about 100 times as much as making synthetic ones.'

Esters with a fruity smell

One of the suppliers of ingredients to The Body Shop is a Manchester-based company called Fragrance Oils. One of its products is a blackcurrant perfume concentrate that contains the ester ethyl butanoate. The company's perfumery director, Philip Harris, has been familiar with this chemical for a very long time: 'I remember buying strongly flavoured sweets called pineapple chunks, which tasted more or less exclusively of ethyl butanoate.'

'Ethyl butanoate has a strong pineapple aroma, but it's also reminiscent of all sorts of fruity aromas, so we use it in blackcurrant, strawberry, raspberry, apple, mango . . . everything fruity!'

'It's quite simply made from ethanol and butanoic acid. The only trouble is that the reaction can go in reverse. In the presence of alkali the ester can hydrolyse back to these starting products. As butanoic acid is extremely smelly, this isn't so good. We have to avoid using it in alkaline products.'

'I've always found it amazing that such an unpleasant smelling material could be used to produce such a delicious fruity smell.'

From fruit esters to soaps

Tony Moreton also uses esters with larger molecules found in various nuts. 'They are formed from glycerol and long-chain fatty acids. They are oily or waxy so are water resistant, soften the skin, and help retain moisture.'

'We can use these fruit esters to produce soap. Synthetic versions of these kinds of esters would be very expensive to make, so in this case we use the natural material.'

Philip Harris and Farzana Rujidawa working in front of the smelling booths at Fragrance Oils. Philip designed many of The Body Shop's fruit-based fragrances.

It is possible to have molecules with more than one ester link between alcohol and acid. Important examples are fats and oils. These compounds release more energy when oxidised than carbohydrates. This makes them important to plants and animals as an energy store.

The structures of fats and oils

The alcohol in fats and oils is **glycerol**. This is a compound with three —OH groups.

The carboxylic acids in fats and oils are often called **fatty acids**. These are compounds with a long hydrocarbon chain attached to a carboxylic acid group.

Find out about

✓ structures of fats and oils
✓ saturated and unsaturated fats

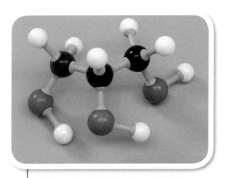

The general structure of a compound in which glycerol has formed three ester links with three fatty acid molecules. In natural fats and oils the fatty acids may all be the same or they may be a mixture.

Glycerol, which is also called propan-1,2,3-triol.

Saturated and unsaturated fats

Animal **fats** are generally solids at room temperature. Butter and lard are examples. **Vegetable oils** are usually liquid, as illustrated by corn oil, sunflower oil, and olive oil.

Chemically the difference between fats and oils arises from the structure of the carboxylic acids. Stearic acid is typical of the acids combined in animal fats. All the bonds in its molecules are single bonds. Chemists use the term 'saturated' to describe molecules like this because the molecule has as much hydrogen as it can take. These saturated molecules are straight.

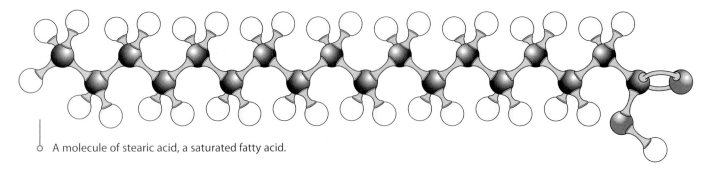

A molecule of stearic acid, a saturated fatty acid.

Esters made of glycerol and saturated fats have a regular shape. They pack together easily and are solid at room temperature.

Oleic acid is typical of the acids combined in vegetable oils. There is a double bond in each molecule of this acid. Oleic acid is unsaturated. The double bond means that the molecules are not straight. It is more difficult to pack together molecules made of glycerol and unsaturated fats. This means that they are liquid at room temperature.

Key words
- glycerol
- fatty acids
- fats
- vegetable oils

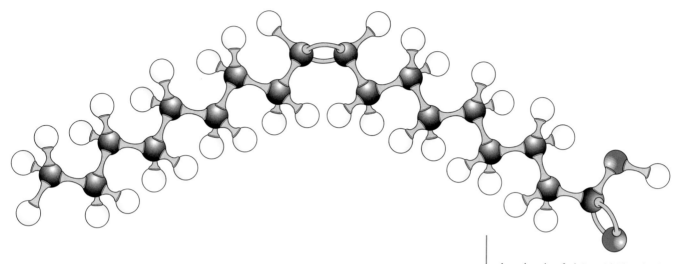

A molecule of oleic acid. The double bond means that there are carbon atoms that do not form four bonds with other atoms. Because there is not as much hydrogen as there would be with all single bonds, these molecules are 'unsaturated'.

Making soap from fats and oils

An ester splits up into an acid and an alcohol when it reacts with water. Chemists call this type of change hydrolysis. 'Hydro-lysis' is derived from two Greek words meaning 'water-splitting'.

$$\text{ester} + \text{water} \longrightarrow \text{acid} + \text{alcohol}$$

In the absence of a catalyst, this is a very slow change.

A strong alkali, such as sodium hydroxide, is a good catalyst for the hydrolysis of esters. Hydrolysis of fats and oils by heating with alkali produces soaps. Soaps are the sodium or potassium salts of fatty acids.

Questions

1 Chemists sometimes describe fats and oils as 'triglycerides'. Why is this an appropriate name for these compounds?

2 The molecular formula of an acid can be written C_xH_yCOOH. What are the values of x and y in:
   a stearic acid?
   b oleic acid?

3 Manufacturers state that some spreads are high in polyunsaturated fats. Suggest what the term 'polyunsaturated' means.

Fats, oils, and our health

The chemistry of fats and oils has triggered food scares. 'Saturated' fats and 'trans' fats are thought to be bad for people, while 'unsaturated' fats (especially polyunsaturated fats) and some 'omega' fatty acids are good. Many people use these terms with little idea of what they mean and limited understanding of the effects that these fats and fatty acids have on our health.

Edible oils from plants.

Spreads made from vegetable oils.

Hydrogenated vegetable oil

Margarine was originally a cheap substitute for butter. It can be made from vegetable oils that have been altered to 'harden' them so that they are solid at room temperature.

The first margarines were made by bubbling hydrogen through an oil with a nickel catalyst. The hydrogen hardened the oil by adding to the double bonds and turning it into a saturated fat.

If both parts of the hydrocarbon chain are on the same side of the double bond between carbon atoms, it is **cis**. Nearly all naturally occurring unsaturated fatty acids contain **cis** double bonds. If the two parts of the chain are on the opposite sides of the double bond, it is **trans**. The shape of a **trans**-unsaturated molecule is a bit like a saturated fatty acid. They are not as runny as **cis**-molecules.

This is a relatively cheap and easy process. But, research in the 1960s showed that these saturated fats could contribute to heart disease.

Trans and *cis* fats

Some margarine tubs, and bottles of vegetable oil, give information about *cis*- and *trans*-fatty acids. This refers to the arrangement of the atoms either side of the double bond in unsaturated fatty acids.

Trans-fatty acids can form during the hydrogenation process used to make some 'hard' margarines. In the 1990s an American scientist, Walter Willet, found evidence that too much *trans*-fat could aggravate heart disease. Not all scientists agreed with him, and the research continues.

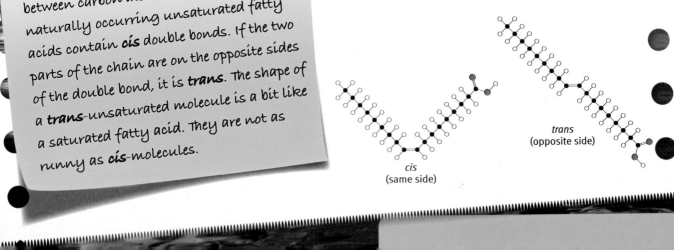

cis
(same side)

trans
(opposite side)

Hardening without hydrogen

Food scientists have found ways to turn vegetable oils into solid spreads without adding hydrogen. The fatty acids in vegetable oils are polyunsaturated. This means they contain many double bonds. The molecules of these fatty acids are not straight because of all the double bonds. So they do not pack together easily.

Imagine what would happen if you could swap the fatty acid chains around so that they all stack together more neatly and make a denser material. This is exactly what modern margarine makers do – using a catalyst, they make the fatty acids rearrange themselves. David Allen works for one of the suppliers to a big supermarket chain: 'It's a bit like musical chairs in that they all change places. Instead of music you have a catalyst, or an enzyme, and the right conditions.'

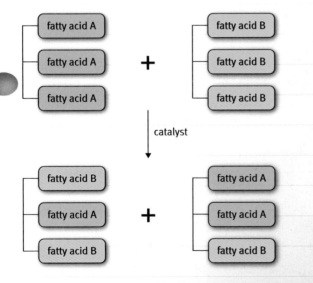

In the presence of a catalyst the fatty acids can swap places between molecules of fats and oils. This results in a mixture. The diagram shows just two of the possible products. This can raise the melting point by several degrees.

Omega-3 and omega-6 oils

Omega (ω) is the last letter in the Greek alphabet. The letter is used in a naming system that counts from the last carbon atom in the chain of a fatty acid molecule – the carbon atom furthest from the —COOH group. If you count in this way, omega-3 fatty acids have the first double bond between carbon atoms 3 and 4. Omega-6 fatty acids have the first double bond between carbon atoms 6 and 7.

Some of these omega compounds are essential fatty acids because our bodies need them but cannot make them. People need to take them in through their diet. According to Professor John Harwood of Cardiff University: 'You need a ratio of about three times omega-6 to one omega-3. But most people in Western countries take in far too much omega-6 and not enough omega-3 – more like a ratio of 15 to 1.'

'Omega-3 acids are found in oily fish and can reduce pain in joints. They are also important in the developing brains of the very young and in the brains of the very old, and have implications for heart disease. Omega-6 acids are found in margarines.'

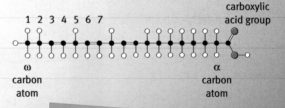

Linolenic acid has three double bonds. They are all cis. This form of linolenic acid is an omega-3 fatty acid. Another form of linolenic acid is an omega-6 fatty acid. Omega-6 acid has double bonds between carbon atoms numbered 6 and 7, 9 and 10, and 12 and 13.

Topic 3: Energy changes in chemistry

The thermite reaction is highly exothermic. The energy released causes the iron produced in the reaction to be molten. It can be used to weld rail tracks together.

A fireball from detonating gunpowder. Explosions are very fast reactions. They need to be carefully controlled to make sure they are safe.

When a reaction takes place, atoms are rearranged and bonds are broken and made. When this happens, energy is taken in and given out. It is important for chemists to understand the energy changes that occur during a reaction so that they can control how fast the reaction happens.

Energy in and out

Some chemical reactions take in energy, while others release energy. Exothermic reactions give out energy and are put to use all the time. An exothermic reaction between petrol and air causes energy to be released, making a car engine work. Scientists need to understand these energy changes in order to put them to good use in a controlled way.

How fast?

It is important for anyone trying to control changes to understand how fast a reaction will happen. Reactions that are too slow tie up equipment and people's time for too long. This costs money. But reactions that are too fast can be hazardous.

Catalysts can be used to speed up reactions that are too slow. Understanding how catalysts work is enabling scientists to make the chemical industry more sustainable.

Molecular theories

Chemists explain their observations with the help of theories about the behaviour of atoms and molecules. Atoms and molecules are too small to see, so chemists use models to help develop their theories.

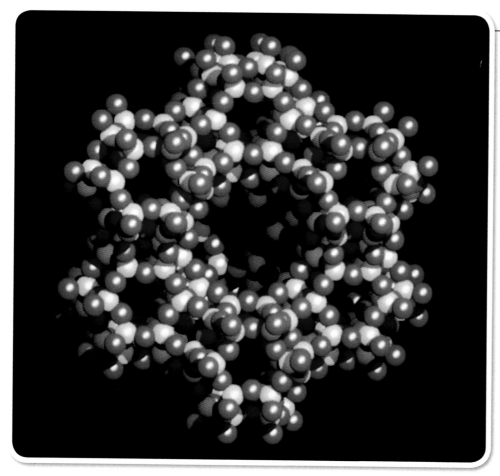

Computer graphic of a model of a zeolite crystal. The yellow atoms are either silicon or aluminium atoms. The red atoms are oxygen. Zeolites are catalysts used to control reactions in the petrochemical industry. Chemists can make synthetic zeolites with crystal structures designed to catalyse particular reactions.

All chemical changes give out or take in energy. The study of energy changes is central to the science of explaining the extent and direction of a wide variety of changes. Understanding these energy changes also helps chemists to control reactions.

In C6 Section E, you were introduced to **exothermic** and **endothermic** reactions and used **energy-level diagrams** to try and explain the energy changes.

Exothermic reactions

Many reactions, such as burning and respiration, are exothermic. They give out energy to the surroundings.

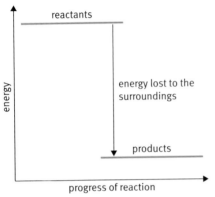

Energy-level diagram for an exothermic reaction.

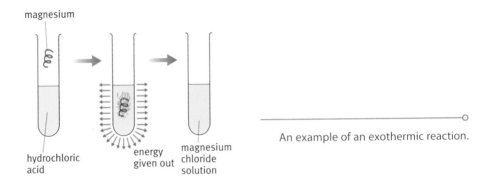

An example of an exothermic reaction.

In an exothermic reaction, the energy of the products is less than the energy of the reactants.

Endothermic reactions

Endothermic reactions, such as photosynthesis, take in energy from the surroundings.

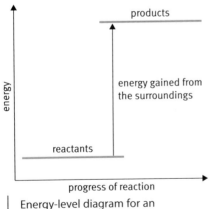

Energy-level diagram for an endothermic reaction.

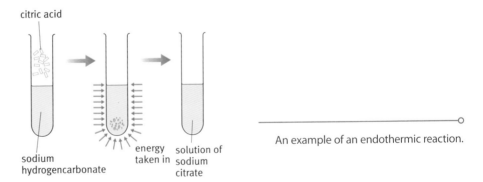

An example of an endothermic reaction.

In an endothermic reaction, the energy of the products is greater than the energy of the reactants.

How much energy?

There is growing interest in hydrogen as a fuel because water is the only product of its reaction with oxygen. This is a highly exothermic reaction, but at room temperature the two gases do not react. It takes a hot flame or an electric spark to heat up the mixture enough for the reaction to start.

This is because, in all reactions, regardless of whether they are exothermic or endothermic, some of the chemical bonds in the reactants have to be broken before new chemical bonds in the products can be formed.

Think of chemical bonds as tiny springs. In order to get hydrogen to react with oxygen, the tiny springs joining the atoms in the molecules have to be stretched and broken. This takes energy, as you will know if you have ever tried to stretch and break an elastic band.

The product is water. This is created as new bonds form between oxygen atoms and hydrogen atoms. Bond formation releases energy – just like relaxing a spring. So what decides whether a chemical reaction is exothermic or endothermic? It is the difference between the energy taken in to break bonds and the energy given out as new bonds form.

The strength of the chemical bonds that break and form during a reaction determines the size of the overall energy change, and whether it is exothermic or endothermic.

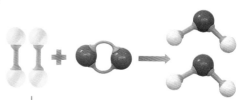

Two H—H bonds and one O=O bond break when hydrogen reacts with oxygen. The atoms recombine to make water as four new O—H bonds form.

Two H—H bonds and one O=O bond break when hydrogen reacts with oxygen. The atoms recombine to make water as four new O—H bonds form.

Questions

1 Classify these changes as exothermic or endothermic:
   a petrol burning
   b water turning to steam
   c water freezing
   d sodium hydroxide neutralising hydrochloric acid.

2 Turning 18 g ice into water at 0 °C requires 6.0 kJ of energy. Use an energy-level diagram to show this change.

More energy is given out when the bonds form than is taken in when the bonds break, and so the reaction overall is exothermic. The energy given out keeps the mixture hot enough for the reaction to continue.

Energy change calculations

The overall energy change that takes place during a chemical reaction can be calculated if the strength of all the chemical bonds in the reactants and the products are known. So, to calculate the energy change that takes place during the formation of steam from hydrogen and oxygen, the following data is needed. The units of **bond strength** are kilojoules (kJ).

$$H_2(g) + O_2(g) \longrightarrow 2H_2O(g)$$

Bond	Energy change for the formula masses (kJ)
H—H	434
O=O	498
O—H	464

Question

3 Hydrogen burns in chlorine.
   $$H_2(g) + Cl_2(g) \longrightarrow 2HCl(g)$$

   a Which bonds are broken during the reaction?
   b Which bonds are made during the reaction?
   c Use the data in the table to calculate the overall energy change for the reacting masses shown in the equation.

Bond	Energy change for the formula masses (kJ)
H—H	434
Cl—Cl	242
H—Cl	431

   d Is this reaction exothermic or endothermic?
   e Draw an energy-level diagram for the reaction.

From the energy-level diagram, we can see that during the reaction, two H—H and one O=O bonds are broken, and four O—H bonds are formed.

So the energy needed to break the bonds = 2 × (H—H) + 1 × (O=O)

$$= (2 \times 434) + 498 = 1366 \, kJ$$

The energy given out as the new bonds are formed = 4 × (O—H)

$$= 4 \times 464 = 1856 \, kJ$$

Overall energy change

= energy needed   –   energy given out as new
   to break bonds   bonds are formed

$$= 1366 - 1856 = -490 \, kJ$$

The negative sign shows that this reaction is exothermic. Remember that in an exothermic reaction, the products have less energy than the reactants.

Molecular collisions

In a mixture of hydrogen gas and oxygen gas the molecules are constantly colliding. Millions upon millions of collisions happen every second. If every collision led to a reaction, there would immediately be an explosive reaction.

Find out about

✔ **collisions between molecules**
✔ **activation energies**

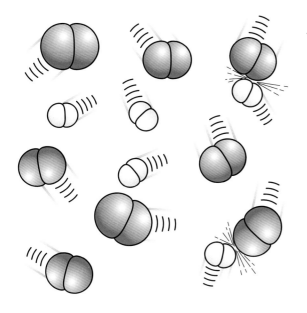

A mixture of hydrogen and oxygen molecules. The molecules that are colliding may react to form new molecules, but only if they have enough energy to start breaking bonds.

Activation energies

It is not enough for the hydrogen and oxygen atoms to collide. Bonds between atoms must break before new molecules can form. This needs energy. For every reaction, there is a certain minimum energy needed before the process can happen. This minimum energy is called the **activation energy**. It is like an energy hill that the reactants have to climb before a reaction will start. The higher the hill, the more difficult it is to get the reaction started.

The collisions between molecules have a range of energies. Head-on collisions between fast-moving particles are the most energetic. If the colliding molecules have enough energy, the collision is 'successful', and a reaction occurs.

Fast and slow reactions

The course of a reaction is like a high-jump competition. The bar is set at a height such that only a few competitors with enough energy can jump it and land safely the other side. The chemical equivalent is shown in the diagram on the next page.

Question

1 a Concentration is one of four factors that affect the rates of chemical reactions. Identify the three other factors that affect rates.
   b Give examples of measurements that chemists make to collect data to show how changes in concentration affect the rate of a reaction.
   c What is the theory that chemists use to explain how changes in concentration affect reaction rates?
   d Use this example to explain the difference between data and an explanation.

progress of the reaction

The activation energy for a reaction. The size of the activation energy is usually less than the energy needed to break all the bonds in the reactant molecules because new bonds start forming while old bonds are breaking, returning energy to the reaction mixture.

Key word

✓ **activation energy**

In this diagram for an exothermic reaction, the activation energy can be thought of as the height of the high-jump bar, and the products as the landing area.

If the high-jump bar is low, many competitors are successful. If it is high, the success rate is much less. In chemical reactions, if the activation energy is low, a high proportion of collisions have enough energy to break bonds, and the reaction is fast even at low temperatures.

Reactions in which the activation energy is high are very slow at room temperature, because only a small fraction of collisions have enough energy to cross the activation energy barrier. Heating the mixture to raise the temperature gives the molecules more energy. In the hot mixture, more molecules have enough energy to react when they collide.

Using a catalyst provides an alternative route for a chemical reaction with a lower activation energy. The energy of the reactions and the energy of the products does not change, but the activation energy is smaller. This means a higher proportion of collisions have enough energy to cross the activation energy barrier.

Questions

2 a Why is a spark or flame needed to light a Bunsen burner?
  b Why does the gas keep burning once it has been lit?

3 a Adding a catalyst to a reaction mixture means that the activation energy for the change is lower. Explain why this speeds up the reaction even if the temperature does not change.
  b Copy the energy-level diagram on this page and add in a new line to show the effect of adding a catalyst.

Chemistry in action

The explosives expert

All chemists secretly love controlled explosions, even if they do not admit it openly. The word 'control' is important. To be useful, explosions have to be controlled. Designing and understanding that control is part of Jackie Akhavan's job.

Two types of explosive

'There are two types of high explosive,' explains Jackie. 'Primary explosives have low activation energies, while secondary explosives have higher activation energies.'

Therefore it takes less energy to initiate primary explosives. They are more sensitive to an external stimulus such as friction or impact. This makes them more dangerous to handle than secondary explosives. Secondary explosives are more difficult to initiate.'

New explosives and detonators

Jackie is a polymer chemist. She has worked on making polymer-bonded secondary explosives. 'A polymer explosive can be manufactured into sheets that resemble plasticine. The explosive can be wrapped around an old bomb or a pipe, and a detonator pushed into the sheet. On initiation, the explosive cuts the metal into two pieces.'

Jackie has also been involved in new ways of providing the activation energy to make detonators start explosions. This used to be done using an electrical current, but these types of detonator are vulnerable to initiation by unwanted electromagnetic radiation from overhead pylons or thunderstorms. 'We've developed a new detonator that is secondary initiated with a laser pulsed through a fibre-optic cable. It is safe to handle and can't be set off by unwanted electromagnetic radiation.'

Jackie Akhavan works for Cranfield University as an explosives chemist. Her work has applications in quarrying and mining, bomb disposal, demolition, and fireworks.

Safety
Safety is always important in chemistry and is essential in Jackie's work: 'I am not allowed to detonate an explosion myself as I don't have the specific training – even though I understand the chemistry.' It is illegal as well as dangerous to carry out unauthorised experiments with explosive chemicals.

Topic 4: Reversible reactions and equilibria

Changing the temperature of tubes containing a mixture of nitrogen compounds determines which way and how far the reaction goes. When the tube is warmed, more of the brown NO_2 gas forms and the gas in the tube becomes darker. When the tube is cooled, more of the colourless N_2O_4 gas forms and the gas in the tube becomes paler.

Water and ice are at equilibrium at the melting point of the ice and the freezing point of the water. Molecules of ice are escaping into the water (melting) and molecules of water are being captured onto the surface of the ice (freezing).

There are many questions that scientists try to answer when explaining changes to chemicals and materials. This topic tackles the challenging questions 'Which way?' and 'How far?'

Which way?

'Which way?' is an important question for chemists to ask if they are going to control reactions to get the right results.

Cooks also have to understand how to control conditions to get the direction right, to make sure they produce a good meal. Otherwise they might serve up runny jelly or frozen smoked salmon. Not what the customer ordered!

How far?

'How far?' is an important question for anyone trying to get the maximum yield from a chemical reaction.

The study of carboxylic acids in Topic 2D shows that these are weak acids. They do ionise, but only to a slight extent.

Answering the question 'How far?' helps to explain why some acids, like organic acids, are weak, while other acids, such as the mineral acids, are strong.

Chemists have to be able to answer the questions 'Which way?' and 'How far?' in order to design pH-balanced shampoos and other toiletries. Controlling the pH of shampoos helps to protect the skin and eyes.

Find out about

✔ **reactions that go both ways**
✔ **factors affecting the direction of change**

Questions

1 a Write a symbol equation to show water turning into steam.
  b Write another equation to show steam condensing to water.
  c Write a third equation to show the changes in parts a and b as a single, reversible change.

2 The pioneering French chemist Lavoisier heated mercury in air and obtained the red solid mercury oxide. He also heated mercury oxide to form mercury and oxygen.
  a How can both of these statements be true?
  b Why should you not try to repeat the experiment?

3 a Write an equation to show the reversible reaction of carbon monoxide gas with steam to form carbon dioxide and hydrogen.
  b In your equation, what happens in the forward reaction?
  c In your equation, what happens in the backward reaction?

Some changes go only in one direction. For example, the reactions that happen to a raw egg in boiling water cannot be reversed by cooling the egg. To produce a soft-boiled egg, a cook has to check that it stays in the water for just the right amount of time. Other processes in the kitchen are easily reversed. A table jelly sets as it cools but becomes liquid again on warming. Chemists, like cooks, have to understand how to control conditions to get reactions to go far enough and in the right direction.

Burning methane in air is an example of an **irreversible change**. The gas burns to form carbon dioxide and water. It is then pretty well impossible to turn the products back into methane and oxygen.

Reversible changes of state

In contrast, melting and evaporating are familiar **reversible processes**. Heating turns water into steam, but water re-forms as steam condenses on cooling.

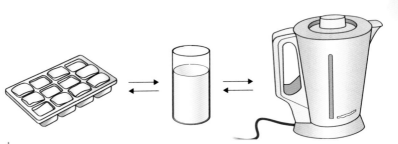

Two familiar reversible processes.

Heating turns ice into water:

$$H_2O(s) \longrightarrow H_2O(l)$$

Ice reforms if water cools to 0 °C or below:

$$H_2O(l) \longrightarrow H_2O(s)$$

Combining these two equations gives:

$$H_2O(s) \rightleftarrows H_2O(l)$$

Many chemical reactions are also reversible. A reversible reaction can go forwards or backwards depending on the conditions. The direction of change may vary with the temperature, pressure, or concentration of the chemicals.

Temperature and the direction of change

Heating decomposes blue copper sulfate crystals to give water and anhydrous copper sulfate, which is white:

$$CuSO_4.5H_2O(s) \longrightarrow CuSO_4(s) + 5H_2O(l)$$

Add water to the white powder after cooling, and it changes back into the hydrated form. As it does so it turns blue again and gets very hot:

$$CuSO_4(s) + 5H_2O(l) \longrightarrow CuSO_4.5H_2O(s)$$

Temperature also affects the direction of change in the formation of ammonium chloride. At room temperature ammonia gas and hydrogen chloride gas react to form a white solid, ammonium chloride:

$$NH_3(g) + HCl(g) \longrightarrow NH_4Cl(s)$$

Gentle heating decomposes ammonium chloride back into ammonia and hydrogen chloride:

$$NH_4Cl(s) \longrightarrow NH_3(g) + HCl(g)$$

Concentration and the direction of change

This equation describes the reaction between iron and steam:

$$3Fe(s) + 4H_2O(g) \longrightarrow Fe_3O_4(s) + 4H_2(g)$$

The change from left to right (from reactants to products) is the forward reaction. The change from right to left (from products to reactants) is the backward reaction.

The forward reaction is favoured if the concentration of steam is high and the concentration of hydrogen is low.

Key words
- irreversible change
- reversible process

Clouds of solid ammonium chloride form where ammonia and hydrogen chloride gases meet above concentrated solutions of the two compounds on glass stoppers.

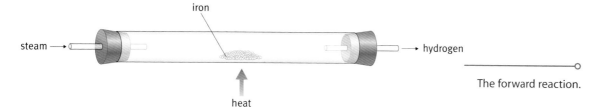

The forward reaction.

The backward reaction is favoured if the concentration of hydrogen is high and the concentration of steam is low:

$$Fe_3O_4(s) + 4H_2(g) \longrightarrow 3Fe(s) + 4H_2O(g)$$

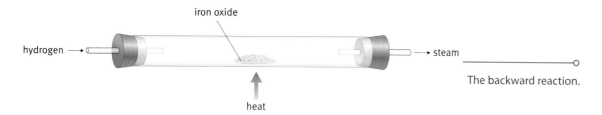

The backward reaction.

Find out about

- ✓ chemical equilibrium
- ✓ dynamic equilibrium
- ✓ strong and weak acids

Equilibrium

Reversible changes often reach a state of balance, or **equilibrium**. A solution of litmus in water at pH 7 is purple because it contains a mixture of the red and blue forms of the indicator. Similarly, melting ice and water are at equilibrium at 0 °C. At this temperature, the two states of water coexist with no tendency for all the ice to melt or all the water to freeze.

When reversible reactions are at equilibrium, neither the forward nor the backward reaction is complete. Reactants and products are present together and the reaction appears to have stopped. Reactions like this are at equilibrium. Chemists use a special symbol in equations for reactions at equilibrium: $\rightleftharpoons$

So at 0 °C,

$$H_2O(s) \rightleftharpoons H_2O(l)$$

The question 'How far?' asks where the equilibrium point is in a reaction. At equilibrium the reaction may be well to the right (mainly products), well to the left (mainly reactants), or at any point between these extremes.

Reaching an equilibrium state

A mixture of two solutions of iodine helps to explain what happens when a reversible process reaches a state of equilibrium.

Iodine is slightly soluble in water but much more soluble in a potassium iodide solution in water. The solution with aqueous potassium iodide is yellow–brown. Iodine is also soluble in organic solvents (such as hexane, a liquid alkane), in which it forms a violet solution. Aqueous potassium iodide and the organic solvent do not mix.

Approaching the equilibrium state starting with all the iodine in the liquid alkane.

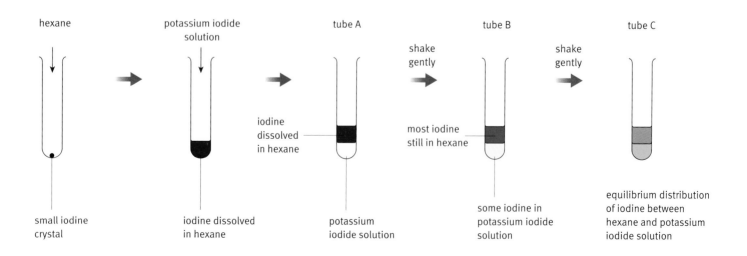

hexane	potassium iodide solution	tube A	tube B	tube C

iodine dissolved in hexane

shake gently

most iodine still in hexane

shake gently

equilibrium distribution of iodine between hexane and potassium iodide solution

small iodine crystal — iodine dissolved in hexane — potassium iodide solution — some iodine in potassium iodide solution

Graph 1 shows how the iodine concentrations in the two layers change with shaking. In tube C, the iodine is distributed between the organic and aqueous layers and there is no more change. In this tube there is an equilibrium:

$$I_2(\text{organic}) \rightleftharpoons I_2(\text{aq})$$

Graph 1

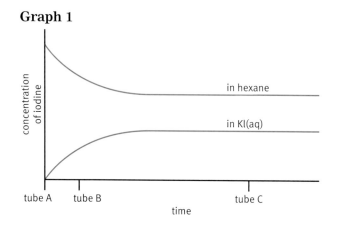

The change of concentration of iodine with time in the mixture, starting with all the iodine in the liquid alkane.

The same equilibrium can be reached starting with all the iodine dissolved in potassium iodide solution rather than hexane.

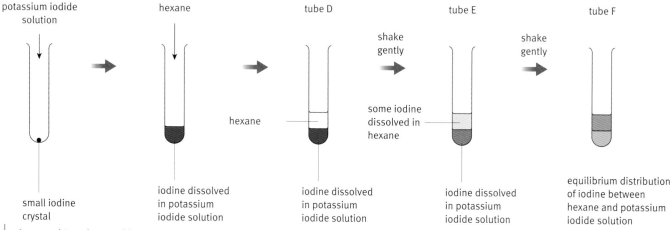

Approaching the equilibrium state starting with all the iodine in the aqueous layer.

Graph 2 shows how the iodine concentration in the two layers change with shaking.

Tube F looks just like tube C. Tube F is also at equilibrium: equilibrium mixtures in the two tubes are the same. This illustrates two important features of equilibrium processes:

- At equilibrium, the concentrations of reactants and products do not change.
- An equilibrium state can be approached from either the 'reactant side' or the 'product side' of a reaction.

Graph 2

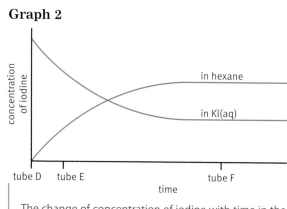

The change of concentration of iodine with time in the mixture, starting with all the iodine in the aqueous layer.

Dynamic equilibrium

The diagram below gives a picture of what happens to the iodine molecules if you shake a solution of iodine in an organic solvent with aqueous potassium iodide (see tube A on page 152).

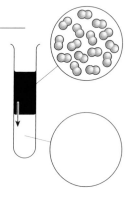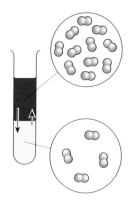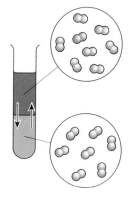

Iodine molecules reaching dynamic equilibrium between two solvents. The solvent molecules are far more numerous. They are not shown.

All the iodine starts in the upper, organic layer. At first, when the solution is shaken, movement is in one direction (the forward reaction) as some molecules move into the aqueous layer. There is nothing to stop some of these molecules moving back into the organic layer. This backward reaction starts slowly because the concentration in the aqueous layer is low. So to begin with, the overall effect is that iodine moves from the organic to the aqueous layer. This is because the forward reaction is faster than the backward reaction.

As the concentration in the organic layer falls, the rate of the forward reaction goes down. As the iodine concentration in the aqueous layer rises, the rate of the backward reaction goes up. There comes a point at which the two rates are equal. At this point both forward and backward reactions continue, but there is no overall change because each layer is gaining and losing iodine at the same rate. This is **dynamic equilibrium**.

Questions

1 Under what conditions are these in equilibrium:
   a water and ice?
   b water and steam?
   c salt crystals and a solution of salt in water?

2 a Why do iron and steam not reach an equilibrium state when they react as shown in the forward reaction diagram on page 151?
   b Suggest conditions in which a mixture of iron and steam would react to reach an equilibrium state.

   c Which chemicals would be present in an equilibrium mixture formed from iron and steam?

3 Explain in your own words what is meant by the term 'dynamic equilibrium'.

Ammonia

Ammonia, NH_3, is an extremely important and interesting bulk chemical. It is able to both sustain life through increased food production from the use of fertilisers, and to destroy life through its exploitation as an explosive.

Demand for explosives as well as fertilisers has led to the development of chemical processes to 'fix' nitrogen, to produce nitrogen compounds such as ammonia, nitric acids, and nitrates.

Nitrogen gas is all around us in the air but for a long time chemists did not know it was there because it is very unreactive. The low reactivity of nitrogen means that fixing it into nitrogen compounds is not easy.

Producing ammonia

At first, ammonia was obtained from the distillation of coal and the by-products of other industrial processes. However, in the early 20th century, German scientists Fritz Haber and Carl Bosch discovered and developed a new process for making ammonia. They reacted nitrogen from the air with hydrogen. They had achieved **nitrogen fixation**.

During the First World War, the **Haber process** became very important in Germany because ammonia was needed to make explosives. Before the war, explosives were made from nitrates imported from Chile. But the British navy blockade stopped imports and so a different production method was needed.

Today, ammonia is produced in more than 80 countries around the world. About 130 million tonnes of ammonia is produced annually. Over 50% is produced in developing countries such as China and India.

Fertilisers: benefits and costs

The production of ammonia has increased significantly over the past 60 years. More fertilisers are being produced to achieve the increase in food production that is needed to support the world's growing population.

The ability to fix nitrogen has affected society, and has also had an impact on the environment. The increased availability of fertilisers has led to changes in land use. Less land is needed to provide food for more people and so larger towns and cities can be supported. The fixing of nitrogen also affects the natural nitrogen cycle. For example, the overuse of fertilisers such as ammonium nitrate can lead to excess concentrations of nitrogen compounds being washed into the rivers by rain. This can lead to increased growth of algae, which upsets ecosystems.

Find out about

- ✔ **ammonia and the Haber process**
- ✔ **nitrogen fixation**
- ✔ **Le Chatelier's principle**
- ✔ **the influence of green chemistry on the ammonia industry**

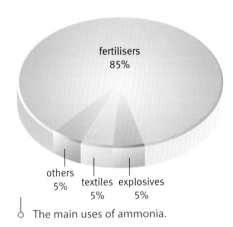

fertilisers 85%

others 5%   textiles 5%   explosives 5%

The main uses of ammonia.

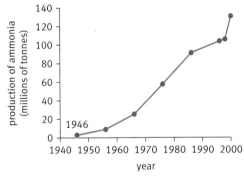

Worldwide production of ammonia. Since the 1960s, production of ammonia has grown at a rapid rate.

Questions

1. What is the main use of ammonia?

2. What impact do you think the Haber process had on the First World War?

The Haber process

The basis of the Haber process is a reversible reaction between nitrogen and hydrogen gas. Nitrogen is obtained from the air, and the main feedstock for hydrogen is natural gas or methane.

$$\text{nitrogen} + \text{hydrogen} \rightleftharpoons \text{ammonia}$$

$$N_2(g) + 3H_2(g) \rightleftharpoons 2NH_3(g)$$

The reactant gases are compressed to about 200 times atmospheric pressure, heated to about 450 °C, and passed over an iron catalyst. Haber and Bosch systematically tested about 20 000 catalysts, before finding the right one. Finally they found an iron ore containing traces of alkali metals that worked.

The atom economy for the Haber process is 100%, since there are no by-products. All the starting atoms end up in the ammonia molecules. But the yield is only 15%. The reaction yield is increased by recycling the unreacted nitrogen and hydrogen gas.

In this reversible reaction, there has to be a compromise between a high yield and a high rate of reaction. The process must be economically viable without using too much energy.

Fritz Haber won the 1918 Nobel Prize for his process. A number of French scientists refused their awards at the time in protest against Haber's war work for Germany.

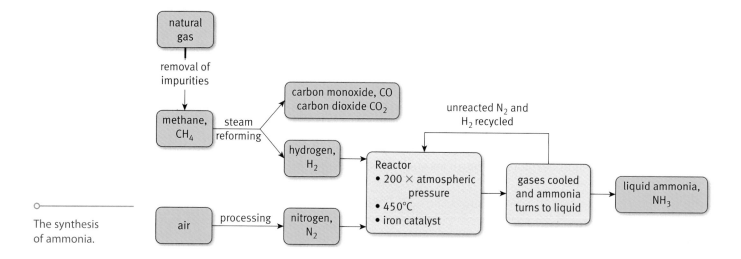

The synthesis of ammonia.

Getting the conditions right

Reversible reactions can reach a state of equilibrium. Changing the conditions of temperature and pressure can alter the proportions of reactants and products in a mixture of chemicals at equilibrium.

The effect on an equilibrium mixture of changing conditions can be predicted using **Le Chatelier's principle**. It states that:

'When the conditions change, an equilibrium mixture of chemicals responds in a way that tends to counteract the change.'

Effect of pressure

In the reaction to make ammonia there are four molecules of gas on the left-hand side of the equation but only two molecules of gas on the right. An equilibrium mixture of the gases responds to an increase in pressure by changing to make more ammonia and less nitrogen and hydrogen. This is what Le Chatelier's principle predicts because reducing the number of molecules tends to lower the pressure.

Effect of temperature

The reaction of nitrogen with hydrogen is exothermic. The reverse reaction, the decomposition of ammonia, is endothermic. Le Chatelier's principle predicts that if the temperature of an equilibrium mixture of the gases rises, then the equilibrium changes in a way that takes in energy because this tends to lower the temperature. So at a higher temperature there is less ammonia and more nitrogen and hydrogen in the equilibrium mixture.

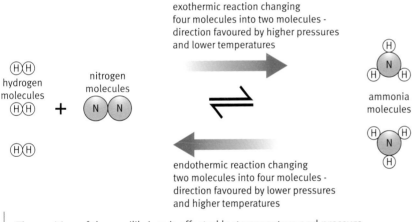

The position of the equilibrium is affected by temperature and pressure. The conditions used for the Haber process are a compromise to achieve a good yield at a reasonable cost.

Conditions in industry

In the Haber process the mixture of gases flows continuously through the reactor. The gases are only in contact with the catalyst for a short time. This means that the mixture never gets all the way to equilibrium.

The conditions chosen for the Haber process in industry are a compromise that balances chemical efficiency with cost and safety. The higher the pressure, the higher the yield of ammonia as the gas mixture approaches an equilibrium state. But high-pressure plants are expensive to build and run. They can also be more hazardous for plant operators. The lower the temperature, the higher the posssible yield of ammonia, but the reaction becomes too slow to be economic.

Questions

3   Suggest possible consequences for the environment of the large-scale manufacture of ammonia.

4   In the Haber process there is a continuous flow of reactants through the reactant chamber, rather than batches of reactants. Explain:
   a   why this has an advantage regarding the amount of reactants used
   b   how the ammonia is separated from the flow of reactants.

5   Suggest reasons why the Haber process can become uneconomic if the operators try to increase the yield of ammonia by:
   a   making the pressure even higher
   b   lowering the temperature.

6   At a pressure of 200 times atmospheric pressure and at 450 °C, an equilibrium mixture of nitrogen, hydrogen, and ammonia contains about 40% ammonia. In an industrial plant working under these conditions the mixture of gases leaving the reactor is only about 15% ammonia. Explain why.

Nitrogen fixation occurs in the nodules of legumes such as clover.

Nitrogen fixation: a really important process

Nitrogen fixation is the process by which nitrogen is taken from its unreactive molecular form (N_2) in the air and converted into nitrogen compounds such as ammonia, nitrate, and nitrogen dioxide.

The growth of all organisms depends on the availability of mineral nutrients, especially nitrogen. Nitrogen is often the **limiting factor** for growth in environments where there is suitable climate and availability of water to support life.

Most organisms are unable to use nitrogen directly from the atmosphere because its **triple bond** makes it so stable. Some organisms are able to fix nitrogen directly from the air. These include different types of bacteria found in the roots of some plants.

Nitrogen is also fixed during chemical reactions that occur in the air during lightning flashes, and by industrial methods such as the Haber process. A significant proportion of all nitrogen fixation is as a result of non-biological processes.

Type of fixation		N_2 fixed (10^{12} g per year, or 10^6 metric tons per year)
non-biological	industrial	about 50
	combustion	about 20
	lightning	about 10
	TOTAL	*about 80*
biological	agricultural land	about 90
	forest and non-agricultural land	about 50
	sea	about 35
	TOTAL	*about 175*

Data from various sources, compiled by DF Bezdicek & AC Kennedy, in *Microorganisms in Action* (eds JM Lynch & JE Hobbie). Blackwell Scientific Publications, 1998.

Fixing nitrogen by organisms

Nitrogen from the air is 'fixed' at normal temperatures and pressures by some organisms. The enzyme **nitrogenase** acts as a catalyst to allow the reaction to take place. Nitrogenase contains clusters of iron, molybdenum, and sulfur (Fe/Mo/S). Nitrogenase converts nitrogen to ammonia:

$$N_2 + 6H^+ + 6e^- \longrightarrow 2NH_3$$

The best known examples of nitrogen fixing in plants are the root nodules of legumes such as peas, beans, and clovers.

The nitrogen cycle

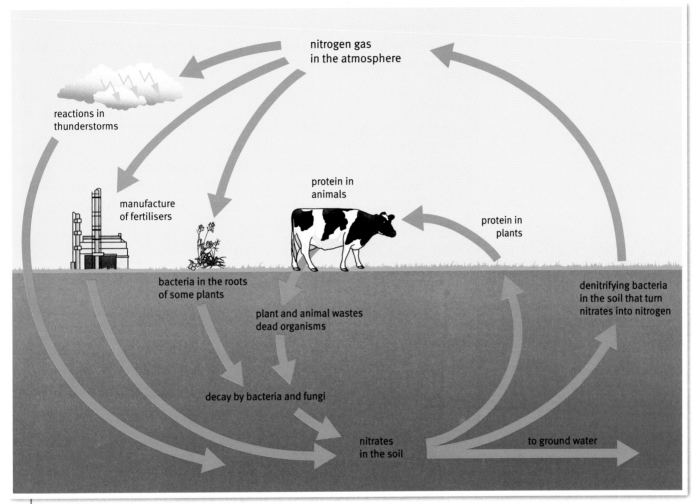

Natural and human activities contribute to the nitrogen cycle in the environment.

The **nitrogen cycle** consists of nitrogen fixation processes, which remove nitrogen from the atmosphere, and denitrification processes, which return nitrogen to the atmosphere.

Industrial nitrogen fixation has significantly increased the amount of fixed nitrogen, disrupting the natural nitrogen cycle. This has led to problems for the environment and human health. High levels of nitrates in rivers and lakes can cause the rapid growth of algae, which can damage ecosystems. Nitrates can also get into drinking water and be harmful to human health.

Restoring the balance in the nitrogen cycle is an important challenge for sustainable development.

Questions

7   Explain why nitrogen fixation is important.

8   Explain why plants can be short of nitrogen when there is so much nitrogen in the air.

9   The total amount of nitrogen fixed per year is about 255×10^{12} g. What percentage of this total is:
    a   non-biological?
    b   industrial?

10 Which process in the nitrogen cycle would need to increase in order to balance non-biological nitrogen fixation?

Can nitrogen fixation become any greener?

Environmental impact of the Haber process

The production of ammonia is a relatively clean process. The only emissions are carbon dioxide and oxides of nitrogen. In a modern plant, both of these gases can be recovered or reduced to very low levels.

Energy use

A major problem with the production of ammonia is the amount of energy needed. More than 1% of all the energy consumed in the world is used for ammonia production. The energy needed to operate the process has decreased over the past 100 years. This is mainly due to the use of more efficient catalysts that allow the reaction to take place at lower temperatures and pressures.

When the Haber process was introduced, the energy used in the production of ammonia dramatically decreased. Application of the principles of green chemistry in more recent years has ensured there is still a downward trend.

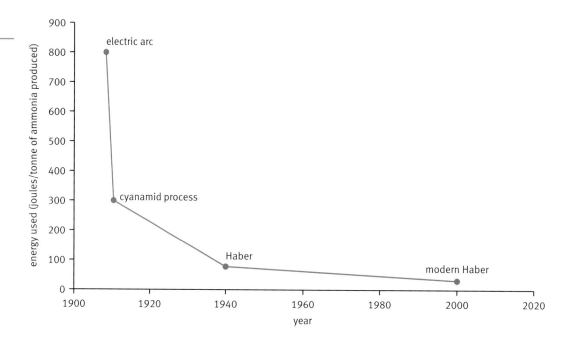

Future feedstocks

Currently, hydrogen is extracted from methane by steam reforming. If fossil fuel sources of methane run low, alternative ways of producing hydrogen will be needed. The electrolysis of water could become a major source of hydrogen. This feedstock would depend on a cheap and renewable electricity supply, such as hydroelectricity or solar power.

Using renewable energy sources for ammonia production would also reduce the amount of greenhouse gases entering the atmosphere.

New catalysts

The search for new catalysts is an important area of current research and development. The higher the catalytic activity of a catalyst, the more efficient it is at synthesising ammonia.

The Kellogg Advanced Ammonia Process (KAAP)

In 1992, M. W. Kellogg and the Ocelot Ammonia Company started ammonia production using a new ruthenium catalyst deposited on an active carbon support. With this catalyst a pressure of 40 times atmospheric pressure can be used for ammonia production, instead of 200 times atmospheric pressure.

The ruthenium catalyst is more active than the original iron-based catalyst and yields of about 20% ammonia can be achieved.

This new technology can be fitted to existing ammonia plants, saving money and energy. The newer catalyst is more expensive, but this is outweighed by other cost savings.

The Haldor–Topsøe catalyst

In 2000, scientists at a Danish company announced the discovery of a new commercially viable catalyst for the Haber reaction. The new compounds contain iron, molybdenum, nitrogen, nickel, and cobalt. They appear to be two or three times more efficient than the current commercial, iron-based catalysts at the same operating conditions.

The new catalysts are cheaper than the ruthenium-based catalysts of the KAAP. The same Haldor–Topsøe team have also produced new ruthenium catalysts that are 2.5 times more active than current ruthenium catalysts.

Learning from nature

Chemists are keen to learn about nitrogen fixation from nature. Studies of the enzyme nitrogenase have shown that it contains clusters of iron, molybdenum, and sulfur.

Chemists have been successful in making similar artificial clusters that show catalytic activity. By producing and using new catalysts that mimic natural enzymes, it may be possible in the future to produce ammonia at room temperature and pressure. This, of course, would lead to even lower energy use during production.

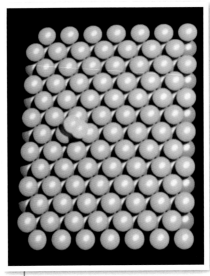

Model of a nitrogen molecule held on a layer of iron atoms at the surface of the usual iron catalyst for making ammonia. Nitrogen and hydrogen molecules react when brought together on the catalyst surface. Replacing iron atoms by ruthenium atoms gives a more effective catalyst.

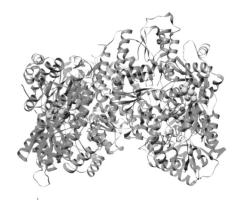

A computer-generated image representing the enzyme nitrogenase.

Questions

11 How are the principles of green chemistry influencing the development of industrial nitrogen fixation? (You may need to look back to page 155 to remind yourself about green chemistry.)

12 The enzyme nitrogenase fixes nitrogen at a pressure of 1 atmosphere, the KAAP ruthenium catalyst fixes nitrogen at 40 times atmospheric pressure, and the iron catalyst of the Haber process fixes nitrogen at 200 times atmospheric pressure.

Explain why processes that give a good yield at a lower pressure are more sustainable.

Topic 5: Chemical analysis

The LGC in Teddington is the UK's largest independent analytical laboratory. Its work covers food and agriculture, oil and chemicals, the environment, health care, life sciences, and law enforcement. It organises proficiency tests to check the performance of analytical laboratories.

The business of analysis

Analytical measurement is important. It is essential to ensure that the things we use in our everyday lives do us good and not harm. Over £7 billion is spent each year on chemical analysis in the UK.

Health and safety

The responsibility for health and safety in a laboratory is shared by everybody. Observing these regulations helps to keep accidents down to a minimum and the risk of injury low. Laboratories have their own health and safety regulations and codes of practice. Many have health and safety officers.

Looking after equipment

Equipment must be kept in good working condition. It has to be serviced regularly. Measuring instruments are checked at regular intervals.

Equipment should be cleaned properly after use and stored correctly. This is particularly important for fragile pieces of equipment such as glassware.

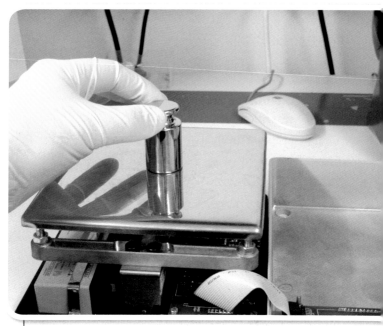

This electronic balance, like all equipment, must be maintained correctly and tested.

Accreditation

Analytical laboratories must show that they can do the job. Like the things tested in them, all laboratories must meet standards. Their standards are checked by the United Kingdom Accreditation Service (UKAS).

Analysts use proficiency tests to assess their work. Each laboratory receives identical samples to analyse. They send their results back to the organisers, who evaluate them. The laboratories are not named in the report, but results are coded so that a laboratory can recognise its results and see how well it has done.

International standards

There are international standards too. The International Olympic Committee (IOC), for example, accredits 27 laboratories to test blood and urine samples from athletes. The laboratories are all over the world and analyse 100 000 samples each year.

An analyst testing for stimulants in one of the laboratories accredited by the IOC.

Find out about

✓ **qualitative and quantitative methods**
✓ **steps in analysis**

Choosing an analytical method

The first step is to pick a suitable method of analysis. A **qualitative** method can be used if the aim is simply to find out the chemical composition of the specimen. However, if the aim is to find out how much of each component is present, then a **quantitative** approach is essential. Each step of the analysis must be carried out as set down in the agreed standard procedures.

Analysts study samples of blood and urine to look for the presence of banned substances in athletes and other sports people. This can include qualitative analysis to identify drugs, and quantitative analysis to find out how much of a banned substance there is in a sample.

Taking a sample

The analysis must be carried out on a **sample** that represents the bulk of the material under test. This can be hard to achieve with an uneven mixture of solids, such as soil, but much easier when the chemicals are evenly mixed in solution, as in urine.

Measuring out laboratory specimens for analysis

Analysts take a sample and measure out accurately known masses or volumes of the material for analysis. It is common to carry out the analysis with two or more samples in parallel to check on the reliability of the final result. These are **replicate samples**.

Dissolving the sample

Many analytical methods are based on a solution of the specimens. With the analysis of acids or alkalis that are soluble in water, this is not a problem. It can be much more difficult to prepare a solution when analysts are working with minerals, biological specimens, or polymers.

Questions

1 What is the difference between a quantitative and qualitative analytical method? Give an example of each method.

2 Suggest reasons why it is important for analysts to follow standard procedures.

3 Samples are often dissolved in a solvent. Why is this?

Measuring a property of the sample in solution

When determining quantities, analysts look for a property to measure that is proportional to the amount of chemical in the sample. With an acid, for example, the approach is to find the volume of alkali needed to neutralise it. The more acid present, the greater the volume of alkali needed to neutralise it.

Calculating a value from the measurements

An understanding of chemical theory allows analysts to convert their measurements to chemical quantities. Given the equation for the reaction, and the concentration of the alkali, it is possible to calculate the concentration of the acid from the volume of alkali needed to neutralise it.

Key words

 ✔ **qualitative**
 ✔ **quantitative**
 ✔ **sample**
 ✔ **replicate sample**

Analysts preparing blood and urine samples for analysis. They are using a type of spectrometer to measure the concentrations of iron and zinc in the samples.

Estimating the reliability of the results

Analysts have to state how much confidence they have in the accuracy of their results. Comparing the values obtained from two or three replicate samples helps.

Find out about

✓ **collecting, storing and analysing samples**

Analysts work with samples of materials. Rarely do they analyse the whole thing. How big the samples need to be depends on the analyses to be carried out.

Representative samples

The samples the analyst chooses must be **representative**. In other words, the samples should give an accurate picture of the material as a whole.

The composition of a homogeneous material is uniform throughout, like a milk chocolate bar.

The composition of a heterogeneous material varies throughout it, like a chocolate bar made in layers.

Scientists have to decide:
- how many samples, and how much of each, must be collected to ensure they are representative of the material
- how many times an analysis should be repeated on a sample to ensure results are reliable
- where, when, and how to collect the samples of the material
- how to store samples and transport them to the laboratory to prevent the samples from 'going off', becoming contaminated, or being tampered with.

Analysing water

Think about analysing water from two different sources. One is bottled water bought at a local supermarket. The other is from a local stream.

Key word
✓ **representative sample**

The bottled water is clear. There are no solids in suspension. It is likely to be tested for dissolved metal salts. The water is homogeneous, so only a single sample is needed. However, to check a batch of bottles, the analyst would take samples from a number of bottles. How much is needed depends on the test. There are no storage or transport problems. The bottle can be opened in the laboratory. This is a straightforward sampling problem.

Water from the stream may be cloudy. It may contain small creatures. It may be tested for a range of things, from the concentrations of dissolved chemicals to the number and variety of living organisms. Samples may vary from one part of the stream to another. They are likely to be heterogeneous. The time of year when samples are collected will have an effect on the water's composition. Also, samples need to be stored and taken back to the laboratory for analysis. This is a complex sampling problem that needs careful planning.

Water from a stream is likely to be heterogeneous. Samples may vary from one part of stream to another.

Bottled water is homogeneous. To test the water in the bottle, only a single sample is needed.

Questions

1 Why must the sample be representative of the bulk material under test?

2 Why is it good practice to take two or more samples?

3 Suggest how an analyst should go about sampling when faced with the following problems. In each case, identify the difficulties of taking representative samples. Suggest ways of overcoming the difficulties.
   a Measuring the concentration of chlorine disinfectant in a swimming pool.
   b Checking the purity of citric acid supplied to a food processor.
   c Detecting banned drugs in the urine of athletes.
   d Monitoring the quality of aspirin tablets made by a pharmaceutical company.
   e Determining the level of nitrates in a farmer's field.

4 Why is the way in which samples are stored important?

Collecting samples

A life of grime

All local authorities have Environmental Health Officers. Most of their work involves checking restaurants, cafés, and food shops, but they do many other things as well, including checking pollution levels. The photograph shows Ralph Haynes of Camden Council in London taking soil samples.

Ralph says: 'There is concern that chromium salts from an old metal plating factory nearby may have contaminated the soil. I am taking 1 kg samples and putting them in plastic containers. I am taking care to label it properly. There is a British Standard on labelling, you know: it's called BS5969.'

'I'm taking care to take a sample from where I can actually see the change in the soil. I'm also going to take a sample from where I can't see it. Then I'm going to take samples from anywhere I think people could be at risk – such as gardens where children play.'

'Soil samples will keep for a while, but I'm also going to take water samples, and these must get to the lab within a couple of days.'

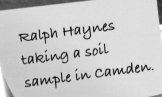

Ralph Haynes taking a soil sample in Camden.

Sporting samples

Sports men and women are often asked to provide urine samples to check if they have been taking drugs. Sometimes these cases hit the headlines, and allegations have been made in the past that urine samples have been tampered with.

The scientists who carry out the analysis at Kings College, London have to be sure that they have the right sample and that it has been correctly stored and labelled.

- First, the athlete has to produce the sample in front of a testing officer, who has to actually see the urine leaving the athlete's body and ensure there has been no cheating.
- With the testing officer watching, the athlete is allowed to pour the sample into two bottles. They seal the bottles themselves so that they feel assured no one else has tampered with them.
- The bottles are labelled with a unique code rather than the athlete's name, so the lab does not know the identity of the athlete. The bottles are sent to the lab by courier in secure polystyrene packaging.
- At the lab, one bottle is analysed immediately and the other stored in the freezer in case there is a query at a later date.

'We send the results to the Sports Council,' says Richard Caldwell, one of the analysts. 'It's someone at the Council who tallies up which bottle was collected from which person. It's quite interesting when we have a positive result and we find out from the press a few months later who it was!'

Labelled urine samples from athletes ready for testing.

Find out about

- ✔ principles of chromatography
- ✔ paper chromatography
- ✔ thin-layer chromatography

There are several types of **chromatography**. At the cheap-and-simple end is paper chromatography, which can be done with some blotting paper and a solvent. At the expensive end is gas chromatography, which involves high-precision instruments. All types of chromatography work on similar principles.

Chromatography can be used to:
- separate and identify the chemicals in a mixture
- check the purity of a chemical
- purify small samples of a chemical.

Principles of chromatography

Chromatography depends on the movement of a **mobile phase** through a fixed medium called the **stationary phase**. The analyst adds a small sample of the mixture to the stationary phase. As the mobile phase moves through the stationary phase, the chemicals in the sample move between the mobile and stationary phases.

For each chemical in the mixture there is a dynamic equilibrium as the molecules distribute themselves between the stationary phase and mobile phase. If a chemical in the mixture is attracted more to the mobile phase it moves faster. If a chemical is attracted more to the stationary phase it moves more slowly. Since each chemical in the mixture is attracted differently they move at different speeds and are separated.

- The chemical moves quickly if the position of equilibrium favours the mobile phase.
- The chemical moves slowly if the position of equilibrium favours the stationary phase.

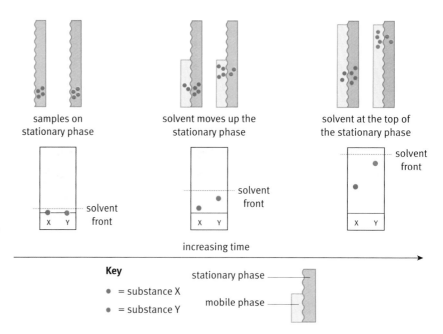

samples on stationary phase

solvent moves up the stationary phase

solvent at the top of the stationary phase

solvent front

X Y

solvent front

X Y

solvent front

X Y

increasing time

Key

● = substance X

● = substance Y

stationary phase

mobile phase

For each chemical there is a dynamic equilibrium for the molecules as they distribute themselves between the two phases. How quickly substances move through the stationary phase depends on the position of equilibrium.

Paper and thin-layer chromatography

Paper chromatography and thin-layer chromatography (TLC) are used to separate and identify substances in mixtures. The two techniques are very similar.

These techniques do not require expensive instrumentation, but are limited in their use. Paper chromatography is very rarely used. TLC is 'low technology', but it can be useful before moving on to more complex techniques. TLC is quick, cheap, and only requires small volumes of solution. A large number of samples can be run at once.

Organic reactions are monitored to find out at what point the reaction is complete, and purification can begin. TLC is simple and quick, so it is often used to monitor the progress of organic reactions and to check the purity of products.

Forensic laboratories may use TLC to analyse dyes extracted from fibres and when testing for controlled drugs, cannabis in particular.

Stationary and mobile phases

In paper chromatography the stationary phase is the paper, which does not move. In TLC the stationary phase is an absorbent solid supported on a glass plate or stiff plastic sheet.

In both paper chromatography and TLC, the mobile phase is a solvent, which may be one liquid or a mixture of liquids. Substances are more soluble in some solvents than others. For example, some substances dissolve well in water, while others are more soluble in petrol-like, hydrocarbon solvents. With the right choice of solvent, it becomes possible to separate complex mixtures.

Chemists call solutions in water **aqueous** solutions. The term **non-aqueous** describes solvents with no water in them.

Questions

1 Describe in your own words how chromatography works.

2 Name two substances that dissolve better in water than in hydrocarbon (or other non-aqueous) solvents.

Key words
- reference materials
- chromatogram
- solvent front
- locating agent
- retardation factor (R_f)

Chromatography plates must be spotted carefully. Small, concentrated spots are needed. Their starting position should be marked.

Preparing the paper or plate

The sample is dissolved in a solvent. This solvent is not usually the same as the mobile phase.

A small drop of the solution is put on the paper, or TLC plate, and allowed to dry, leaving a small 'spot' of the mixture.

If the solution is dilute, further drops are put in the same place. Each is left to dry before the next is added. This produces a small spot with enough material to analyse. The separation is likely to be poor if the spot spreads too much.

One way of identifying the chemicals in the sample is to add separate spots of solutions of substances suspected of being present in the unknown mixture. These are called **reference materials**.

Running the chromatogram

The analyst adds the chosen solvent (the mobile phase) to a chromatography tank and covers it with a lid. After the tank has stood for a while, the atmosphere inside becomes saturated with solvent vapour.

The next step is to place the prepared paper or TLC plate in the tank, checking that the spots are above the level of the solvent.

The solvent immediately starts to rise up the paper or plate. As the solvent rises, it carries the dissolved substances through the stationary phase. Covering the tank ensures that the solvent does not evaporate.

The chromatography paper, or TLC plate, is taken from the tank when the solvent gets near the top. The analyst then marks the position of the **solvent front**.

A chromatography tank. The sample spots on the paper or plate must be above the level of the solvent.

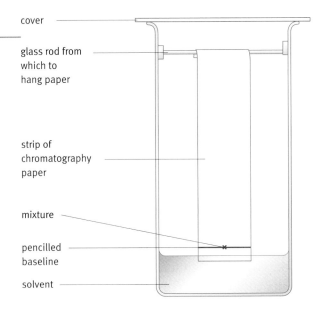

cover

glass rod from which to hang paper

strip of chromatography paper

mixture

pencilled baseline

solvent

Locating substances

There is no difficulty marking the positions of coloured substances. All the analyst has to do is outline the spots in pencil and mark their centres before the colour fades.

There are two ways to locate colourless substances:
- Develop the chromatogram by spraying it with **a locating agent** that reacts with the substances to form coloured compounds.
- Use an ultraviolet lamp with TLC plates that contain fluorescers, so that the spots appear violet in UV light.

Interpreting chromatograms

Chemicals may be identified by comparing spots with those from standard reference materials.

A chemical may also be identified by its **retardation factor** (R_f). This does not change, provided the same conditions are used. It is calculated, using the following formula, by measuring the distance travelled by the substance:

$$R_f = \frac{\text{distance moved by chemical}}{\text{distance moved by solvent}} = \frac{y}{x}$$

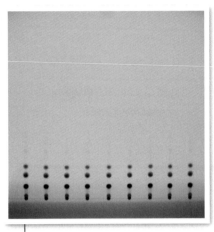

'Invisible' spots can often be seen under a UV lamp.

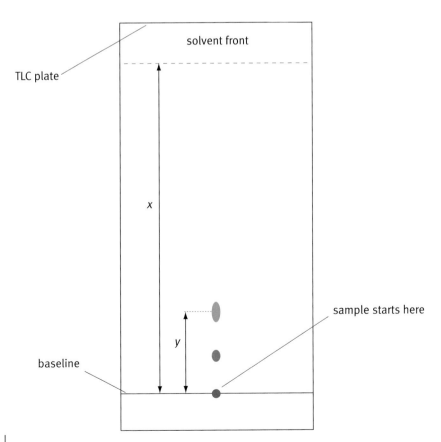

Retardation factors (R_f) can be calculated by measuring the distances travelled by chemicals in the sample and by the solvent.

Questions

3 Why is it sometimes necessary to 'develop' a chromatogram? How can this be done?

4 Why is it sometimes useful to use thin-layer chromatography plates that have been impregnated with fluorescers?

5 What are reference materials used for?

6 Paper chromatography is used to separate a mixture of a red and a blue chemical. The blue compound is more soluble in water while the red chemical is more soluble in the non-aqueous chromatography solvent. Sketch a diagram to show the chromatogram you would expect to form.

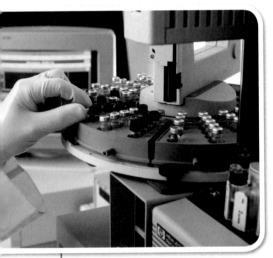

This scientist uses GC to check the quality of water from a river.

Gas chromatography (GC) is used to separate complex mixtures. The technique separates mixtures much better than paper or thin-layer chromatography (TLC).

This technique is also more sensitive than paper chromatography or TLC, which means it can detect small quantities of compounds. That is why it is usually preferred to paper chromatography or TLC. The technique not only identifies the chemicals in a mixture but also can measure how much of each is present.

Understanding the limits of detection for a technique can be very important, otherwise an analyst can report that a contaminant is absent when it is in fact present, but at too low a concentration to be detected. Careful research has been necessary to find out the detection limits for such chemicals as pesticide residues in food.

Stationary and mobile phases

The principles of GC are the same as for paper chromatography and TLC. A mobile phase carries a mixture of compounds through a stationary phase. Some compounds are carried through more slowly than others. This is because they have different boiling points or a greater attraction for the stationary phase. Because they travel at different speeds, the compounds can be separated and identified.

The mobile phase is a gas such as helium. This is the **carrier gas**.

The stationary phase is a thin film of a liquid on the surface of a powdered solid. The stationary phase is packed into a sealed tube,

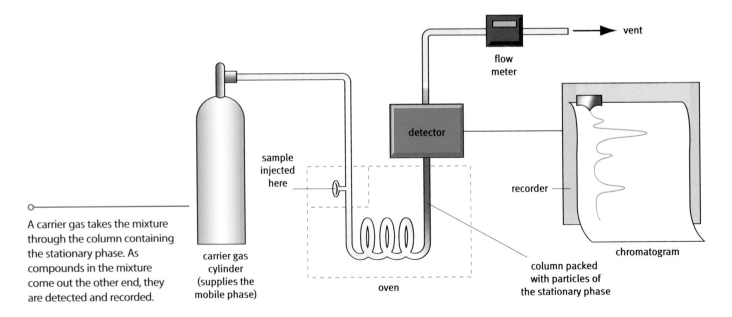

A carrier gas takes the mixture through the column containing the stationary phase. As compounds in the mixture come out the other end, they are detected and recorded.

which is the column. The column is long and thin. Some columns are 25 m long but only 0.25 mm in diameter.

Only very small samples are needed. The analyst uses a syringe to inject a tiny quantity of the sample into the column. Samples are generally gases or liquids.

The column is coiled inside an oven, which controls the temperature of the column. This means that it is possible to analyse solids if they can be injected in solution and then turn to a vapour at the temperature of the column.

Separation and detection

Once the column is at the right temperature, the carrier gas is turned on. Its pressure is adjusted to get the correct flow rate through the column. The analyst injects the sample at the start of the column where it enters the oven. The chemicals in the sample turn to gases and mix with the carrier gas. The gases pass through the column.

In time, the chemicals from the sample emerge from the column and pass into a detector. The chemicals can be identified using mixtures of known composition.

Interpreting chromatograms

The detector sends a signal to a recorder or computer when a compound appears. A series of peaks, one for each compound in the mixture, make up the chromatogram. The position of a peak is a record of how long the compound took to pass through the column. This is its **retention time**. The height of the peak indicates how much of the compound is present.

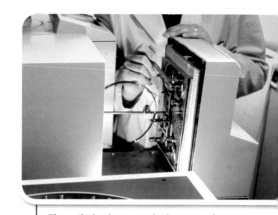

The coiled column inside the oven of a GC instrument. The detector is connected to a computer and the chromatogram appears on the screen.

Questions

1 Look at the chromatogram on this page.
   a How many components have been separated?
   b Estimate the retention time of each component.
   c Which component was present in the largest quantity? Which one was present in the smallest quantity?

2 Why is it important to understand the detection limits of a technique?

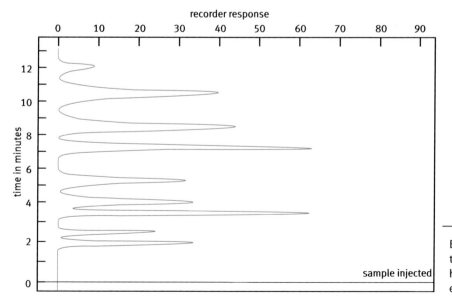

Each compound in the mixture appears as a peak in the chromatogram. The time it takes to get through helps the scientist to identify it. The height of the peak enables the scientists to say how much there is.

Chemical archaeology

Analytical chemist Anna Mukherjee carrying out a GC analysis at the University of Bristol.

Richard Evershed is a professor at Bristol University. He has used gas chromatography all his career: 'During my PhD, I used gas chromatography to study the chemical messages insects use to communicate. After my PhD, I moved to the University of Bristol, where I used the same technique to look at the organic chemicals preserved in ancient rocks originating from organisms that lived many millions of years ago.'

Ancient traces

Richard recognised that gas chromatography could also be used to identify the remains of fats, waxes, and resins preserved at archaeological sites.

He has used this technique to analyse organic residues trapped in the walls of very old cooking pots to find out what people ate in the past. He uses gas chromatography to separate the mixture of fats and waxes in the residues. By gradually increasing the temperature of the gas chromatography column, he is able to separate compounds with different boiling points. When the temperature reaches the boiling point of a chemical, it turns into gas and is carried by the carrier gas to a flame, where it burns to produce an electrical signal. The separated compounds appear as a series of peaks on the chromatogram.

Richard says: 'We made a real breakthrough when we found that we could identify traces of butter in 6000-year-old pottery from prehistoric Britain. This showed us that milking animals is a very ancient practice.'

Analysis of the chemicals absorbed into old pots gives clues to the food that our ancestors cooked.

A whiff of cabbage

Traces of cooked cabbage can survive for a long time. Richard found this to be true when investigating a set of pots dating from late Saxon times. The pots are over a thousand years old. 'I've found traces of cabbage preserved in the pot wall. It's the natural wax you can see on the surface of the cabbage, which is released during boiling. We can extract the same waxes from modern supermarket cabbages, and the gas chromatography traces look pretty much identical.'

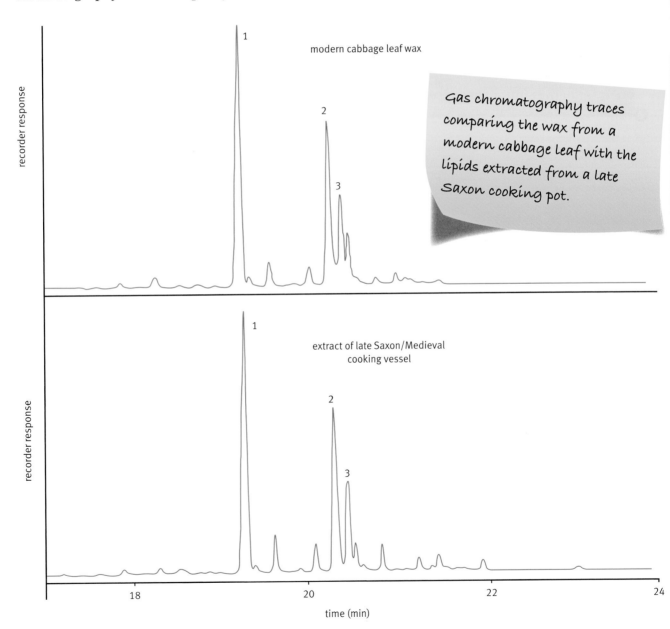

Gas chromatography traces comparing the wax from a modern cabbage leaf with the lipids extracted from a late Saxon cooking pot.

Find out about

- ✓ acid–alkali titrations
- ✓ standard solutions

Key words

- ✓ titration
- ✓ pipette
- ✓ end point
- ✓ burette
- ✓ standard solution

A **titration** is a quantitative technique based on measuring the volumes of solutions that react with each other. Chemists use titrations to measure concentrations and to investigate the quantities of chemicals involved in reactions. Titrations are widely used because they are quick, convenient, accurate, and easy to automate.

Titration procedure

In a typical titration, an analyst uses a **pipette** (or a burette) to transfer a fixed volume of liquid to a flask. In an acid–base titration to find the concentration of an acid, this might be 20 cm³ of the solution of acid.

Next, the analyst adds one or two drops of a coloured indicator. The indicator is chosen to change colour sharply when exactly the right amount of alkali has been added to react with all the acid. The indicator works because there is a very sharp change of pH at this point, which is called the **end point.**

wear eye protection

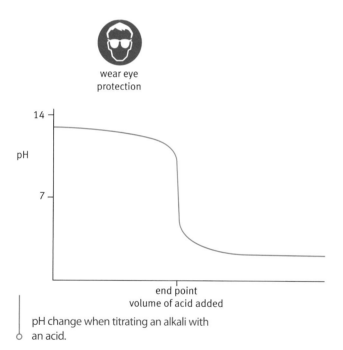

pH change when titrating an alkali with an acid.

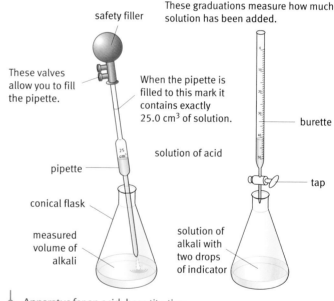

Apparatus for an acid–base titration.

The analyst has a **burette** ready containing a solution of acid with a concentration that is known accurately. Then the analyst runs the acid from a burette into the alkali a little at a time until the indicator changes colour. Reading the burette scale before and after the titration shows the volume of alkali added.

It is common to do a rough titration first to get an idea where the end point lies, and then to repeat the titration more carefully, adding the acid drop by drop near the end point. The analyst repeats the titration two or three times as necessary to achieve consistent values for the volume of alkali added.

Remember

1 litre = 1 dm³ = 1000 cm³

$$\text{concentration} \atop (\text{g/dm}^3) = \frac{\text{mass (g)}}{\text{volume (cm}^3)}$$

Preparing accurate solutions

The accuracy of a titration can be no better than the accuracy of the solutions used to make the measurements. If chemists know the concentration of a solution accurately, they call it a **standard solution**, because it can be used in analysis to measure the concentrations of other solutions.

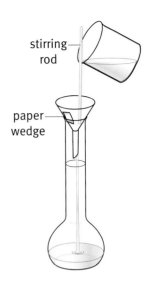
stirring rod
paper wedge

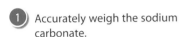
stirring rod

① Accurately weigh the sodium carbonate.

② Dissolve the solute in a small amount of solvent, warming it if necessary.

③ Transfer the sodium carbonate solution to a graduated flask.

wash bottle

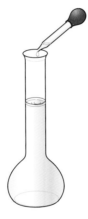

④ Rinse all the solution into the flask with more solvent.

⑤ Add solvent drop by drop to make up the volume to the mark on the flask

⑥ Stopper and shake the flask.

↧ The procedure for making up a standard solution with an accurately known concentration.

Questions

1 What is the concentration of these solutions in grams per litre (g/dm³):

  a a solution of sodium carbonate made by dissolving 4.0 g of the solid in water and making the volume up to 500 cm³ in a graduated flask?

  b a solution of citric acid made by dissolving 2.25 g of the solid in water and making the volume up to 250 cm³ in a graduated flask?

2 What is the mass of solute in these samples of solutions?

  a A 10 cm³ sample of a solution of silver nitrate with a concentration of 2.55 g/dm³.

  b A 25 cm³ sample of a solution of sodium hydroxide with a concentration of 4.40 g/dm³.

Titrating acids in food and drink

Rachel measures the mass of a sample of blueberry juice.

Rachel Woods is the quality control manager for Danisco, a company that manufactures ingredients for food and soft drinks. Acids are very important in her work. Some acids occur naturally in the fresh ingredients; others are added as preservatives or to improve flavour.

The quantity of acid in any food or drink is important. Think of a soft drink – too much acid and it tastes sour; too little and it might be insipid. With just the right amount it tastes refreshing and fruity, and just the right amount of acid makes a drink seem more thirst-quenching and satisfying.

Automated titrations

One of the most important acids in Rachel's work is citric acid. She regularly has to test ingredients and finished products to check their citric acid content. She uses a titration machine. Here she is testing a sample of blueberry juice. First, using a dropping pipette, she takes a sample of the juice from the container into a beaker. It is the same beaker in which she will carry out the titration, which makes things so much quicker and simpler. She has weighed exactly 4.30 grams.

She adds boiled water to the juice to bring it up to the $300 \, cm^3$ mark. She does not use water straight from the tap as it has dissolved calcium hydrogencarbonate in it. Boiling the water removes this. For many titrations distilled water is necessary, but for these food samples ordinary boiled water is fine.

All Rachel has to do is put the pH probe and tube from the burette into the beaker and put it on the stand.

Rachel sets up her automatic titration machine. The burette tube in the middle fills from the reservoir of alkali on the right.

It has a magnetic stirrer, so she does not even have to swirl the flask. She presses a button, and the burette tube starts to fill from the reservoir bottle. The concentration of her sodium hydroxide, NaOH, solution is $8.0\,g/dm^3$.

When the burette is full, it slowly pumps the NaOH solution into the beaker. Because blueberry juice contains a natural indicator, you can see a colour change from purply–red to dark-blue–grey as it reaches the end point.

The exact point is not easy to see, but that does not matter, as the machine works by measuring the pH of the solution. It measures the quantity of NaOH required to bring the blueberry juice up to a pH of 8.3. Not that Rachel has to measure that volume – far from it: all she has to do is look at the readout on the screen. It shows a little graph and calculates the percentage of citric acid in the juice. This sample is 6.08% citric acid, which is exactly what it should be, and using the machine, Rachel can test as many samples as she needs very quickly and simply.

The beaker with the blueberry juice in the titration machine. A magnetic stirrer mixes the juice with the alkali added by the burette. The probe dipping into the solution measures the pH.

The hands-on method

Not all of Rachel's titrations can be done on the machine. Here she is using the traditional method to test the concentration of a sample of butanoic acid.

Butanoic acid (C_3H_7COOH) is an important part of butter and cheese flavours, so it is used in things like cheese-and-onion crisps, and some margarines. Used in this way, butanoic acid is great, but unfortunately in large quantities it smells terrible.

It is not Rachel's favourite titration, but she is so used to it she manages to keep smiling. Butanoic acid is associated with fats, so it is not soluble in water. Instead it is dissolved in ethanol.

Rachel fills the burette with the acid solution. She keeps her eye level with the zero mark on the burette. She wants the meniscus to sit exactly on the line.

The next job is to pipette exactly 20.0 cm³ of warm potassium hydroxide, KOH, solution into a clean flask. The concentration of the alkali is accurately known. Again Rachel keeps her eye level with the mark on the pipette as she uses the valve on the filler to adjust the level. A tiny drop of solution is always left in the end of the pipette, but Rachel resists the temptation to blow it out. As she adds a few drops of the indicator, phenolphthalein, the alkaline solution turns a stunning shade of shocking pink.

Now the titration begins. With her right hand she swirls the flask, and with her left hand she gently releases the tap on the burette to let 1 cm³ of the acid into the flask at a time. She keeps her eye on the flask all the time. Because she does this titration so regularly, she knows when the end point is coming up. It happens suddenly. First the solution in the centre of the flask goes colourless, then the pink colour disappears altogether. At that precise point Rachel closes the tap on the burette and takes a note of the reading: 40.2 cm³. She repeats the titration at least once more.

Rachel uses a pipette to run a measured volume of the standard potassium hydroxide into a titration flask.

Interpreting the results

Relative formula masses: $C_3H_7COOH = 88$ and $KOH = 56$

The equation for the reaction in the titration flask is

$$C_3H_7COOH + KOH \longrightarrow C_3H_7COOK + H_2O$$
$$88\,g \qquad 56\,g$$

Concentration of the potassium hydroxide solution = 11.2 g/dm³

In 20.0 cm³ of the KOH solution there is

$$\frac{20}{1000} \times 11.2\,g = 0.224\,g$$

If 56 g KOH reacts with 88 g of the acid, then 0.224 g reacts with

$$\frac{0.224}{56} \times 88\,g = 0.352\,g \text{ butanoic acid}$$

This amount of acid was present in 40.0 cm³ = 0.040 dm³ of butanoic acid solution. So the concentration of the butanoic acid solution is

$$\frac{0.352\,g}{0.040\,dm^3} = 8.80\,g/dm^3$$

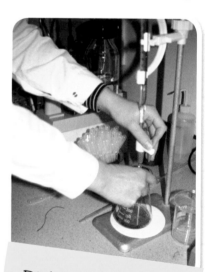

Rachel runs the butanoic acid from the burette into the flask during the titration.

Scientists need to be able to make sense of analyses and tests. This means that they have to be able to interpret their significance and say what they show. Scientists must also judge how confident they are about the accuracy of results.

Measurement uncertainty

All measurements have an uncertainty. This means that scientists usually give results within a range. For example, they may analyse the purity of a drug and give the answer as 99.1 ± 0.2%. This means that the average value obtained from analyses of several samples was 99.1%. The precise value is uncertain. The scientists are confident that the true value lies between 98.9% and 99.3%. To show this, they quote the results as 99.1 (the mean) ± 0.2%.

Errors of measurement are not mistakes. Mistakes are failures by the operator and include such things as forgetting to fill a burette tip with the solution, or taking readings from a sensitive balance in a draught. Mistakes of this kind lead to outliers in results, and should be avoided by people doing practical work.

Types of uncertainty

There are two general sources of **measurement uncertainty**: systematic errors and random errors.

Find out about

✔ **systematic and random sources of uncertainty**
✔ **accuracy and precision**

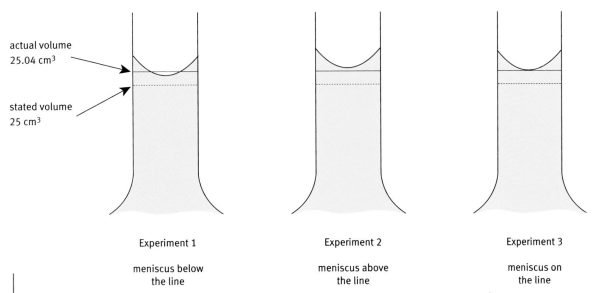

actual volume
25.04 cm³

stated volume
25 cm³

Experiment 1	Experiment 2	Experiment 3
meniscus below the line	meniscus above the line	meniscus on the line

Systematic and random errors in the use of a pipette. The manufacturing tolerance for a 25-cm³ grade B pipette is ±0.06 cm³. This can give rise to a systematic error. Every time an analyst uses the pipette, the meniscus is aligned slightly differently with the graduation mark. This gives rise to random error.

Random error means that the same measurement repeated several times gives different values. This can happen, for example, when making judgements about the colour change at an end point or when estimating the reading from a burette scale.

Systematic error means that the same measurement repeated several times gives values that are consistently higher than the true value, or consistently lower. This can result from incorrectly calibrated measuring instruments, or from making measurements, at a consistent, but wrong, temperature.

It is difficult to determine accurately the volume of liquid in a burette if the meniscus lies between two graduation marks.

The material used to prepare a standard solution may not be 100% pure.

A 250 cm^3 volumetric flask may actually contain 250.3 cm^3 when filled to the calibration mark owing to permitted variation in the manufacture of the flask.

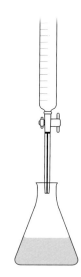

It is difficult to make an exact judgement of the end point of a titration (the exact point at which the colour of the indicator changes).

The burette is calibrated by the manufacturer for use at 20 °C. When it is used in the laboratory the temperature is 23 °C. This difference in temperature will cause a small difference in the actual volume of liquid in the burette when it is filled to a calibration mark.

The display on a laboratory balance will only show the mass to a certain number of decimal places.

Sources of uncertainty in analysis by titration.

An analysis or test is often repeated to give a number of measured values, which are then averaged to produce the result.

- **Accuracy** describes how close this result is to the true or 'actual' value.
- **Precision** is a measure of the spread of measured values. A big spread indicates a greater uncertainty than a small spread.

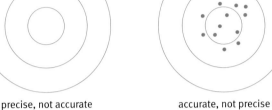
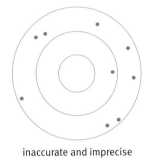
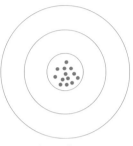

precise, not accurate   accurate, not precise   inaccurate and imprecise   precise and accurate

Accuracy and precision are not the same thing.

Conclusions

The conclusions scientists draw from their work must be valid and justifiable.

- Valid means that the techniques and procedures used were suitable for what was being analysed or tested.
- Justifiable means that conclusions reached are backed by sound, reliable evidence.

Questions

1 An analyst determined the percentage of potassium in three brands of plant fertiliser for house plants by making five measurements for each brand.

These are the results of measuring the percentage by mass of potassium in three brands:
A 4.93, 4.89, 4.71, 4.81, 4.74
B 6.76, 7.91, 6.94, 6.71, 6.86
C 4.72, 4.76, 4.68, 4.70, 4.69
  a Determine the mean and range for each brand.
  b What conclusions can you draw about the three brands?

2 Why would the results be inaccurate if an analyst used hot solutions in graduated glassware?

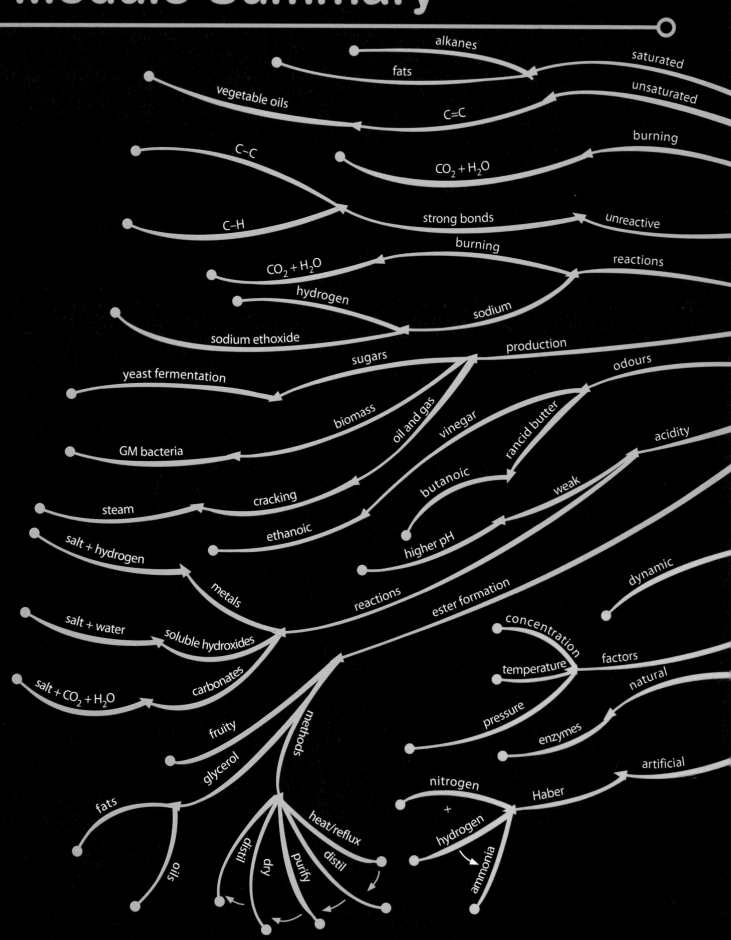

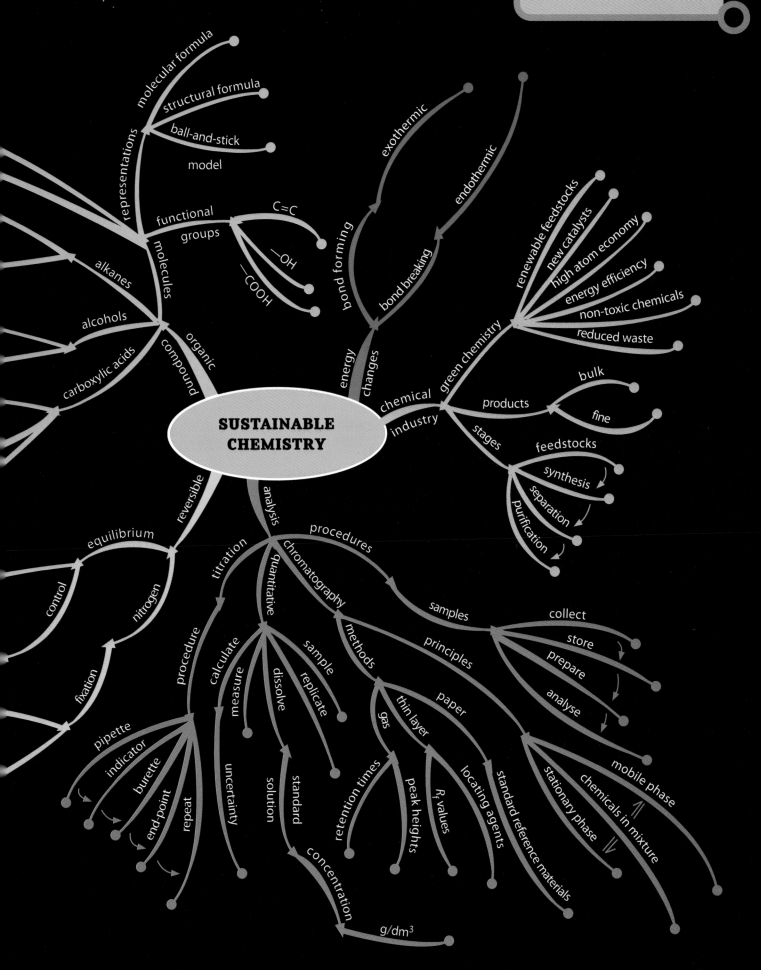

SUSTAINABLE CHEMISTRY

representations
- molecular formula
- structural formula
- ball-and-stick
- model

functional groups
- C=C
- —OH
- —COOH

molecules

organic compound
- alkanes
- alcohols
- carboxylic acids

reversible
- equilibrium
  - control
  - nitrogen
  - fixation

energy changes
- bond forming
  - exothermic
- bond breaking
  - endothermic

chemical industry
- green chemistry
  - renewable feedstocks
  - new catalysts
  - high atom economy
  - energy efficiency
  - non-toxic chemicals
  - reduced waste
- products
  - bulk
  - fine
- stages
  - feedstocks
  - synthesis
  - separation
  - purification

analysis
- procedures
- titration
- chromatography
- quantitative

quantitative
- calculate
- measure
- sample
- dissolve
- replicate

procedure
- pipette
- indicator
- burette
- end-point
- repeat
- uncertainty
- solution
- standard
- concentration
  - g/dm³

chromatography
- methods
  - gas
  - thin layer
  - paper
- principles
- samples
  - collect
  - store
  - prepare
  - analyse
- retention times
- peak heights
- R_f values
- locating agents
- standard reference materials
- stationary phase
- mobile phase
- chemicals in mixture

Science Explanations

Green chemistry

The chemical industry is reinventing many of the processes used to convert raw materials into useful products.

You should know:

- how to distinguish between bulk and fine chemicals produced by the chemical industry
- the importance of research to develop new products and processes
- the importance of regulations to control the chemical industry and the uses of its products
- the main stages in the industrial production of useful chemicals
- how the principles of green chemistry help to make the industry more sustainable
- why catalysts are important and how they affect the rates of reactions
- the contribution that enzymes can make to green chemistry
- how to use balanced symbol equations to calculate theoretical yields and atom economies.

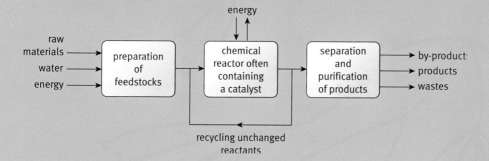

Alcohols, carboxylic acids, and esters

Chemists make sense of this great variety of compounds by classifying them according to their functional groups.

You should know:

- how to translate between molecular, structural, and ball-and-stick representations of simple molecules
- the names, formulae, and structures of the simpler examples of alkanes, alcohols, and carboxylic acids

- how to write and interpret symbol equations for organic reactions
- that the characteristic properties of organic molecules arise from their functional groups
- the functional groups of alcohols and carboxylic acids
- the difference between saturated and unsaturated compounds
- that some organic compounds, such as carboxylic acids and esters, have distinctive odours and tastes
- what happens when alkanes burn in air and why alkanes are unreactive towards aqueous reagents
- how the properties of ethanol compare with the properties of water and with those of alkanes
- the reactions of alcohols with air and with sodium
- that ethanol can be made by fermentation and is then concentrated by distillation
- which factors control the optimum conditions for making ethanol by fermentation

- the conditions that favour the use of genetically modified bacteria to make ethanol from biomass
- that there is a synthetic route from oil or natural gas to ethanol, and be able to evaluate the sustainability of this route compared with processes based on fermentation
- that carboxylic acids react like other acids with metals, alkalis, and carbonates
- why carboxylic acids are described as weak acids
- the conditions under which carboxylic acids and alcohols form esters
- the techniques used, and the reasons for each stage, in the procedure for making a simple ester from a carboxylic acid and an alcohol
- how fats are related to glycerol and fatty acids, and how fats differ from vegetable oils
- why living organisms make fats
- examples of the uses of some organic compounds such as methanol, ethanol, ethanoic acid, and simple esters.

Energy changes in chemistry

Chemists explain exothermic and endothermic reactions in terms of the energy changes when chemical bonds break and form.

You should know:

- how to draw and interpret energy-level diagrams for exothermic and endothermic reactions
- that energy is needed to break chemical bonds, and that energy is given out as bonds form
- how to use data on the energy needed to break bonds to determine the overall energy change for a reaction between simple molecules
- what is meant by the term activation energy.

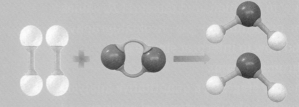

Two H—H bonds and one O═O bond break when hydrogen reacts with oxygen. The atoms recombine to make water as four new O—H bonds form.

Many important processes are reversible and reach a state of equilibrium, which can be controlled by varying the conditions of concentration, temperature, and pressure.

You should know:

- that reversible reactions can reach a state of dynamic equilibrium
- why it is important that there are natural and artificial ways to fix nitrogen
- how and why the conditions for the Haber process are chosen to give the optimum yield
- why it is desirable to find new ways to manufacture ammonia.

Analysis

Analysis is important in checking the quality of food, in detecting pollution, in diagnosing diseases, and in gathering evidence that can help to convict criminals.

You should know:

- why standard procedures are needed for the collection, storage, and preparation of samples for analysis
- how different methods of chromatography separate mixtures as a mobile phase moves through a stationary phase
- why standard reference materials and locating agents are used in chromatography
- the similarities and differences between paper and thin-layer chromatography
- how to calculate and interpret R_f values
- the procedure for gas chromatography, and how to interpret simple gas chromatograms
- the key stages in a quantitative analysis
- how to make up a standard solution and calculate its concentration in g/dm^3
- how to carry out a titration, interpret the data, and assess the degree of uncertainty in the calculated result.

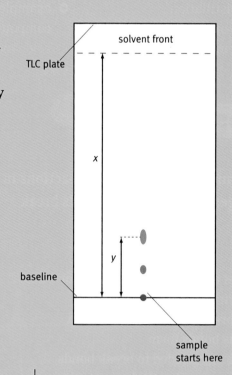

Retardation factors (R_f) can be calculated by measuring the distances travelled by chemicals in the sample and by the solvent.

Ideas about Science

Data: its importance and limitations

Scientists can never be sure that a measurement tells them the true value of the quantity being measured. Data is more reliable if it can be repeated. In the context of chemical analysis by chromatography or titration, you should be able to:

- explain the importance of repeating measurements
- estimate the true value from a set of repeated measurements and suggest the range in which the true value probably lies
- discuss and defend the decision to discard or retain an outlier.

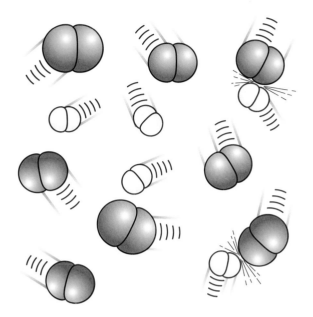

Developing scientific explanations

Scientific explanations are based on data but they go beyond the data and are distinct from it. You should be able to:

- distinguish statements about energy changes, rates, and equilibria, which report data from statements of explanatory ideas
- recognise data or observations that are accounted for by (or conflict with) an explanation
- identify where creative thinking is involved in the development of an explanation illustrated, for example, by explanations of the effect of catalysts on rates or of dynamic equilibrium.

Making decisions about science and technology

Science helps us find ways of using natural resources in a more sustainable way. You should be able to:

- identify benefits and costs of making chemicals such as ammonia and ethanol
- suggest reasons why the choice of method for making a chemical depends on the social or economic context
- explain how the principles and practices of green chemistry contribute to sustainable development
- use data, such as atom economies and yields, to compare the sustainability of alternative processes.

Review Questions

1 Below are the structural formulae of three organic compounds.

A

$$H-\overset{\overset{\displaystyle H}{|}}{\underset{\underset{\displaystyle H}{|}}{C}}-\overset{\overset{\displaystyle H}{|}}{\underset{\underset{\displaystyle H}{|}}{C}}-\overset{\overset{\displaystyle H}{|}}{\underset{\underset{\displaystyle H}{|}}{C}}-H$$

B

$$H-\overset{\overset{\displaystyle H}{|}}{\underset{\underset{\displaystyle H}{|}}{C}}-\overset{\overset{\displaystyle H}{|}}{\underset{\underset{\displaystyle H}{|}}{C}}-OH$$

C

$$H-\overset{\overset{\displaystyle H}{|}}{\underset{\underset{\displaystyle H}{|}}{C}}-\overset{\displaystyle C}{\overset{\nearrow O}{\searrow OH}}$$

a Write the molecular formula of each of the compounds.

b From the compounds above, identify:

   i an alkane

   ii an alcohol

   iii a compound that reacts with calcium carbonate to produce carbon dioxide gas

   iv a compound that is used as a solvent and a fuel

   v a compound that is made by fermentation

   vi two compounds that combine to make an ester.

2 This question is about two alkanes, butane and propane. Both of these alkanes are useful fuels.

a The molecular formula of butane is C_4H_{10}. Draw its structural formula.

b A chemist bubbles butane gas through acidic and alkaline solutions. Explain why butane does not react with the substances in the solutions.

c Butane burns in air to produce carbon dioxide and water. Write a balanced symbol equation for the burning reaction. Include state symbols.

d The equation for the reaction of propane with oxygen is given below.

$$C_3H_8 + 5O_2 \longrightarrow 3CO_2 + 4H_2O$$

Calculate the mass of carbon dioxide produced when 58 g of butane is burned in a good supply of air.

3 This question is about carboxylic acids.

a Give one use of ethanoic acid.

b Ethanoic acid reacts with magnesium to make magnesium ethanoate and one other product. Give the name of the other product.

c Copy and complete the word equation below for the reaction of butanoic acid with sodium hydroxide.

   butanoic acid + sodium hydroxide $\longrightarrow$

d Explain why carboxylic acids are called weak acids.

e The table below gives the pH values of samples of hydrochloric acid and ethanoic acid. The concentration of each acid sample is the same. Identify which of the two acids – X or Y – is ethanoic acid, and give a reason for your choice.

Acid	pH
X	1.0
Y	2.9

4 Every year, UK chemical companies produce more than 1 million tonnes of ammonia by the Haber process.

a **i** Explain why ammonia is manufactured on such a large scale.

ii The feedstocks for the Haber process are hydrogen and nitrogen. State the source of each of these gases.

b The equation for the Haber process reaction is:

$$N_2(g) + 3H_2(g) \rightleftharpoons 2NH_3(g)$$

i Use ideas about molecules and equilibrium to explain why increasing the pressure increases the yield of ammonia.

ii The lower the temperature, the higher the yield of ammonia. Explain why a relatively high temperature of 450 °C is chosen for the Haber process.

5 Gas chromatography (GC) is a useful analytical technique. The diagram below outlines the instrument used.

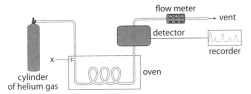

a Name the substance that is the mobile phase in the diagram above.

b A sample of a mixture is injected at X. Describe what happens to the sample as it moves through the instrument to the detector.

c A student injects a sample into a GC instrument. He obtains the chromatogram below.

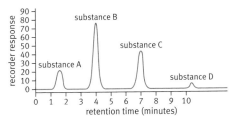

i How many substances were present in the sample?

ii Which substance passes through the column most quickly?

iii Which substance has the shortest retention time?

iv Which substance is present in the mixture in the smallest amount?

6 A technician makes up some solutions.

a First, she dissolves exactly 1.00 g of sodium hydroxide in water and makes up exactly 250 cm³ of solution. Calculate the concentration of the solution, in g/dm³.

b Next, the technician needs to make up 500 cm³ of sodium carbonate solution of concentration 10.6 g/dm³. What mass of sodium carbonate does she need?

7 Hydrogen reacts with fluorine. The equation for the reaction is:

$$H_2(g) + F_2(g) \longrightarrow 2HF(g)$$

Use the data in the table to calculate the energy change for the reacting masses in the equation above.

Process	Energy change for the formula masses (kJ)
Breaking one H–H bond	434 needed
Breaking one F–F bond	158 needed
Forming one H–F bond	562 given out

8 The sustainability of a chemical process depends on many factors. Describe and explain six of these factors.

P7 Studying the Universe

Why study the Universe?

Physics offers an important way of looking at the world. Studying the whole Universe helps us know *where* the Earth is and *when* it is too because, it turns out, the Universe has a history. Though it may seem odd, explaining what happens in stars requires an understanding of matter at the microscopic scale, right down to the smallest subatomic particles. Everything in the physical world is made from a few basic building blocks.

What you already know

- The Solar System includes planets, asteroids, minor planets, and comets, all orbiting the Sun.

- The energy of the Sun is the result of nuclear fusion in the core of the star.

- The Universe began with a 'big bang', and after 14 thousand million years it is still expanding.

Find out about

- what we can see in the night sky
- how telescopes work and how they are used to map the Universe
- the life stories of stars
- how the astronomy community works together.

The Science

In the 1830s, the French philosopher Auguste Comte suggested that there were certain things that we could never know. As an example, he gave the chemical composition of the stars. By 1860, two years after his death, physicists had interpreted the spectrum of starlight and identified the elements present. In this module, you will look at how physicists have gradually extended our understanding of stars and galaxies.

Ideas about Science

How can scientists be sure? Scientists make careful observations of the Solar System and Universe. They use their imaginations to explain the data. Then they test their ideas by sharing them with the wider science community.

Topic 1: Naked-eye astronomy

This sailor is demonstrating the use of an astrolabe, an astronomical instrument invented over 2000 years ago. The instrument measures the angle of a star above the horizon. It was used for navigation, astronomy, astrology, and telling the time.

Astronomy is the oldest science in the world. Ancient civilisations – for example, the Chinese, Babylonians, Egyptians, Greeks, and Mayans – practised naked-eye astronomy long before the invention of telescopes in the 17th century. They built costly observatories for both practical and religious reasons.

Everything beyond the Earth moves across the sky, from horizon to horizon. Calendars and clocks were based on cycles in these movements: day and night, the phases of the Moon, and seasonal changes in the Sun's path. Long-distance travellers, on sea and on land, navigated using the positions of familiar stars.

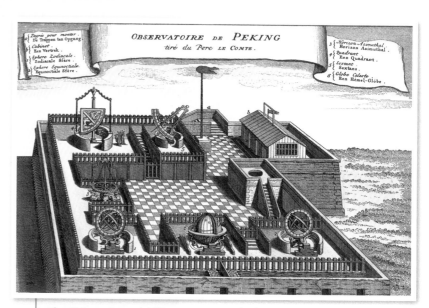

The Chinese Imperial Observatory was built in 1442. Instruments similar to astrolabes were used to measure the positions of objects in the sky.

Day-time astronomy

You do not have to stay up all night to make valid astronomical observations. You can see the Sun cross the sky every day from East to West, moving at a steady rate. That is an observation that any scientific theory of the Universe must account for. You may also have noticed that the Moon follows a similar path, sometimes by day and sometimes by night.

Around the pole

The stars also move across the night sky. Their movement is imperceptible, but it is revealed by long-exposure photography. The photo in the margin below shows that the stars appear to rotate about a point in the sky directly above one of the Earth's poles.

Eclipses

Sometimes it is rare and unusual events that reveal something important. When the Sun passes behind the Moon in a total eclipse, you can see the Sun's gaseous corona.

The Sun sets – a time-lapse photograph.

During a total eclipse of the Sun, the outer atmosphere, or corona, becomes visible. Its appearance changes from one eclipse to the next.

This photograph shows the motion of the stars across the sky. The exposure time was 10.5 hours.

Find out about

- ✔ observations with the naked eye
- ✔ phases of the Moon
- ✔ how stars change position during the night
- ✔ the difference between sidereal and solar days
- ✔ how astonomers describe positions in the sky

The Moon is shown here at intervals of three days. The Sun is off to the right. Notice that it is the half of the Moon facing the Sun that is lit up.

Key words

- ✔ phases of the Moon
- ✔ constellation

The phase of the Moon changes as it orbits the Earth.

The spinning observatory

The Sun and Moon move across the sky in similar but slightly different ways:

- The Sun appears to travel across the sky once every 24 hours (on average).
- The Moon moves very slightly slower, reappearing every 24 hours and 49 minutes.

Arctic Sun. A series of photographs over 24 hours shows the Sun's position in the sky each hour during a single day in the Arctic summer.

People are, of course, deceived by their senses. The Sun is not moving round the Earth. It is the Earth that is spinning on its axis. That is why the Sun rises and sets every day, and why we experience day and night.

The situation with the Moon is more complex. The spinning of the Earth makes the Moon cross the sky. But the Moon is also slowly orbiting the Earth, from West to East. One complete orbit takes about 28 days.

Even without taking into account the fact that the Earth orbits the Sun, you can use these ideas to explain the changing **phases of the Moon**.

The Moon's phases

At any time, half of the Moon is lit up by the Sun's rays, just like the Earth. The view from the Earth depends on where the Moon is around its orbit.

- When the Moon is on the opposite side of the Earth to the Sun, an observer on the Earth can see the whole of its illuminated side. This is a full Moon.
- When the Moon is in the direction of the Sun, the side that is in darkness faces the Earth. This is a new Moon.

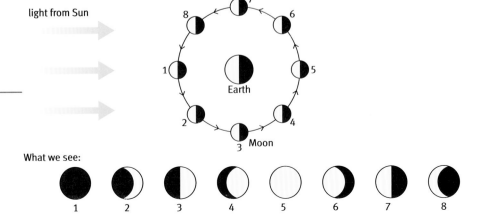

light from Sun

What we see:

Mapping the sky: constellations

The stars are always seen in the same patterns. Most civilisations have identified 'pictures' in the stars and given them names. The stars within each **constellation** (group of stars) are usually separated by huge distances and have no connection with one another. Different civilisations have 'joined the dots' differently, so they have different constellations. Many of the constellation names we use today originated with the ancient Greeks. Astrologers use the movements of planets across constellations to tell fortunes, but this is superstition and there is no scientific evidence that it works.

The Southern Cross, photographed from Cuba.

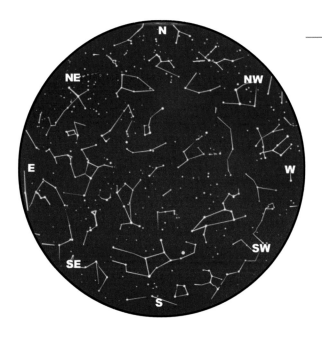

Star charts from newspapers and websites show which stars and planets can be seen at a given time and date. First-magnitude stars are the brightest and can most easily be seen.

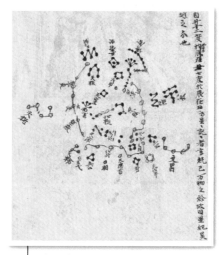

This Chinese star map was probably drawn in the seventh century. The stars are joined in much smaller groups than in European maps.

Seasonal skies

Some constellations seen on a winter night are different from those of a summer night. This is because the Earth travels halfway round its orbit in six months. You see the stars that are in the opposite direction to the Sun, so after six months you will see the opposite half of the sky.

Each day, a star seen from Earth will rise four minutes earlier. After six months, those extra minutes add to twelve hours, so that a star that is rising at dusk in June will be setting at dusk in December.

Questions

1 Draw a diagram to show the relative positions of the Earth, Sun, and Moon when the Moon is at first quarter (half-illuminated as seen from Earth).

2 Imagine that the Earth suddenly starts to spin in the opposite direction. What difference would this make to:
   a the path of the Sun and Moon across the sky?
   b the Moon's phases?

The spinning, orbiting observatory

Earth-bound observers see the sky from a rotating planet. That is why the stars appear to move across the night sky. Their apparent motion is slightly different from the Sun's.

- The stars appear to travel across the sky once every 23 hours 56 minutes.

That is four minutes less than the time taken by the Sun. The difference arises from the fact that the Earth orbits the Sun, once every year.

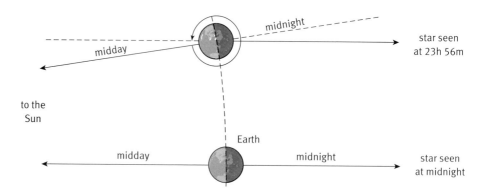

Imagine looking up at a bright star in the sky. 23 hours 56 minutes later, it is back in the same position. This tells you that the Earth must have turned through 360° in this time, and you are facing in the same direction in space.

Repeat the above observation, this time looking at the Sun. After 23 hours 56 minutes, the Earth has turned through 360°, but the Sun has not quite reached the same position in the sky. The diagram shows that, in the course of a day, the Earth has moved a short distance around its orbit. Now it must turn a little more (4 minutes' worth) for the Sun to appear in the same direction as the day before.

Days are measured by the Sun. The average time it takes to cross the sky is 24 hours, and this is called a **solar day**. We could choose to set our clocks by the stars (although this would be very inconvenient). Then a day would last 23 hours 56 minutes; this is called a **sidereal day** ('sidereal' means 'related to the stars').

The celestial sphere

Long ago people described the stars as though they were lights on the inside of a spinning bowl, with the observer on the Earth at the centre. A better description extends the bowl to be a complete sphere. This **celestial sphere** has an axis running from the Pole Star through the axis of the Earth. The celestial equator is an extension of the Earth's equator.

You can think of the Sun and stars as fixed. We view them from a spinning, orbiting planet.

Key words
- ✔ solar day
- ✔ sidereal day

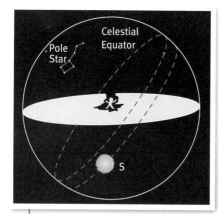

The celestial sphere is an imaginary sphere with the Earth at its centre and the stars fixed to the surface of the sphere.

How can we locate objects in the sky?

By international agreement, the sky is divided up into regions named after constellations. Astronomers use these to describe positions in the sky.

To give positions more precisely, astronomers use angles.

Imagine standing in a field, looking at a star. Two angles are needed to give its position:

- Start by pointing at the horizon, due North of where you are. Turn westwards through an angle until you are pointing at the horizon directly below the star. That gives you the first angle.
- Now move your arm upwards through an angle, until you are pointing directly at the star. That gives you the second angle.

But the stars move across the sky every 24 hours, and are in different directions depending on where on the Earth's surface you are standing. So astronomers use a system that will work wherever you are and whatever the time of day and year.

The equatorial coordinate system uses a reference point in the sky (this point is called the vernal equinox point). The position is defined using two angles – **right ascension** and **declination**. The diagram below shows how these are used.

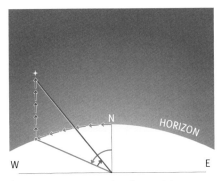

Two angles describe the position of a star.

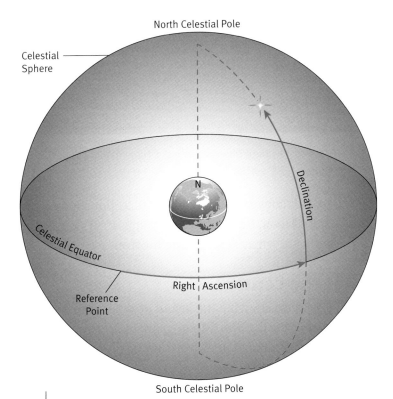

Right ascension measures the angle east from the vernal equinox point. The angle is commonly measured in hours, minutes, and seconds. Declination measures the angle of the star above or below the celestial equator. The angle is usually measured in degrees and minutes.

Questions

3 a If the Earth orbited the Sun more quickly – in, say, 30 days – would the difference between sidereal and solar days be greater or less?

   b Work out the time difference between sidereal and solar days.

4 Why would it be 'inconvenient' if we set our clocks according to sidereal time?

5 a Draw a diagram to explain why you see some different constellations in winter and summer.

   b Use your diagram to explain why there are some stars that can never be seen from the UK, but that can be seen from places in the southern hemisphere.

6 Suggest how measuring the angles of stars above the horizon could help with navigation.

Find out about

- ✓ **how planets move against the star background**
- ✓ **how planets' motion can be explained**

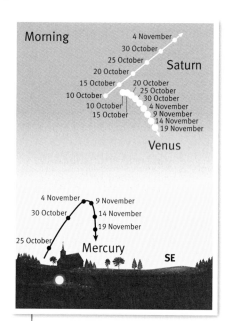

The pattern of movements of planets in the sky is different from that of stars. This diagram shows the pattern of movement of three planets just before sunrise.

This geocentric (Earth-centred) map was published in Germany in 1524.

Heavenly wanderers

Five **planets** can be seen with the naked eye from Earth – Mercury, Venus, Mars, Jupiter, and Saturn. These were recognised as different from stars long, long ago because they appear to move, very slowly, night by night, against the background of 'fixed stars'. The diagram on the left shows the changing positions in the sky of three planets at dawn over a few weeks in one recent year. Any scientific theory of the planets must be able to explain their observed motion.

Mercury and Venus are only ever seen at dawn or dusk, fairly close to the horizon near the setting or rising Sun.

The planets appear as bright objects in the sky. Here Mercury, Venus, and Saturn are visible as well as the crescent Moon.

The planets generally move in an East–West direction along a similar path to the Sun and Moon. But at times they appear to slow down and go into reverse; this is known as **retrograde motion**.

What is at the centre?

Before about 1600, maps showing the layout of the Universe placed the Earth at the centre, with the Sun, Moon, planets, and stars orbiting around it. But to explain the planets' retrograde motion, their **orbits** would need to be very complicated.

In 1543, the Polish astronomer Copernicus suggested that Earth, along with the five known planets, orbited the Sun. This idea was rejected by many people at the time, but its success at explaining many observations meant that eventually it became accepted.

Planets' motion explained

In our present-day model of the **Solar System**, Earth is a planet. The planets orbit the Sun, and their orbits all lie in approximately the same plane. Each planet takes a different amount of time to orbit the Sun. The planets furthest from the Sun take the longest time.

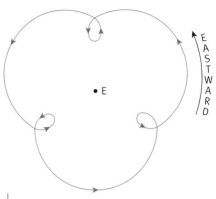

This diagram shows the sort of orbit a planet would need to have if it orbited the Earth in a way consistent with the observations.

Earth is one of eight major planets that orbit the Sun. Pluto is a dwarf planet; its orbit is tilted and is a different shape. (In this picture, the planets and Sun are not drawn to scale.)

Key words

- ✓ **planets**
- ✓ **retrograde motion**
- ✓ **orbits**
- ✓ **Solar System**

To explain retrograde motion, recall that both the Earth and the planets are orbiting the Sun. An observer looking towards Mars sees it against a backdrop of the fixed stars. Its position against this backdrop depends on where the Earth and Mars are in their orbits.

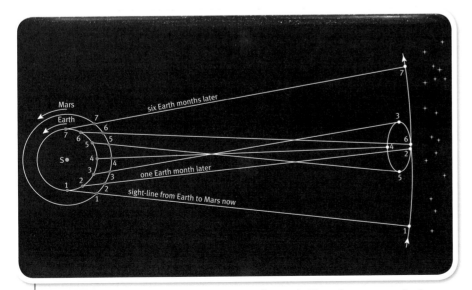

From months 1 to 3, Mars appears to move forwards. Then, for two months, it goes into reverse before moving forwards again.

Questions

1 Mercury is the closest planet to the Sun. It is only ever seen at dawn or dusk, close to the Sun in the sky. Draw a diagram to explain why.

2 Suggest reasons why people rejected the Sun-centred idea and why it took a long time to be accepted.

Find out about

✓ why solar and lunar eclipses happen

✓ angular size

✓ the effect of the Moon's orbital tilt

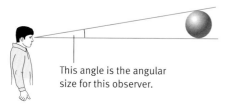

This angle is the angular size for this observer.

Angular size is the angle between two lines drawn from an observer to each side of an object. It depends on the object's actual size and its distance away.

Key words

✓ **solar eclipse**
✓ **lunar eclipse**
✓ **angular size**

Eclipses involve both the Sun and the Moon.

- In a **solar eclipse**, the Moon blocks the Sun's light.
- In a **lunar eclipse**, the Moon moves into the Earth's shadow.

Astronomers can predict when an eclipse of the Sun will occur. A solar eclipse happens just a few times each year. And a total eclipse at any particular point on the Earth is a rare event.

The predictability of eclipses shows that they must be related to the regular motions of the Sun and Moon. Their rarity suggests that some special circumstances must arise if one is to occur.

The first way to explain a solar eclipse is to think of the Sun and Moon and their apparent motion across the sky. The Sun moves slightly faster across the sky than the Moon, and its path may take it behind the Moon. For us to see a total eclipse, the Sun must be travelling across the sky at the same height as the Moon. Any higher or lower and it will not be perfectly eclipsed.

The fact that the Moon precisely blocks the Sun is probably a coincidence. The Sun is 400 times the diameter of the Moon, and it is 400 times as far away. So, by coincidence, they both have the same **angular size** (about 0.5°).

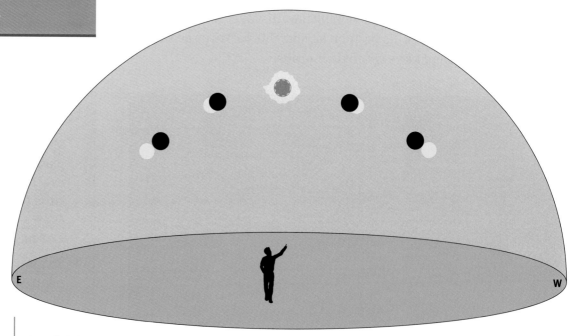

Provided the Sun's path across the sky matches the Moon's, a total eclipse may be seen.

Umbra and penumbra

The diagram below shows a different way of explaining eclipses, both solar and lunar. Both the Earth and the Moon have shadows – areas where they block sunlight. Because the Sun is an extended source of light, these shadows do not have hard edges. There is a region of total darkness (the umbra) fringed by a region of partial darkness (the penumbra). The Earth's shadow is much bigger than the Moon's.

• When the Moon's umbra touches the surface of the Earth, a solar eclipse is seen from inside the area of contact.

• When the Moon passes into the Earth's umbra, a lunar eclipse is seen.

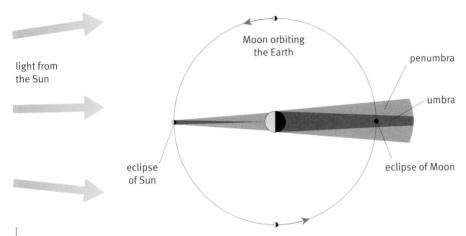

The umbra and penumbra for an eclipse of the Sun and an eclipse of the Moon.

Why the rarity?

The Moon orbits the Earth once a month, so you might expect to see a lunar eclipse every month, followed by a solar eclipse two weeks later. You do not – eclipses are much rarer than this. The reason is that the Moon's orbit is tilted relative to the plane of the Earth's orbit by about 5°. Usually the Earth, Sun, and Moon are not in a line so no eclipse occurs.

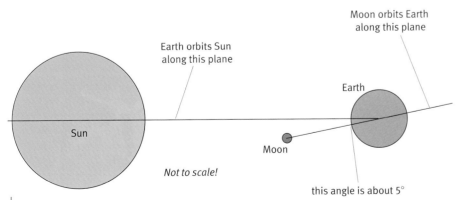

The Moon's orbit is tilted relative to the plane of the Earth's orbit around the Sun. The effect is exaggerated here.

Questions

1 At times, the Moon's orbit takes it further from Earth so that it looks smaller in the sky. If it is in front of the Sun, the result is that we see a ring of bright sunlight around the black disc of the Moon. This is an annular eclipse. Construct a diagram like the one on this page to show why this happens.

2 What is the phase of the Moon at the time of:
   a a solar eclipse?
   b a lunar eclipse?

3 Explain why a person on Earth is more likely to see a lunar eclipse than a solar eclipse.

Eclipse trips

Today, solar eclipses are big business. Thousands of people select their holiday dates to coincide with an eclipse. Tour operators organise plane-loads of eclipse spotters, and cruise liners sail along the track of the eclipse. Guest astronomers give lectures to interested audiences. And, provided the clouds hold off, hundreds of thousands of satisfied customers will get a view of a spectacular natural phenomenon.

The moment of total eclipse. For a few tens of seconds, the Moon blocks the Sun's bright disc and the solar corona (the Sun's hot atmosphere) is visible. Photograph by Fred Espenak.

Scientific expeditions

For centuries, astronomers have travelled to watch eclipses for scientific purposes. They have helped us to learn about the dimensions of the Solar System, and about the Sun and Moon. Take the question of the corona. For a long time, scientists had been unable to agree whether the corona was actually part of the Sun, or a halo of gas around the Moon, illuminated by sunlight during an eclipse.

The picture on the right shows a scientific expedition that travelled to India to observe and record the total solar eclipse of 12 December 1871. They took photographs from which it was possible, for the first time, to develop a scientific description of the Sun's corona (outer atmosphere).

A scientific purpose?

But is it worth studying eclipses today? Are there good scientific reasons to take tonnes of scientific equipment off to some distant land? One person who thinks so is Fred Espenak, an astrophysicist at NASA's Goddard Space Flight Centre. His interest is in the atmospheres of planets, moons, and the Sun.

Preparing to observe a solar eclipse in 1871.

Fred uses an infrared spectrometer to examine radiation coming from planetary atmospheres. A spectrometer is a device that splits radiation into its different frequencies. For example, a prism splits light into the colours of the spectrum from red (lowest frequency) to violet (highest frequency). By studying the frequencies that are present, it is possible to deduce the chemical composition of the source of the radiation. One of Fred's experiments, to measure atmospheric flow, was carried out on the Space Shuttle.

A young Fred Espenak, preparing to observe an eclipse in 1983. He is now a veteran of over 20 eclipse expeditions.

A solar eclipse lets Earth-bound observers see the Sun's corona. This is a mysterious part of the Sun, extending far out into space. The mystery is its temperature. We see the surface of the Sun, which is hot, at about 5500°C, but the corona is far hotter – perhaps 1.5 million degrees. Measurements during eclipses may help to explain how this thin gas become heated to such a high temperature.

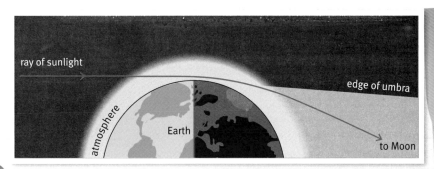

ray of sunlight
atmosphere
Earth
edge of umbra
to Moon

During a lunar eclipse, light from the Sun is refracted as it passes through the Earth's atmosphere, and lights up the Moon.

And lunar eclipses? Fred's main interest is in examining the light that reaches the Moon through the Earth's atmosphere at this time. The quality of the light can be a good guide to the state of the Earth's atmosphere, indicating pollution from such causes as forest fires and volcanoes.

A composite image of the Moon moving in and out of eclipse. The central image shows the Moon lit up by sunlight that has been refracted through the Earth's atmosphere. Photograph by Fred Espenak.

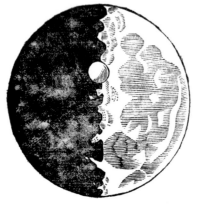
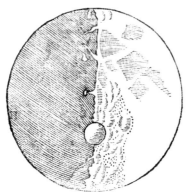
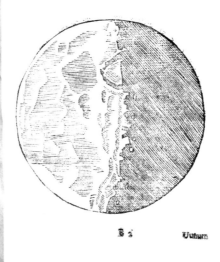

Galileo made these sketches of the Moon in 1610, and saw that the edge of the shadow between the Moon's light and dark sides was sometimes irregular (top) and sometimes smooth (bottom). He deduced that this was due to mountains on the Moon, challenging the existing worldview that said the heavens were perfect and unchanging.

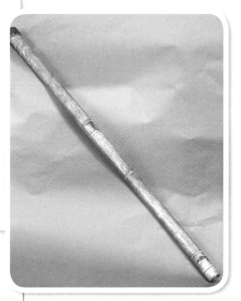

This telescope is a replica of one made by Galileo. It uses lenses to focus light. His best telescopes had a magnification of about 30 times.

In the autumn of 1609, Galileo made his first observations of the Moon using a telescope. He was not the first person to use a telescope to look at the night sky. But the observations Galileo made, and his interpretation of them, had repercussions down the centuries. He changed the way people thought about the Universe.

Everything that we know about the Universe beyond the Solar System comes from using telescopes. By studying electromagnetic radiation from very distant objects, astronomers can discover a surprising amount of information about things that are much too far away to visit.

Seeing the light

The first telescopes used visible light. These are known as **optical telescopes**. Some are designed for people to look through, but most modern optical telescopes record the image using electronic detectors.

Knighton Observatory in mid-Wales is part of the Spaceguard Foundation. It keeps an eye out for comets and asteroids that might collide with Earth.

Greenwich Observatory in south-east London was built by the British Navy in the 17th century. They had suffered defeat at the hands of the Dutch because the enemy were able to navigate better. Dutch astronomy was in advance of the English, giving them better star charts of the night sky, which were used to work out the ship's position.

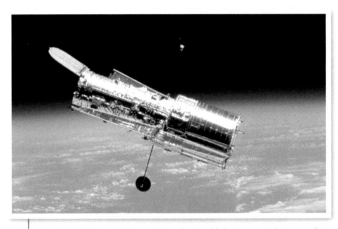

Launched into orbit in 1990, the Hubble Space Telescope has given us a more detailed view of the Universe than ever before.

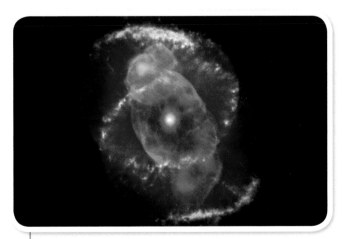

The Hubble Space Telescope made this image in 2004. It shows the Cat's Eye nebula, in which thin layers of hot gas have been thrown off the surface of a dying star.

This reflecting telescope is at the Calar Alto Observatory, over 2000 m above sea level in southern Spain. Light passes through the ring (diameter 3.5 m) and reflects off the curved, shiny mirror at the back.

Key word

✓ **optical telescopes**

A telescope makes distant objects appear larger and closer, so that more detail can be seen. Also, it has a bigger **aperture** than a human eye. This means it collects more radiation, allowing fainter objects to be studied.

Modern telescopes can produce lasting images using electronic detectors or photographic film. Also, images of faint objects can be made by collecting radiation over a long time.

Beyond the visible

Since the mid-20th century, astronomers have developed telescopes to study radiation in all parts of the electromagnetic spectrum. Each requires a suitable detector and a means of focusing the radiation. These telescopes have produced results that came as a complete surprise, leading to major changes in people's ideas about stars and the Universe.

Jocelyn Bell with part of one of the charts produced by the radio telescope, showing the trace produced by a pulsar.

Pulsars

In October 1967, Jocelyn Bell was working with Anthony Hewish in Cambridge. She was involved in making a survey of radio sources in the sky.

> 'Six or eight weeks after starting the survey I became aware that on occasions there was a bit of "scruff" on the records, which did not look exactly like man-made interference. Furthermore I realised that this scruff had been seen before on the same part of the records – from the same patch of sky.

> Whatever the source was, we decided that it deserved closer inspection, and that this would involve making faster chart recordings. As the chart flowed under the pen, I could see that the signal was a series of pulses, and my suspicions that they were equally spaced were confirmed as soon as I got the chart off the recorder. They were 1.3 seconds apart.'

Jocelyn Bell and Anthony Hewish had discovered pulsars. These are distant objects that send out radio waves that vary with an extremely regular pulse.

Jocelyn Bell and Anthony Hewish used a radio telescope. The wires in the field form an aerial that detects radio waves. There are 1000 posts spaced over 4.5 acres.

The Effelsberg radio telescope in Germany. With a diameter of 100 m, it gathers radio waves from distant objects in the Universe, including galaxies other than our own. The dish is scanned across the sky to generate an image.

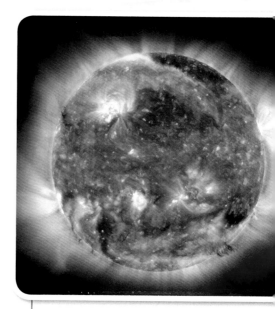

The orbiting SOHO (Solar and Heliospheric Observatory) made this image of ultraviolet radiation from the Sun. It reveals details of the hot atmosphere that traces the shape of the Sun's magnetic field.

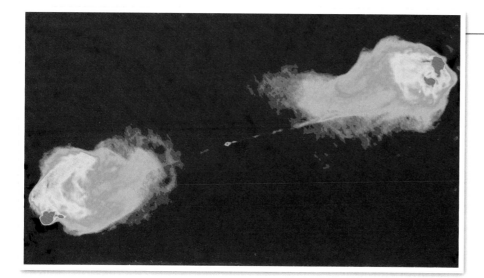

This image shows radio emission from a galaxy called Cygnus A, one of the brightest radio objects in the sky. With an optical telescope, all you observe is the tiny central dot, which is a distant galaxy. The radio waves come from clouds stretching a quarter of a million light-years either side of the galaxy.

Infrared radiation is mostly absorbed by Earth's atmosphere. The orbiting Spitzer telescope observes infrared radiation from space. This infrared image was taken with the Spitzer telescope. The green indicates clouds of warm gas between stars. The small red spots are hot balls of gas on their way to becoming stars, and the darker patch on the left is the remains of an exploded star.

Questions

1 Different telescopes make use of different types of electromagnetic radiation. List the telescopes shown on these two pages, together with the radiation that each gathers.

2 Telescopes 'make things visible that cannot be seen with the naked eye'. Is that true for all of the telescopes shown here?

3 Look at the image of the Moon on page 208 and think about how the Moon appears to the naked eye when you see it in the night sky. What extra features has Galileo been able to identify by using a telescope?

Making an image

A telescope makes an image of a distant object that is clearer and more detailed than the view with the naked eye. To understand how telescopes work, you need to learn how images are formed.

The simplest way to make an image uses just a small pinhole in a sheet of card. Light that is scattered, or given out, by an object passes through the pinhole and makes an image on a screen. This is a **real image**. A real image can be recorded using a light-sensitive electronic detector or photographic film. You can see a real image on a screen without having to look towards the object.

Find out about

- ✔ **how to make an image using a pinhole camera**
- ✔ **how to draw diagrams of light rays to explain image formation**

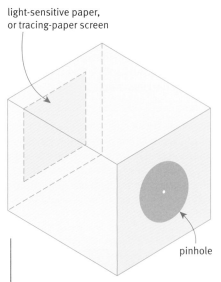

light-sensitive paper, or tracing-paper screen

pinhole

You can use a pinhole camera, made from a box with a pinhole at one end, to take photographs using light-sensitive paper or film. Alternatively, use a tracing-paper screen so that you can see the image from outside.

This picture was taken with a pinhole camera.

Ray diagram

A **ray diagram** helps explain how a pinhole produces a real image on a screen.

- Straight lines with arrows show the direction of light rays travelling from the object.

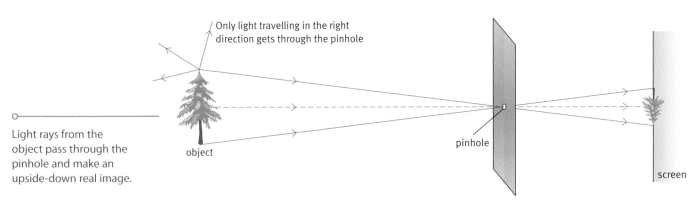

Only light travelling in the right direction gets through the pinhole

pinhole

object

Light rays from the object pass through the pinhole and make an upside-down real image.

screen

- Rays leave the object in all directions, but only those travelling towards the pinhole get through and light up the screen.
- As the pinhole is very small, each point on the object produces a tiny spot of light on the screen. Together, all these spots make up the image.

A ray diagram for a pinhole camera can help you predict and explain:

- why the image is upside down
- what happens to the image if the screen is moved away from the pinhole
- what happens if you enlarge the pinhole.

Pinhole telescope?

You can use a pinhole to make an image of the Sun. The image is faint because the aperture is small – only a small amount of light passes through the pinhole.

This long-exposure photograph was taken with a pinhole camera. It shows the path of the Sun over six months.

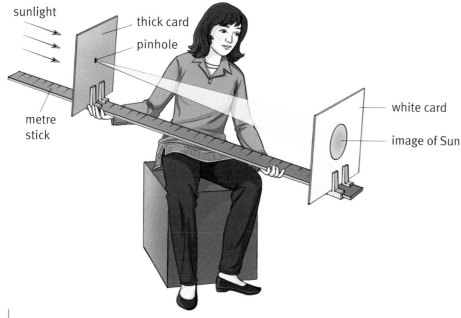

SAFETY: Face away from the Sun so that it shines over your shoulder.
Do not look directly at the Sun.

Key words

- ✔ **real image**
- ✔ **ray diagram**

Questions

1 **a** Draw two ray diagrams to explain what happens to the image in a pinhole camera if the screen is moved further away from the pinhole.

   b Predict what happens to the image if the distance between pinhole and screen is doubled.

2 By drawing a ray diagram, predict what you would see on the screen of a pinhole camera that had several pinholes.

3 Explain why a pinhole image of stars other than the Sun would not be much use to astronomers.

4 Suggest reasons why the pinhole photograph of the Sun's path above has some dark streaks and patches.

Find out about

- ✔ **how a converging lens makes a real image**
- ✔ **the focal length and power of a lens**
- ✔ **refraction**

The earliest and simplest telescopes used lenses. To understand these telescopes, you need first to understand what lenses do.

The focal length of a converging lens

The picture below shows how you can make a miniature image of a distant object using a single **converging lens**. If you position the screen correctly, you will see a small, inverted image of a distant scene.

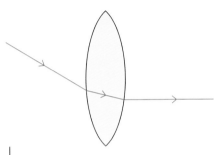

A ray of light bends as it passes at an angle from one material to another. This effect is called **refraction**.

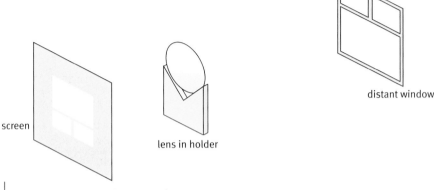

distant window

screen

lens in holder

Using a converging lens to make an image on a screen.

Rays of light enter the lens. Because of the lens shape they are refracted (they change direction), first on entering the lens and again on leaving.

A ray diagram shows this. A horizontal line passing through the centre of the lens is called the **principal axis**. Rays of light parallel to the axis are all refracted so that they meet at a point. This is why converging lenses are so called: they cause parallel rays of light to converge.

How a converging lens focuses parallel rays of light.

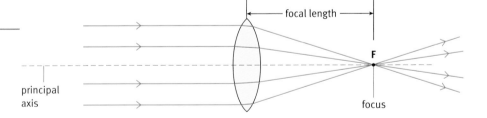

focal length

principal axis

F

focus

Lenses are cleverly designed. The surface must be curved in just the right way in order for the rays to meet at a point, the **focus** (F).

When early astronomers made their own telescopes, they had to grind lenses from blocks of glass. If the glass was uneven, or if the surface was not smooth or was of the wrong shape, the telescope would give a blurred, poorly focused image. It is said that much of Galileo's success was achieved because he made high-quality lenses so that he could see details that other observers could not.

The distance from the centre of the lens to the focus is called the **focal length** of the lens. The longer the focal length of a lens, the larger (actual physical size) will be the real image that the lens produces of a distant object.

Estimating the focal length

You can compare lenses simply by looking at them. For lenses of the same material:

- a lens with a long focal length has surfaces that are not very strongly curved
- a lens with a short focal length has surfaces that are more strongly curved.

To estimate the focal length of a converging lens, stand next to the wall on the opposite side of the room to the window. Hold up the lens and use it to focus an image of the window on the wall. Measure the distance from the lens to the wall – this will give you a good estimate of the focal length.

The power of a lens

A lens with a short focal length bends the rays of light more. Its **power** is greater. So short focal length equals high power, and long focal length equals low power. As one increases, the other decreases, they are inversely proportional.

Here is the equation used to calculate power when you know the focal length:

$$\text{power (in } \textbf{dioptres, D}) = \frac{1}{\text{focal length (in metres)}}$$

So if a lens has a focal length of 0.5 m, its power is

$$\frac{1}{0.5} = 2 \text{ dioptres}$$

If you look at the reading glasses sold in chemists' shops, or at an optician's prescription, you will see the power of the lens quoted in dioptres.

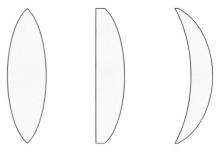

converging lenses

All converging lenses are fatter in the middle than at the edges.

Questions

1 The focal length of a lens is measured between which two points?

2 A lens has a focal length of 20 cm. What is its power?

3 A pair of reading glasses has lenses labelled +1.5D (D stands for dioptres). What is their focal length?

Key words
- ✔ converging lens
- ✔ principal axis
- ✔ focus
- ✔ focal length
- ✔ power
- ✔ dioptres

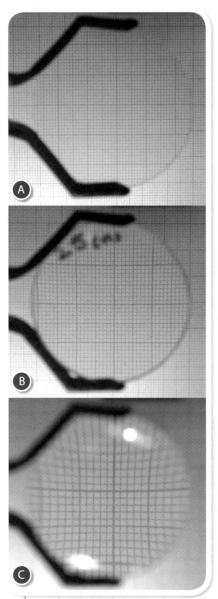

Three lenses with different focal lengths.

More about lenses

To astronomers, most objects of interest are so distant that they are 'at infinity'. When light reaches a lens from such a distant point, all the rays entering the lens are parallel. Parallel rays at an angle to the principal axis converge to one side of the principal focus.

light from top of object

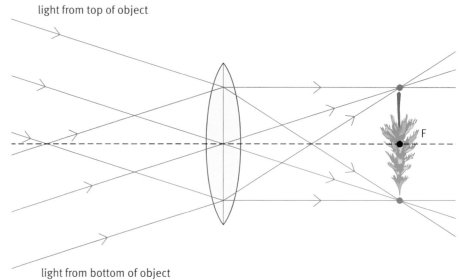

light from bottom of object

This ray diagram shows how a converging lens makes a real image of a distant object.

If you look through a converging lens at a very nearby object, you see an image that appears to be behind the lens. It is bigger than the object and the right way up. The lens is acting as a magnifying glass.

If you look through a diverging lens you see a virtual image that appears smaller than the object and the right way up. A diverging lens on its own cannot make a real image.

Questions

4 Look at the three lenses A, B, and C in the photograph. (The lenses are made from the same material.)
  a Put them in order starting with the one with the shortest focal length.
  b Which one has the greatest power?
  c How are their shapes different?

5 Suppose that you adapted a pinhole camera so that it had a large aperture and a converging lens instead of the pinhole. What differences would this make to the image of a distant object?

More about refraction

Light changes direction when it passes at an angle from one material to another. This is called **refraction**. To understand why refraction happens, it is helpful to look at the behaviour of water waves.

Waves can be studied using a ripple tank. Waves are created on the surface of water and a lamp projects an image of the waves on to a screen.

Waves in water of constant depth are equally spaced. This shows that waves do not slow down as they travel. The wave speed stays the same. As the wave travels, it loses energy (because of friction). Its amplitude gets less but not its speed.

Refraction

If waves cross a boundary from a deeper to a shallower region, they are closer together in the shallow region. The wavelength is smaller. This effect is called refraction. It happens because water waves travel slower in shallower water. The frequency (f) is the same in both regions, so the slower wave speed (v) means that the wavelength (λ) must be less (as $v = f\lambda$).

If the waves are travelling at an angle to the boundary between the two regions, their direction also changes. You can work out which way they will bend by thinking about which side of the wave gets slowed down first.

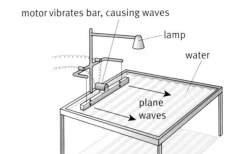

A ripple tank producing a steady stream of plane waves.

Plane waves travelling at constant speed.

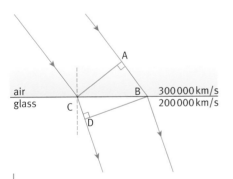

Light is refracted because its speed is different in the two media. Light travels the distance AB in air in the same time as it travels the distance CD in glass.

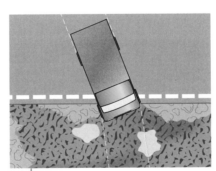

A model to help explain refraction. The truck goes more slowly on the muddy field. One wheel crosses the boundary first – so one side slows down before the other. This makes the truck change direction.

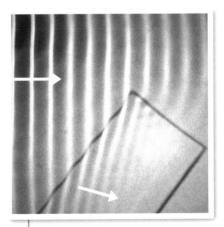

Refraction of water waves at a boundary between deep and shallow regions.

Question

6 When a ray of light passes from air into glass, it slows down.
   a Explain what happens to its frequency and to its wavelength.
   b Draw a diagram to show how the direction of the light changes as it passes at an angle from air into glass.

Key word

✓ **refraction**

Find out about

- ✓ **the lenses used in telescopes**
- ✓ **the magnification produced by a telescope**
- ✓ **how bigger apertures give brighter images**

Just two lenses

Telescopes evolved from the converging lenses used for correcting poor eyesight. These were in use before 1300, though you had to be quite 'well off' to afford a pair of spectacles in those days. The lenses were biconvex; that is, they were convex (bulging outwards) on both sides. (The word 'lens' is Latin for 'lentil', which has the same shape.)

Such lenses work as magnifying glasses, producing an enlarged image when you look through them at a nearby object. For medieval scholars, whose eyesight began to fail in middle age, spectacles meant that they could go on working for another 20 or 30 years.

The Dutch inventor Hans Lippershey is credited with putting two converging lenses together to make a telescope. There is a story that in 1608, his children held up two lenses and noticed that the weathercock on a distant building looked bigger and closer. Lippershey tested their observation, and went on to offer his invention to the Dutch military.

In fact, Lippershey failed to get a patent on his device. Other 'inventors' challenged his claim, and the Dutch government decided that the principle of the telescope was too easy to copy, so that a patent could not be granted.

Telescopes rapidly became a fashionable item, sold widely across western Europe by travelling salesmen. That is how one came in to Galileo's hands in Padua, near Venice, in 1609.

A telescope that uses two converging lenses.

Hans Lippershey and his children. Their play with lenses led to the invention of the telescope.

DIY telescope

A telescope using lenses to gather and focus the light is called a refracting telescope, or a **refractor**. You can make a telescope using almost any two converging lenses mounted in a line.

- The **eyepiece lens** is next to your eye. This is the stronger of the two lenses.
- The **objective lens** is nearer to the object you are observing. This is the weaker lens.

You will only get a clear image if the two lenses have the correct separation, and this depends on the distance to the object. You will need to adjust the separation so that you get a clear view. This is called **focusing**.

This is what you can see through the telescope shown on the opposite page. The image is upside down.

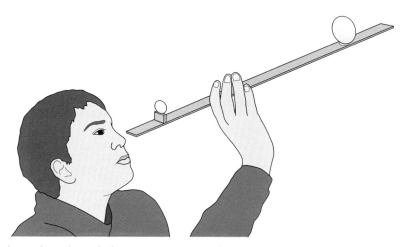

Looking through the eyepiece, you should see an **inverted** (upside-down) **image** of a distant object.

Key words

- ✓ **eyepiece lens**
- ✓ **objective lens**
- ✓ **focusing**
- ✓ **inverted image**

Ray diagram of a telescope

You can use what you have learned about lenses to explain how a telescope made of two converging lenses works. The diagram below shows what happens.

- The objective lens collects light from a distant object.
- Parallel rays of light enter the objective lens from a point on the distant object.
- Each set of parallel rays is focused by the objective lens, so a real image is formed.
- The eyepiece is a magnifying glass, which is used to look at the real image. A strong lens is used for the eyepiece because it magnifies the image more.

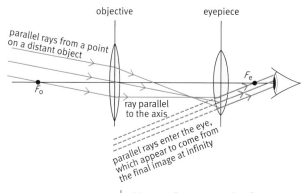

How a telescope made of two converging lenses works.

Questions

1 Why do you think Lippershey offered his invention to the Dutch military?

2 Why do telescopes and binoculars used by bird-watchers need a focusing knob?

Brighter and better

Without a telescope, you can see up to 3000 stars in the night sky. A small telescope can increase the number of visible stars to about 30 000, because it gathers more light.

The objective lens of a telescope might be 10 cm across; its **aperture** is 10 cm. On a dark night the pupil of your eye might be 5 mm across.

The amount of radiation gathered by a telescope depends on the collecting area of its objective lens. To see the faintest and most distant objects in the Universe, astronomers require telescopes with very large collecting areas.

Here is one way to gather a lot of light – build four identical telescopes. This quadruplet telescope is part of the European Southern Observatory in Chile. Each has an aperture of 8 m, so when combined they equal a single telescope with an aperture of 16 m.

Bigger and better

A telescope does not make distant stars look bigger – nearly all of them are so far away that they still appear as points of light. But it can reveal detail in objects that are either much bigger than stars (such as galaxies or clouds of glowing gas) or much closer (such as planets).

When you look at the Moon it appears quite small in the sky. Its image on the retina of your eye is quite small. Look at the Moon through a telescope, and it looks enormous. The telescope produces a greatly enlarged image on your retina.

Suppose your telescope is labelled 50 ×. This is saying that its **magnification** is 50. There is more than one way of thinking about this:

- the telescope makes the Moon seem 50 times bigger than its actual size
- the telescope makes the Moon seem to be at only 1/50th of its actual distance away
- the telescope makes the Moon's angular size look 50 times bigger.

To the naked eye, the Moon has an angular size of about half a degree (0.5°). With the telescope this is increased to 25°. The telescope has an **angular magnification** of 50.

From the ray diagram of the telescope on page 219 you can see that the angle between the rays from the eyepiece and the principal axis is larger than the angle between the rays from the object and the principal axis. This means that any **extended object**, for example the Moon, which looks small to the naked eye, will look much larger through the telescope.

A telescope does not make a distant star look bigger – it remains a point of light. However, the telescope spreads out a group of stars by magnifying the angles between them. This makes it possible to see two stars that are close together as separate objects.

Calculating magnification

The magnification produced by a refracting telescope depends on the lenses from which it is made.

$$\text{magnification} = \frac{\text{focal length of objective lens}}{\text{focal length of eyepiece lens}}$$

Suppose you choose two lenses with focal lengths 50 cm and 5 cm:

$$\text{magnification} = \frac{50 \text{ cm}}{5 \text{ cm}} = 10$$

> **Key words**
> - ✓ aperture
> - ✓ magnification
> - ✓ angular magnification
> - ✓ extended object

Questions

3 Look at the equation for magnification above. Use it to explain why a telescope made with two identical lenses will be useless.

4 Calculate the magnification provided by a telescope made with focal lengths 1 m and 5 cm.

5 You are asked to make a telescope with as large a magnification as possible. You have a boxful of lenses. How would you choose the two most suitable lenses?

6 Show that four telescopes of diameter 8 m gather as much light as one telescope of diameter 16 m.

Find out about

✓ **how radiation can be separated into different frequencies**

Analysing radiation

Astronomy is not only about making images that show the size and shape of objects. By analysing the make-up of radiation received, astronomers can find out more about its source. As you will learn later in this module, radiation can provide important clues about the temperature of an object and its chemical composition. To get this information, astronomers use a **spectrometer** to measure the amount of radiation received at different frequencies. For visible light, different frequencies correspond to different colours.

Dispersion

If a beam of white light passes through a triangular block (a **prism**), the emerging ray is coloured. This is called a **spectrum**. Newton carried out a famous series of experiments with prisms. He concluded that white light is really a mixture of the colours of the spectrum. This splitting of white light into colours is called **dispersion**.

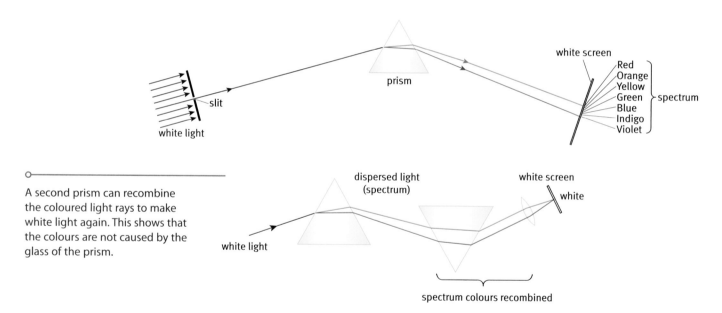

A second prism can recombine the coloured light rays to make white light again. This shows that the colours are not caused by the glass of the prism.

Newton did not know what caused the different colours, but scientists were later able to deduce that the colour of light depends on its frequency. (It therefore also depends on its wavelength, as the two are linked.) The visible band extends from red through to violet. Red has the lowest frequency (longest wavelength) and violet has the highest frequency (shortest wavelength).

Dispersion happens because light of different frequencies travels through glass (and other transparent media) at different speeds. The differences are small but they are enough to split the light up so that different colours are refracted through different angles. In glass, violet slows down more than red light, so it is refracted through a bigger angle.

Spectrometers

A spectrometer containing a prism can be attached to an optical telescope so that it produces a spectrum showing all the frequencies that are present in light.

The Pleiades is a group of bright stars. With a spectrometer, the light from each star is broken up into a spectrum.

The colours you see reflected from a CD arise because the surface has a very fine spiral track that carries the recorded information, and neighbouring sections of the track act as a grating.

An alternative design of spectrometer uses a **grating**, which is a set of very narrow evenly spaced parallel lines ruled on a thin sheet of glass or on a shiny surface. When light shines on the grating, different colours emerge at different angles to produce several spectra.

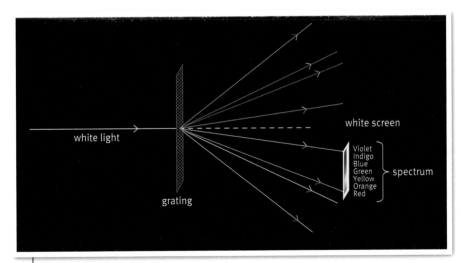

A grating produces a series of spectra.

Astronomers observing other parts of the electromagnetic spectrum also use spectrometers. Their telescopes have detectors that are only sensitive to a particular frequency. For example, radio telescopes have receivers that are tuned to specific frequencies rather like the receivers in a radio or TV.

Key words

- ✓ **spectrometer**
- ✓ **prism**
- ✓ **spectrum**
- ✓ **dispersion**
- ✓ **grating**

Questions

1. What are the main differences between the spectra produced by a prism and by a grating?

2. Draw a diagram to show plane waves being refracted by a prism. (Look back at the photographs of waves in ripple tanks on page 217.)

Find out about

- ✓ the advantages of reflecting telescopes over refractors
- ✓ how mirrors collect light in reflecting telescopes

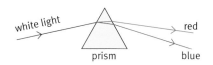

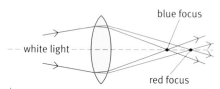

The fact that light refracts light of different colours by different amounts is useful for spectrometers but is a problem for simple lenses.

Why not lenses?

The first telescopes were **refractors** – they used lenses to refract and focus light. But most modern astronomical telescopes are **reflectors** that focus light and other electromagnetic radiation using curved mirrors.

A simple converging lens focuses different colours (frequencies) of light at slightly different points. Used as the objective lens of a telescope, it will produce an unclear image.

It is fairly easy to make small lenses that are specially designed to reduce the problem with colour. These are used in telescopes with objectives a few centimetres in diameter.

For large telescopes, lenses have some further disadvantages:
- The largest objective lens possible has a diameter of about 1 metre. Any larger and the lens would sag and change shape under its own weight, making it useless for focusing light.
- It is very difficult to ensure that the glass of a large diameter lens is uniform in composition all the way through.
- A large converging lens is quite fat in the middle. Some light is absorbed on its way through, making faint objects appear even fainter.
- Glass lenses only focus visible light. Radiation in other parts of the electromagnetic spectrum is either completely absorbed (for example, ultraviolet) or goes straight through (for example, radio).

On reflection

To focus light, a mirror must be curved. To bring parallel rays of light to a point, a mirror must be **parabolic**.

A ray diagram shows how a parabolic mirror forms a real image. It is simple to construct because each ray has to obey the law of reflection:

angle of incidence = angle of reflection

Reflecting telescopes

The first design for a reflecting telescope was proposed in 1636, not long after Galileo's refracting telescope. It used a parabolic mirror as the telescope objective.

Mirrors have several advantages over lenses, and are used in nearly all large professional telescopes.
- A mirror reflects rays of all colours in exactly the same way.
- It is possible to support a mirror several metres in diameter so that it does not sag. Its weight can be supported from the back as well as the sides.

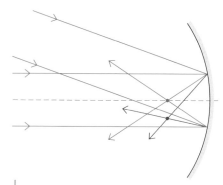

Rays parallel to the axis of the reflector are reflected to the focus. Parallel rays from another direction are focused at a different point.

- A mirror can be made very smooth so that the image is not distorted.
- By choosing suitable materials, reflectors can be made to focus most types of electromagnetic radiation.

The Arecibo radio telescope in Puerto Rico is a reflector built into a natural crater. Hanging above the dish is the detector, which is moved around to collect the reflected radio waves coming from different directions in space.

The Arecibo radio telescope is built into a natural crater. It cannot be steered about.

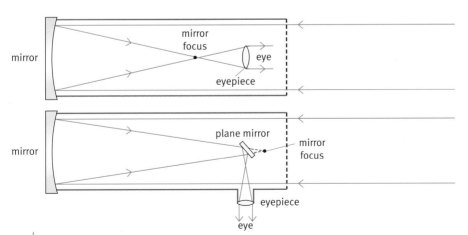

A problem with a reflecting telescope is where to place the observer. In the top diagram, the observer must be inside the telescope. In a different design, a small plane mirror close to the focus of the objective reflects light out of the telescope to an external eyepiece. Many other solutions are in common use.

Questions

1 Sketch a curved mirror. Draw two rays of light striking the mirror parallel to the axis and show how the mirror brings the rays to a focus.

2 Write down three advantages of using a reflector telescope rather than a refractor telescope.

Find out about

- ✔ **what happens to waves when they go through an aperture**
- ✔ **why radio telescopes are in general much bigger than optical ones**

Clear image

Most modern professional telescopes are very big. You have already considered one reason for this: they need to collect a lot of radiation in order to detect faint objects. But there is another reason: it is to make the image clearer so that more detail can be seen.

If an image is blurred, you cannot resolve (distinguish) much detail. To get a clear image you need a telescope with good **resolving power**.

Radio telescopes have to be much bigger than optical ones to get the same resolving power. To understand why, you need to study what happens to waves when they go through an aperture.

Waves through an aperture

When waves hit a barrier, they bend a little at the edge and travel into the shadow region behind the barrier. This effect is called **diffraction**. The longer the wavelength of the wave, the more it diffracts.

At a gap between two barriers, waves bend a little at both edges. If the width of the gap is similar to their wavelength, the waves beyond the gap are almost perfect semicircles. If the gap is really tiny, much less than the wavelength of the waves, the waves do not go through at all.

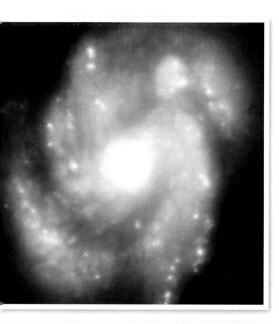

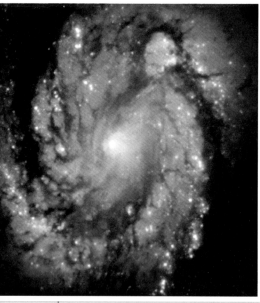

Two views of a region of the night sky, taken with telescopes with different resolving powers.

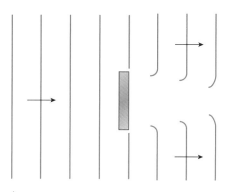

Diffraction occurs when waves meet an obstacle. The edges of the waves bend round the obstacle, into the shadow region behind.

Plane waves arrive at this harbour mouth. The waves inside the harbour are semicircular, because of diffraction at the narrow gap between the two piers.

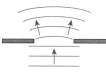

Waves spread out as they pass through the aperture.

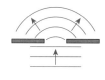

A narrower aperture has more effect.

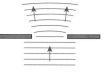

A smaller wavelength gives less diffraction.

The effect is greatest when the aperture is similar to the wavelength of the waves.

Diffraction and resolving power

When a beam of radiation arrives from a very distant object ('at infinity'), it consists of plane waves all travelling in one direction. But when the beam goes through the aperture of a telescope (or the pupil of your eye), diffraction occurs and the waves spread out to give a blurred image.

Even a very small amount of diffraction causes slight blurring. So to reduce diffraction effects, astronomers design telescopes with apertures much larger than the wavelength of the radiation they want to gather.

For optical astronomers, diffraction is not too big a problem because the wavelength of light is so small. More blurring is usually caused by 'twinkling' as light passes through the atmosphere.

Diffraction is much more of a problem for radio astronomers. The wavelengths they use are normally a few centimetres. Even a radio telescope a mile across does not have very good resolving power.

To get a big aperture, radio telescopes often have an array of several small dishes linked together. This arrangement can have the same resolving power as a single telescope with an aperture equal to the distance across the array.

The Very Large Array in New Mexico, USA, is the world's largest radio telescope. It has 27 dishes that can be moved along the 21-km-long arms of a Y-shaped track.

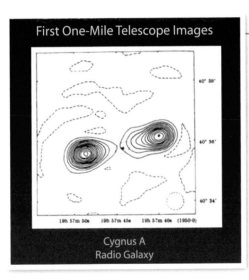

This image of the galaxy Cygnus A was made in the 1960s with a one-mile radio telescope (its dishes were spread out over a distance of one mile). It is shown as a contour map with lines joining points of equal brightness. Compare it with the image of the same galaxy on page 211.

Key words
- ✓ **resolving power**
- ✓ **diffraction**

Questions

1. Draw diagrams to show what happens to a plane wave as it passes through a gap in a barrier that is:
   a bigger than its wavelength
   b about the same size as its wavelength.

2. Look at the two radio images of the galaxy Cygnus A on this page and on page 211. In which image are the details better resolved?

3. An astronomer finds that she can scarcely resolve two images. Which of these will improve the situation:
   a using a telescope with a smaller aperture?
   b observing radiation of a shorter wavelength?
   Explain your answer.

Find out about

✓ **which electromagnetic radiation can get through the atmosphere**
✓ **how light pollution affects astronomy**

Some telescopes are built on high mountains. Others are carried on spacecraft in orbit around the Earth. This is partly because some types of electromagnetic radiation are absorbed by the atmosphere.

- The atmosphere **transmits** (allows through) visible light, microwaves, radio waves, and some infrared.
- Other radiation, including X-rays, gamma rays, and much infrared, is **absorbed**.

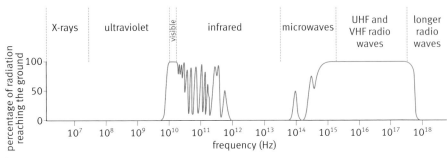

Graph showing the percentage of radiation reaching the Earth's surface across the electromagnetic spectrum.

The Hubble Space Telescope orbits above the Earth, avoiding the effects of atmospheric absorption and refraction of light. As well as gathering visible light, Hubble also gathers ultraviolet and infrared radiation.

Twinkle, twinkle

If you look up at the stars in the night sky, you are looking up through the atmosphere. Even when the sky appears clear, the stars twinkle. This shows an important feature of the atmosphere.

The stars, of course, shine more or less steadily. Their light may travel across space, uninterrupted, for millions of years. It is only on the last few seconds of its journey to your eyes that things go wrong. The twinkling, or scintillation, is caused when starlight passes through the atmosphere.

The atmosphere is not uniform. Some areas are more dense, and some areas are less dense. As a ray of light passes through areas of different densities, it is refracted and changes direction. The atmosphere is in constant motion (because of convection currents and winds), so areas of different density move around. This causes a ray to be refracted in different directions, and is the cause of scintillation.

Some astronomical telescopes record images electronically. Computer software allows them to reduce or remove completely the effects of scintillation from the images they produce.

Dark skies, please

A telescope 'sees' stars against a black background. However, many astronomers find that the sky they are looking at is brightened by **light pollution**. Much of this is light that shines upwards from street lamps and domestic lighting. **Scattered** by the atmosphere, the light enters any nearby telescope.

Another consequence is that it has become difficult to see the stars at night from urban locations. People today are less aware of the changing nature of the night sky, something that was common knowledge for our ancestors.

In 2006, the city authorities in Rome decided that enough was enough. To reduce light pollution and to save energy, it was decided to switch off many of its 170 000 street lights, thereby cutting its lighting bill by 40%. Illumination of its ancient monuments has been dimmed, as well as lights in shop and hotel windows.

The Campaign for Dark Skies, supported by amateur and professional astronomers, campaigns to reduce light pollution. But it is not only light radiation that affects astronomers. Electrical equipment can produce weak radio waves, particularly when being switched on and off. And radio waves used for broadcasting and mobile phones can interfere with the work of radio telescopes, so certain ranges of frequencies must be left clear for astronomical observations.

Key words

- ✓ **transmits**
- ✓ **absorbed**
- ✓ **light pollution**
- ✓ **scattered**

These two maps show the amount of light pollution across the United Kingdom in 1993 and 2000. The red areas indicate where most light is emitted, the dark-blue areas where the least is emitted. You can see that the red areas have grown over the seven years between surveys. But the biggest change is in the countryside. Here the light pollution, although at lower levels than in towns and cities, has increased across large areas of England.

Questions

1 Some astronomers want to study radiation with a frequency around 10^9 Hz. Use information from the graph to explain whether they could do this with a ground-based telescope.

2 Suggest how information from a space telescope could be sent to astronomers on the ground.

3 Do you think it is important to reduce light pollution? Give reasons for your point of view.

Astronomers working together at ESO

There are parts of the sky that are not visible from the northern hemisphere. So 14 European countries have joined together to do astronomical research in an organisation known as the European Southern Observatory (ESO). Together they operate observatories at three sites in the Atacama Desert, high up in the Andes mountains of Chile. Two of ESO's sites are on mountain tops at heights of about 2500 m above sea level. The third observatory, which ESO is building together with other international partners, is the ALMA array of radio telescopes on a 5000-m-high plateau. These remote locations are chosen because the atmosphere is both clear and dry there. This reduces the effects of absorption and refraction of radiation, and of light pollution.

Remote control

Each year, astronomers make observations for about 500 projects using the ESO telescopes. Half of them do this from their home base in Europe. ESO does this by making great use of the power of computers and the Internet. The telescopes in Chile are remote: it takes two days of travel to reach them, and two days to get home again. So many of the astronomers who need observations to be made send in their requests, and these are programmed into the ESO control system. Local operators ensure that the observations are made, and the results are sent back to Europe.

Aerial view of ESO's Paranal Observatory, Chile. The summit of Cerro Paranal is at an altitude of 2600 m.

One benefit of this is to avoid the 'weather lottery'. ESO telescope sites were chosen for their excellent weather but some observations are so sensitive that they require the clearest of skies that these places have to offer. Imagine travelling of Chile for three nights' observing, only to find that the skies were not quite clear enough! ESO's computer control ensures that your observations are postponed to a later date, while another astronomer's observations are brought forward to take advantage of the available time.

ESO's flagship telescope is the Very Large Telescope (VLT) on the 2600-m-high mountaintop of Cerro Paranal in Chile. It is not just one, but an array of four giant telescopes, each with a main mirror 8.2 m in diameter. The next step beyond the VLT is to build a European Extremely Large Telescope (E-ELT) with a main mirror 42 m in diameter. The E-ELT will be "the world's biggest eye on the sky" — the largest telescope in the world to observe visible light and infrared light, and ESO is currently drawing up detailed design plans.

The ESO Very Large Telescope (VLT) on Cerro Paranal in Chile.

The Paranal Residencia accommodates visiting astronomers. The central area is naturally lit through a dome in the ceiling. At the centre of the dome, an umbrella-shaped blackout curtain automatically opens at sunset, to avoid artificial light escaping and interfering with astronomical observations. The curtain closes automatically at sunrise.

Control room for the ESO Very Large Telescope.

ESO people

Douglas Pierce-Price is a British astronomer based at the ESO headquarters in Germany.

How many people work for ESO?

In 2010 ESO employs about 740 staff members around the world (primarily at our headquarters in Germany and in Chile). Included in this are about 180 local staff recruited in Chile, thus providing work with high skill levels for local people.

You don't have to be an astronomer to work at ESO: we also employ engineers, including software engineers, as well as technical and administrative staff. In addition, there are currently opportunities annually for about 40 students and 40 research fellows who are attached to the organisation. These opportunities are open either to students enrolled in a Ph.D. programme or Fellows who have achieved their Ph.D. in astronomy, physics, or a related discipline.

What is it like to live and work in a desert on top of a mountain?

When working at ESO's Very Large Telescope (VLT) on Cerro Paranal, the observatory staff live and work in the Residencia, a futuristic building built partly underground and with a 35-metre-wide glass dome in the roof. It is part of the VLT's 'base camp' facility, situated a short distance below the summit of Cerro Paranal.

Astronomical conditions at Paranal are excellent, but they come at a price. It's a forbidding desert environment; virtually nothing can grow outside. The humidity can be as low as 10%, there are intense ultraviolet rays from the Sun, and the high altitude can

Douglas Pierce-Price

leave people short of breath. The nearest town is two hours away, so there is a small paramedic clinic at the base camp.

Living in this extremely isolated place feels like visiting another planet. Within the Residencia, a small garden and a swimming pool are designed to increase the humidity inside. The building provides visitors and staff with some relief from the harsh conditions outside: there are about 100 rooms for astronomers and other staff, as well as offices, a library, cinema, gymnasium, and cafeteria.

Up all night

Monika Petr-Gotzens is a German astronomer working at the European Southern Observatory. She is studying how stars form in dense clusters. She is particularly interested in the formation of binary stars. These are pairs of stars that orbit one another. Almost half of all stars are in binary pairs.

Monika uses both radio telescopes and optical (light) telescopes in her work.

What is it like to work with a telescope at the top of a mountain?

The Observatory sites are in such isolated places where, during new-moon, the nights are the darkest nights I have ever seen, and the work at the mountain top is accompanied by a natural, amazing silence that one can only experience at these very remote sites. When standing outside the telescope domes you hear only a low drone from the telescope while it changes its pointing position. It is here, on the telescope platform, that one gets the feeling of being part of a very special mission.

The way that we observe with telescopes today is quite different from the image that many people have of an astronomer standing in the cold with their eye to a telescope, looking towards the sky. The control over the telescope and instrument is 100% computer based, and carried out from a control room. The control room is about 100 m away from the telescope, and you don't even see the telescope during your observation, unless you actively walk into the dome. So it isn't the freezing cold that keeps you awake during the observing night, but the smell of coffee and cookies.

What part do computers play in your work?

Modern astronomy without computer control is unthinkable. It sharpens our view of the Universe by directing the telescope very accurately. Computers also process the data gathered by the telescope to give much higher quality images and measurements.

Astronomers today usually work in collaborative teams. Why is this?

International collaborations are very important. Nowadays, it is not a single clever observation that solves one of the grand questions of the Universe. They are answered through major efforts. For example, very deep surveys of stars or galaxy fields across large areas of the sky. It is often impossible for

Monika Petr-Gotzens

individuals to deal with the huge amount of data accumulated from such surveys.

The ESO telescopes are sited high on mountains. Why is this?

The factors that influence the choice of site for an observatory depend on the kind of observatory: optical, infrared, millimetre, or radio waves. For optical observatories, a low-turbulent atmosphere (i.e. very good seeing), a dark sky without light pollution, and a high number of clear sky nights are important factors. It's easier for radio telescopes – they can see through clouds to some extent.

The size of the telescope is also important. Independent of the working wavelength, the rule applies that the larger the telescope, the less windy a site must be, to avoid image blur from vibrations caused by wind shake.

On top of that, sites must also have a practical logistical supply. It must be reasonably easy for astronomers to travel to the observatory, and they need accommodation, food, and drink. Natural springs, for example, for the water supply, are an advantage, although not an absolute requirement.

Topic 3: Mapping the Universe

This spiral galaxy looks rather like the Milky Way seen from the outside. It is 25 million light-years away.

Astronomical distances

Astronomy deals with gigantic objects lying at mind bogglingly huge distances. The pictures on these two pages give just a few examples.

Solar System

Neptune is the furthest major planet from the Sun. The radius of its orbit is about 4500 million km. Beyond Neptune there are dwarf planets and other small objects, such as comets, that orbit the Sun so are part of the Solar System. The furthest of these could be as far as one light-year from the Sun.

One light-year (ly) is the distance electromagnetic radiation travels through space in one year. $1 \text{ ly} = 9.5 \times 10^{12} \text{ km}$

Milky Way galaxy

The Sun is one of about 100 thousand million stars that make up the Milky Way galaxy. This disc-shaped collection of stars is about 100 000 light-years across, and the Sun lies about two-thirds of the way out from the centre.

We can't see the Milky Way from the outside, but we can see other galaxies. Like the Milky Way, some are disc shaped with their brightest stars tracing out a spiral shape.

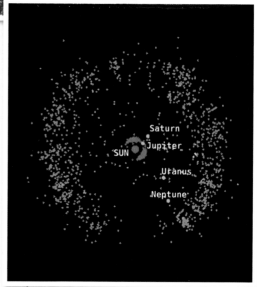

There is more to the Solar System than eight planets and the Sun. This image is created using data about minor planets, asteroids and comets. The four outer planets are blue. Asteroids associated with Jupiter's orbit are pink. The green objects are small objects such as comets and minor planets. The pronounced gap at the bottom is due to lack of data because the sky is obscured by the band of the Milky Way.

Other galaxies

Some galaxies are spirals like the Milky Way, but many are simple oval-shaped collections of stars. Some galaxies have strange shapes that might have been produced when two galaxies collide and merge.

This pair of colliding spiral galaxies is about 400 million light-years away.

This elliptical galaxy is about 300 million light-years away.

The Universe

Since the early 20th century, telescopes have revealed millions of galaxies scattered through space at distances up to 13 *thousand* million light-years. The light we are receiving from them now must have been emitted 13 thousand million years ago – not long after the Big Bang that began the Universe.

How do we know?

In order to understand and explain the Universe and the objects we see in it, we need to know how far away they are. Once an object's distance is known, then astronomers can work out other things, such as how big it is and how much energy it is giving out.

Distance measurement is one of astronomy's major challenges. You can't simply pace out the distance or use a tape measure. Nor (with the exception of the Moon and some nearby planets) is it possible to send a radar pulse and time how long it takes before you detect its echo. So astronomers have had to rely on observations of radiation received on Earth, coupled with ingenuity. In this topic you will learn more about some of the methods they have devised.

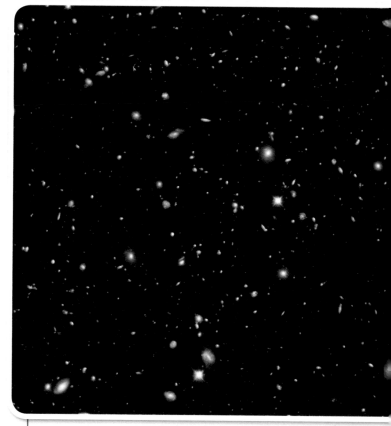

The Hubble Space Telescope has given us a striking view of Universe that contains many billions of galaxies.

Find out about

- ✔ **how distances to nearby stars can be measured**
- ✔ **parallax as an indication of distance**
- ✔ **the parsec as a unit of distance**
- ✔ **how observed brightness can indicate distance**
- ✔ **what determines a star's luminosity**

Parallax angles

The stars are far off. How can we measure their distances? One way is to use the idea of parallax.

Imagine looking across a city park in which there are a number of trees scattered about. You take a photograph. Now take two steps to the right and take another photograph. Your photos will look very similar, but the *relative* positions of the trees will have changed slightly. Perhaps one tree that was hidden behind another has now come into view.

These two photos illustrate the effect of parallax. They show the same view, but the photographer moved sideways before taking the second one. The closest object, the person on the bench, has moved furthest across the image.

Now superimpose the photos one on top of the other and you will see that the closer trees will have shifted their positions in the picture more than those that are more distant. You have observed an effect of **parallax**.

Astronomers can see the same effect. As the Earth travels along its orbit round the Sun, some stars seem to shift their positions slightly against a background of fixed stars. This shifting of position against a fixed background is what astronomers call parallax, and it can be used to work out the distance of the star in question.

The diagram on the left shows how astronomers define the **parallax angle** of a star. They compare the direction of the star at an interval of six months. The parallax angle is *half* the angle moved by the star in this time.

From the diagram, you should be able to see that, the closer the star, the greater is its parallax angle.

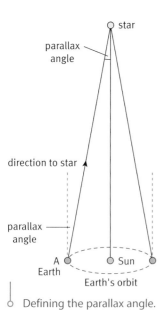

Defining the parallax angle.

The scale of things

In the Middle Ages, astronomers imagined that all of the stars were equally distant from the Earth. It was as if they were fixed in a giant crystal sphere, or perhaps pinholes in a black dome, letting through heaven's light. They could only believe this because the patterns of the stars do not change through the year – there is no obvious parallax effect.

They were wrong. But it is not surprising that they were wrong, because parallax angles are very small. The radius of the Earth's orbit is about 8 light-minutes, but the nearest star is about 4 light-years away – that's over 250 000 times as far.

Parallax angles are usually measured in fractions of a second of arc. There are:

- 360° in a full circle
- 60′ (minutes) of arc in 1°
- 60″ (seconds) of arc in 1′

So a second of arc is $\frac{1}{3600}$ of a degree.

Astronomers use a unit of distance based on this: the **parsec** (pc).

- An object whose parallax angle is 1 second of arc is at a distance of 1 parsec.

$$\text{Distance (parsec)} = \frac{1}{\text{parallax angle (sec)}}$$

Because a smaller angle means a bigger distance:

- An object whose parallax angle is 2 seconds of arc is at a distance of 0.5 parsec.

A parsec is about 3.1×10^{13} km. This is of a similar magnitude to a light-year, which is 9.5×10^{12} km. Typically, the distance between neighbouring stars in our galaxy is a few parsecs.

The European Hipparcos satellite measured the parallax angles of over 100 000 stars out to a distance of about a thousand parsecs.

Key words

- ✓ **parallax**
- ✓ **parallax angle**
- ✓ **parsec**

Questions

1 Draw a diagram to show that a star with a large parallax angle is closer than one with a small parallax angle.

2 How many light-years are there in a parsec?

3 What is the parallax angle of a star at a distance of 1000 pc?

4 If a star has a parallax angle of 0.25 seconds of arc, how far away is it (in parsecs)?

5 Suggest reasons why a satellite was needed to measure very small parallax angles.

6 Suggest why astronomers calculate distances in parsecs, but newspapers and magazines use the light-year when writing about astronomical distances.

Brightness and distance

Measurements of parallax angles allow astronomers to measure the distance to a star. This only works for relatively nearby stars. But there are other methods of finding how far away a star is.

In the late seventeenth century, scientists were anxious to know just how big the Universe was. The Dutch physicist Christiaan Huygens devised a technique for measuring the distance of a star from Earth. He realised that, the more distant a star, the fainter its light would be. This is because the light from a star spreads outwards, and so the more distant the observer, the smaller the amount of light that they receive. So measuring the **observed brightness** of a star would give an indication of its distance.

Here is how Huygens set about putting his idea into practice:
- At night, he studied a star called Sirius, the brightest star in the sky.
- The next day he placed a screen between himself and the bright disc of the Sun. He made a succession of smaller and smaller holes in the screen until he felt that the speck of light he saw was the same brightness as Sirius.
- Then he calculated the fraction of the Sun's disc that was visible to him. It seemed that roughly 1 / 30 000 of the Sun's brightness equalled the brightness of Sirius. His calculation showed that Sirius was 27 664 times as distant as the Sun.

Huygens understood that his method had some problems. Here are three of them:
- First, there was subjectivity in his measurements. He had to judge when his two observations through the screen were the same.
- Second, his method assumed that Sirius and the Sun are identical stars, radiating energy at the same rate.
- Third, he had to assume that no light was absorbed between Sirius and his screen.

Astronomers now know that Sirius is about 500 000 times as distant as the Sun. But at the time, Huygens' measurement was a breakthrough because it used the idea that the Sun would look like other stars if seen from far enough away. Also, Huygens was the first to show that stars lay at such vast distances.

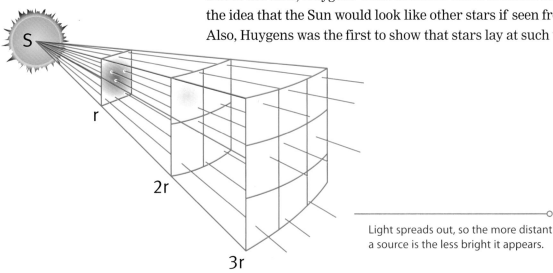

Light spreads out, so the more distant a source is the less bright it appears.

Luminosity

Stars are not all the same. They do not all give out the same amount of light – they have different luminosities.

The **luminosity** of a star is its power output. It is the energy it gives out each second by radiating light and other types of electromagnetic radiation. The Sun's luminosity is about 4×10^{26} W – compare this with the 'luminosity' of a typical electric lamp.

A star's luminosity depends on two factors:
- its temperature – a hotter star radiates more energy per second from each square metre of its surface
- its size – a bigger star has a greater surface radiating energy.

The observed brightness recorded by an astronomer depends on a star's luminosity as well as its distance. Also, any dust or gas between Earth and the star may absorb some of its light.

If astronomers are confident that two stars have the same luminosity, they can use their observed brightness to compare the stars' distances. But rather than relying on subjective judgement like Huygens did, they use sensitive instruments to measure brightness.

Key words
- ✓ **observed brightness**
- ✓ **luminosity**

Questions

7 Suggest at least one other problem with Huygens' method.

8 Explain how two stars having the same observed brightness may have different luminosity.

9 If some starlight is absorbed by dust, explain whether this would make a star appear closer or further away than it really is.

These stars are all roughly 8200 light-years from Earth. They have a range of luminosities, giving a range of observed brightness.

Cepheid variable stars

The Sun and many other stars emit light at a steady rate. But some stars are **variable stars**, meaning that their luminosity varies. Variations in luminosity can provide clues about what's happening in the stars – and can sometimes have other uses too.

In 1784 a young English astronomer, John Goodricke, discovered a new type of variable star. He noticed that a star called δ Cephei (δ = delta) went from dim to bright and back again with a time **period** of about a week, and that this variation was very regular. The graph below shows some modern measurements of the brightness of this star.

Find out about

✓ **why some stars vary regularly in brightness**
✓ **how Cepheid variable stars can be used to measure astronomical distances**

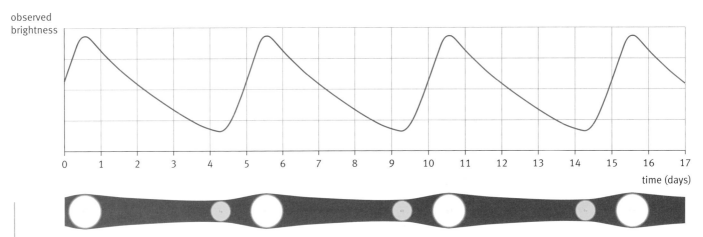

The observed brightness of δ Cephei varies regularly. The variation in its luminosity is caused by its expansion and contraction.

Many stars have been found that vary in this way, and they have been named Cepheid variables, or simply **Cepheids**. It is now thought that a star like this is expanding and contracting so that its temperature and luminosity vary. Its diameter may vary by as much as 30%.

Cepheids and distance measurement

In the early years of the twentieth century, an American astronomer called Henrietta Leavitt made a very important discovery. She looked at Cepheids in a small galaxy close to the Milky Way. She noticed that the brightest Cepheids varied with the longest periods, and drew a graph to represent this.

Because the stars she was studying were all roughly the same distance, Leavitt realised that the stars that appeared brightest were also the ones with the greatest luminosity – they were not brighter simply because they were closer.

Henrietta Leavitt, whose work opened up a new method of measuring the Universe.

Measuring distances

Henrietta Leavitt had discovered a method of determining the distance to star clusters in the Milky Way, and to other galaxies. There are two parts to the method.

Part one:
- find some nearby Cepheids whose distances have been measured using other methods
- measure their brightness and work out their luminosities
- plot a graph of luminosity against period.

Part two:
- look for a Cepheid in a star cluster or galaxy of interest
- measure its observed brightness and period of variation
- from the period, read its luminosity off the graph
- use the luminosity and observed brightness to work out the distance.

The Cepheid method has been used to measure distance to galaxies up to a few **megaparsecs** (Mpc) away. (1 Mpc = 1 million parsecs)

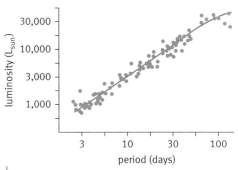

The luminosity of a Cepheid variable star is related to its period.

Questions

1 From the graph on the previous page, deduce the period of variation of δ Cephei.

2 Why did Henrietta Leavitt assume that the stars she was studying were all at roughly the same distance from Earth?

3 Suggest how distances to nearby Cepheids might have been measured.

4 Suggest why Cepheids cannot be used to measure distances beyond a few Mpc.

Key words
- ✔ **variable stars**
- ✔ **period**
- ✔ **Cepheids**
- ✔ **megaparsecs**

Find out about

- ✓ **how stars are distributed in our galaxy**
- ✓ **how measurements of distance revealed the nature of spiral nebulae**

The shape of the Milky Way

On a clear dark night, you can see a faint milky band of light stretching across the sky. This is the Milky Way. With a telescope, you can see that its light comes from vast numbers of faint stars surrounding us in a disc-shaped arrangement.

In 1785, William Herschel attempted to determine the shape of the **galaxy**. Looking through his telescope, he counted all the stars he could see in a particular direction. Then he moved his telescope round a little and counted again. Once he had done a complete circle, he could draw out a map of a slice through the Milky Way.

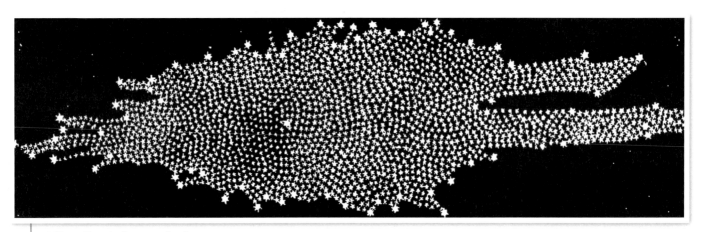

William Herschel's map of a slice through the Milky Way. The Sun is shown near the centre. The more stars seen in a particular direction, the greater the distance to the edge in that direction.

Herschel knew that he was making the following assumptions:

- that his telescope could detect all the stars in the direction he was looking
- that he could see to the far end of the galaxy.

Herschel himself discovered his first assumption to be incorrect when he built a bigger telescope. Astronomers now know that Herschel's second assumption was also incorrect. Dust in the galaxy makes it difficult to see stars in the packed centre of the galaxy.

Sun

Harlow Shapley's idea of the Milky Way galaxy.

Shapley and the nebulae

By the early 20th century, astronomers were starting to use really big telescopes, especially in America. Harlow Shapley worked in California, investigating faint patches of light called nebulae (**nebula** means cloud; nebulae is the plural). Some nebulae are irregular 'blobs' of light, some are roughly circular, while others are spirals. A good telescope reveals that some nebulae are gas clouds but others are clusters of stars.

Thanks to Henrietta Leavitt, Shapley had a new way to measure distances to stars in nebulae. He found that the roughly spherical star clusters (now called **globular clusters**) had distances up to about 100 000 light-years, and that they seemed to lie in a sphere around the Milky Way.

Spiral nebulae – the great debate

Shapley and some other astronomers thought the spiral nebulae were in the Milky Way. Others, including Heber D Curtis (also American) suggested they were 'island universes' a very long way outside the Milky Way.

In 1920, Shapley and Curtis held a public 'great debate'. On the night, Curtis came off better, partly because he was the better speaker.

Then in 1923, American astronomer Edwin Hubble was using a new telescope to study the Andromeda nebula. He spotted a faint Cepheid and found it was almost one *million* light-years away. This was enough to convince astronomers that they were looking at a separate, distant galaxy. Other spiral nebulae were then also found to be galaxies.

This spiral nebula is in the part of the sky belonging to the constellation of Andromeda.

A recent view

Modern optical and infrared telescopes have been used to map the layout of stars in the Milky Way. They show that, like the Andromeda nebula, it is a spiral galaxy.

Key words
- ✓ galaxy
- ✓ nebula
- ✓ globular clusters

This artist's impression of the Milky Way is based on recent optical and infrared measurements.

Questions

1 Suggest reasons why Shapley's evidence seemed stronger than Curtis's on the night of the great debate.

2 What new observations showed that there were objects outside the Milky Way?

Find out about

- **some of the types of object studied by astronomers**
- **typical sizes and distances of some objects studied by astronomers**
- **why supernovae can be used to measure distance**

Key words

- **comet**
- **asteroid**
- **planetary nebula**
- **supernova**
- **supernova remnant**

More than just stars

Astronomers study many different types of object, not just stars and planets. Measurements of their distances and sizes help us to build our picture of the Universe.

Some of these objects are found in the Solar System. In astronomical terms, they are relatively nearby. Other objects of interest are found within the Milky Way galaxy. And others are seen at vast distances far beyond the Milky Way. The images on this page show just some examples of objects discovered and studied by astronomers.

Comets travel around the Sun in very long thin orbits. This is Halley's **comet**, which passes close to Earth every 76 years. At its furthest point, it reaches about 5 thousand million km from the Sun.

In 2010 a Japanese spacecraft returned to Earth after visiting the **asteroid** Itokawa, one of thousands of asteroids orbiting the Sun between Mars and Jupiter.

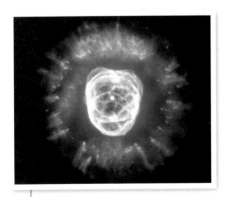

The Eskimo (or Clownface) nebula, about 1000 parsecs (3000 light-years) from Earth, is a **planetary nebula**. This name is misleading because they are nothing to do with planets. They are formed when a dying Sun-like star throws off its outer layers of hot gas. You can often see the remains of the star at the centre of the nebula.

The Crab nebula is about 2000 parsecs from Earth. It is the remains of a dying star that exploded in 1054 ad. The explosion, called a **supernova**, was so powerful that it could be seen in daylight from Earth. At the centre of the nebula is a pulsar (see page 210), all that remains of the original star. The nebula is an example of a **supernova remnant**.

This **quasar** is about 5 hundred million parsecs from Earth. Quasars are some of the most distant objects that can be seen from Earth. They are thought to be galaxies containing gigantic black holes that draw in material from their surroundings, heating it so that it emits vast amounts of radiation.

What can we learn from supernovae?

Supernova explosions are rare. They happen about once per century in a typical spiral galaxy. The most recent one seen in the Milky Way was in 1604 ad, and in 1987 one was observed in a small galaxy close to the Milky Way, about 168 000 light-years from Earth.

Astronomers study supernovae and their remnants in order to learn more about how stars come to an end. But there is another reason too.

Supernova explosions are monitored by measuring how their light output varies with time. One particular type of supernova always produces the same shape graph, and always seems to reach roughly the same peak luminosity. Astronomers can use these supernovae to work out the distances to galaxies where they are observed, in the same way that they use Cepheids to measure distance.

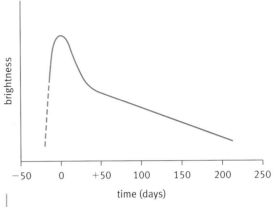

Graph showing how light output from a supernova explosion varies with time.

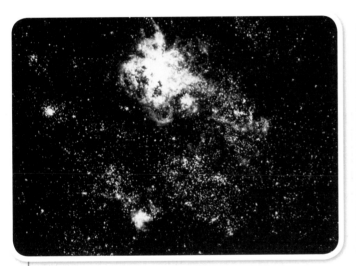

This supernova (shown in the bottom image on the right) was seen in February 1987, two days after it exploded. (The upper image was taken in 1969.) It is the closest supernova that has been seen for over 300 years.

Questions

1 For each object shown on these pages, say whether it is found within the Solar System, within the Milky Way galaxy, or far beyond the Milky Way. Use information from pages 234 and 235 to help you decide.

2 Write a plan for using supernovae to measure distance. Base your plan on the one for Cepheids on pages 240 and 245.

3 Suggest one reason for using supernovae, rather than Cepheids, to measure distances. Suggest at least one problem with using supernovae.

Moving galaxies

Edwin Hubble was fortunate to be working at a time (the 1920s) when the significance of Cepheid variables had been realised. They could be used as a 'measuring stick' to find the distance to other galaxies. At the same time, he was able to use some of the largest telescopes of his day, reflectors with diameters up to 5 metres.

Hubble conducted a survey of galaxies, objects that had not previously been seen, let alone understood, until these powerful instruments became available. In his book *The Realm of the Nebulae* (1936), he described what it was like to see individual stars in other galaxies:

> The observer looks out through the swarm of stars that surrounds him, past the borders and across empty space, to find another stellar system . . . The brightest objects in the nebula can be seen individually, and among them the observer recognises various types that are well known in his own stellar system. The apparent faintness of these familiar objects indicates the distance of the nebula – a distance so great that light requires seven hundred thousand years to make the journey.

Redshift

Hubble used Henrietta Leavitt's discovery to determine the distance of many galaxies. At the same time, he made a dramatic discovery of his own. This was that the galaxies all appeared to be receding (moving away) from us. He deduced this by looking at the spectra of stars in the galaxies. The light was shifted towards the red end of the spectrum, a so-called redshift.

It turned out that, the more distant the galaxy, the greater its **speed of recession** – another linear relationship. Hubble's graph shows that, although his data points are scattered about, the general trend is clear.

Edwin Hubble using the 48-inch telescope at the Mount Palomar observatory.

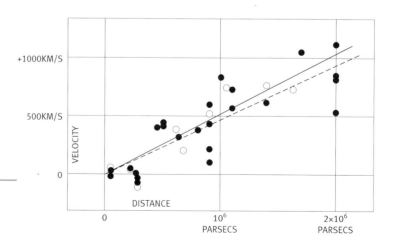

Edwin Hubble's graph, relating the speed of recession of a galaxy to its distance.

The Hubble constant

Hubble's finding can be written in the form of an equation:

speed of recession = Hubble constant × distance

The quantity called the **Hubble constant** shows how speed of recession is related to distance. His first value (from the graph) was about 500 km/s per megaparsec. In other words, a galaxy at a distance of 1 Mpc would be moving at a speed of 500 km/s. A galaxy at twice this distance would have twice this speed.

Other astronomers also began measuring the Hubble constant, using many more distant galaxies. Hubble's first value was clearly too high. For decades, the measurement uncertainties remained high and so there were disputes about the correct value. By 2010, the accepted value of the Hubble constant was 70.6 ± 3.1 km/s per Mpc. This value is based on a large number of measurements, including using many Cepheids and supernovae.

Back to the big bang

Astronomers had discovered that clusters of galaxies are all moving apart from each other. The further they are away, the faster they are moving. It doesn't matter where you are in the Universe, everything appears to moving away – space itself seems to be expanding. Edwin Hubble's discovery:

- the Universe itself may be expanding, and may have been much smaller in the past
- the Universe may have started by exploding outwards from a single point – the big bang.

This is now the widely accepted model of how the Universe began. Scientists use the model to work out how long ago the expansion started. They calculate that the Universe is about 14 thousand million years old.

Questions

1 Calculate the speed of recession of a galaxy that is at a distance of 100 Mpc, if the Hubble constant is 70 km/s per Mpc.

2 Using the same value of the Hubble constant given in question 1, calculate the distance of a galaxy whose speed of recession is 2000 km/s.

3 A galaxy lies at a distance of 40 Mpc from Earth. Measurements show its speed of recession is 3000 km/s. What value does this suggest for the Hubble constant?

Key words

- ✓ speed of recession
- ✓ Hubble constant

Topic 4: Stars

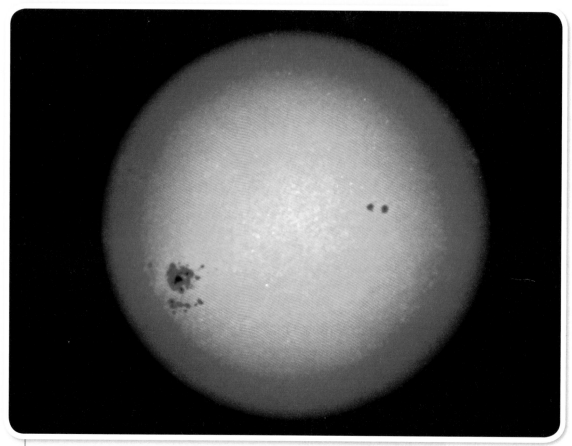

The surface of the Sun is quite dramatic when seen from close up. These are sunspots, cooler areas of the surface. They are still very hot, but perhaps 1000 °C cooler than the average surface temperature of about 5500°C.

Mystery of the Sun

The Sun is our star. By understanding the Sun better, astronomers hope to be able to make more sense of the variety of stars they see in the night sky.

The Sun is much closer than any other star, so it is the easiest star to gather detailed scientific data on. Scientists study its surface and analyse the radiation coming from it. They turn their telescopes on it, and send spacecraft to make measurements from close up.

An energy source

What makes the Sun work? How does it keep pouring out energy, day after day, year after year, millennium after millennium – for billions of years? Why does it burn so steadily? These are questions that have puzzled scientists for centuries.

Some suggestions were that it was powered by volcanoes, that it was burning coal, that it used the energy of comets that fell into it, or simply the energy of the Sun itself as it collapsed inwards under the pull of its own gravity. In this topic you will find out more about the energy source that powers the Sun and other stars.

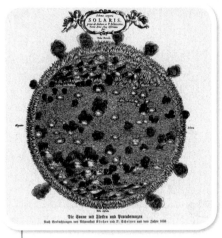

Seventeenth century view – the Sun as an enormous lump of coal.

Composition

In the 1830s, the French philosopher Auguste Comte suggested there were certain things that we could never know. As an example, he gave the chemical composition of the stars. But by 1860 physicists had interpreted the spectrum of starlight and identified the elements present. In this topic you will learn how this works.

The dark lines in this spectrum show which chemical elements are present in the Sun.

Weather from the Sun

The Sun seems to shine steadily, but actually it is a place of violent upheaval. Detailed observations reveal giant bubbles of gas bursting out of the Sun and flying out into space. These are now known as coronal mass ejections (CMEs) and weigh as much as 100 billion tonnes.

CMEs consist of electrically charged particles. When one reaches Earth it can produce dramatic aurora effects in the night sky, but it can also damage electrical communication and power supply systems.

A CME can reach Earth in about four days, travelling at 1.5 million km/h. Light takes just 500 s to make the same journey, so space 'weather forecasts' can give advance warning of a CME's arrival.

In this topic you will learn about some of the processes that take place as stars form, as they shine, and as they end their lives.

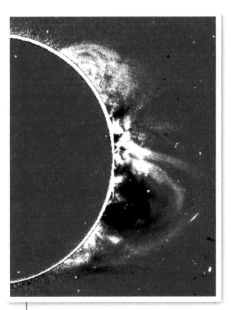

A coronal mass ejection (CME) photographed from the orbiting SOHO solar observatory using an opaque disc to block the Sun's bright disc.

Colour and temperature

A star produces a continuous range of frequencies across the **electromagnetic spectrum**. Most of its radiation is in the infrared, visible and ultraviolet regions of the spectrum, but stars also produce radio waves and X-rays. If you look out at the stars at night, you may get a hint that they shine with different colours – some reddish, some yellow (like the Sun), others brilliantly white. It is more obvious if you look through binoculars or a telescope.

Colour is linked to temperature. Imagine heating a lump of metal in a flame. At first, it glows dull red. As it gets hotter, it glows orange, then yellow, then bluish white.

You might notice that these colours appear in the order of the spectrum of visible light. Red is the cool end of the spectrum, violet the hot end. For centuries, the pottery industry has measured the temperature inside a kiln by looking at the colour of the light coming from inside.

So the colour of a star gives a clue to its surface temperature.

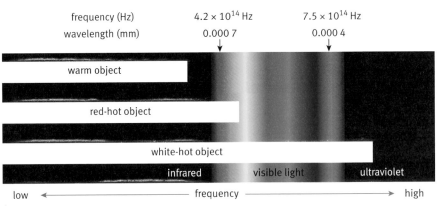

All objects emit some electromagnetic radiation. As the temperature rises, the amount of radiation at high frequencies increases.

Analysing starlight

At one time, astronomers judged the colours of stars and classified them accordingly. However, it is better to analyse stars' light using an instrument called a spectrometer. A spectrometer can be attached to a telescope so that it produces a spectrum, showing all of the frequencies that are present. The photographs show how a spectrometer turns the light from each star into a spectrum.

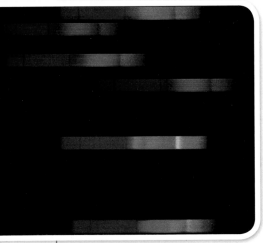

The Pleiades (top) is a group of bright stars about 500 light-years away. With a spectrometer, the light from each star is broken up into a spectrum (bottom image), revealing slight differences in their colour.

Comparing stars

Better still is to turn the spectrum of a star into a graph. The graph below shows the intensity (energy radiated per unit area of a star's surface) for each frequency in the spectrum.

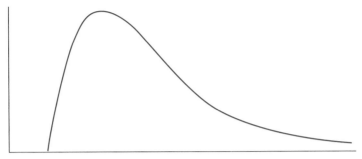

intensity of radiation at each frequency

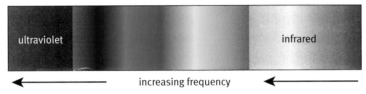

ultraviolet

infrared

← increasing frequency ←

 The graph of the spectrum provides information about intensity as well as showing which frequencies are present.

The Sun's radiation is most intense in the visible part of the spectrum, corresponding to a temperature of about 5500 °C.

The diagram on the right shows the results of comparing the spectra of hotter and cooler stars.

- For a hotter star, the area under the graph is greater; this shows that the luminosity of the star is greater.
- For a hotter star, the **peak frequency** is greater; it produces a greater proportion of radiation of higher frequencies.

These are not special rules for stars; they apply to any hot object.

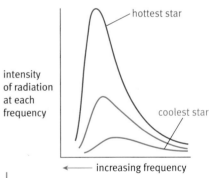

hottest star

intensity of radiation at each frequency

coolest star

← increasing frequency

The spectra of hotter and cooler stars.

Question

1 Stars A and B are the same size, but star A is hotter than star B.
   a Which star has greater luminosity?
   b If you examined the spectra of these stars, which would have the greater peak frequency?
   c Sketch graphs to show how these stars' spectra would differ.

Key words
- ✓ **electromagnetic spectrum**
- ✓ **peak frequency**

Find out about

- absorption and emission spectra as 'fingerprints' of elements
- electron energy levels and photons

The mystery of the Sun

It might seem impossible to find out what the Sun is made of. But it turns out you can do this by examining the light it gives out. If sunlight is passed through a prism or diffraction grating, it is split into a spectrum, from red to violet.

In 1802, William Woolaston noticed that the spectrum of sunlight had a strange feature – there were black lines, showing that some wavelengths were missing from the continuous spectrum. These lines are now called Fraunhofer lines, after Joseph von Fraunhofer who made many measurements of their wavelengths.

The colours of the elements

Fraunhofer knew that sodium burns with a yellow flame. When he looked at the spectrum of light from a sodium flame, Fraunhofer saw that it consisted of just a few coloured lines, rather than a continuous band from red to violet.

A spectrum like this is called an **emission spectrum**, because you are looking at the light emitted by a chemical. Today, we know that each element has a different pattern of lines in its emission spectrum, and that this can be used to identify the elements present.

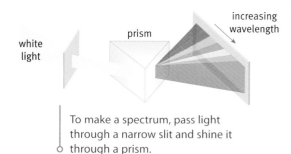

white light → prism → increasing wavelength

To make a spectrum, pass light through a narrow slit and shine it through a prism.

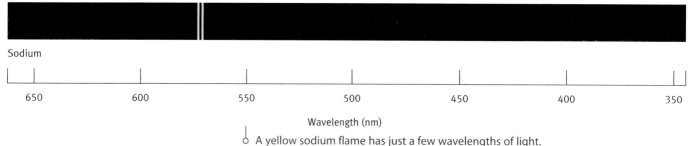

Sodium

| 650 | 600 | 550 | 500 | 450 | 400 | 350 |

Wavelength (nm)

A yellow sodium flame has just a few wavelengths of light.

Making sense of sunlight

The dark lines in the spectrum of sunlight (see opposite) are caused by the absorption of some colours, rather than emission. To understand what is going on, you have to think of the structure of the Sun.

- The surface of the Sun produces white light, with all wavelengths present.
- As this light passes through the Sun's atmosphere, some wavelengths are absorbed by atoms of elements that are present.

As a result, the light that reaches us from the Sun is missing some wavelengths, which correspond to elements in the Sun's atmosphere.

This is an example of an **absorption spectrum**. The wavelengths of the absorption lines reveal which elements have been doing the absorbing. From this, astronomers can identify the elements present in the Sun and in the most distant stars.

Light from the surface of the Sun must pass through its atmosphere before it reaches us.

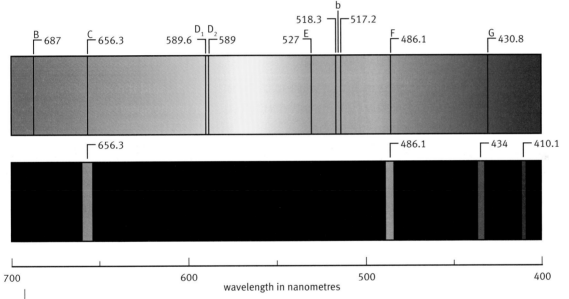

Lines in the emission spectrum of hydrogen (bottom) correspond to some of the dark absorption bands in the Sun's spectrum (top). Other lines in the absorption spectrum are due to other elements in the solar atmosphere, including helium. The numbers are the wavelengths of lines in the hydrogen spectrum in nanometres.

Questions

1 'Light is a messenger from the stars'. Explain how this statement is true.

2 Look at the emission spectrum of hydrogen above. What colours are the main emission lines in this spectrum? Which is the strongest (most intense) line?

A new element

The line spectrum of an element is different from that of every other element – it can be thought of as the 'fingerprint' of the element. In 1868, two scientists used this fact to discover a new element: helium. Norman Lockyer (English) and Jules César Janssen (French) took the opportunity of an eclipse of the Sun to look at the spectrum of light coming from the edge of the Sun. Janssen noticed a line in the spectrum that he had not seen before. He sent his observation to Lockyer, who realised that the line did not correspond to any known element. He guessed that some other element was present in the Sun, and he named it 'helium' after the Greek name for the Sun, 'Helios'. Studies of its spectrum reveal that the Sun is mostly composed of hydrogen and helium, with small amounts of many other elements.

Emitting light

To understand why different elements have different emission spectra, you need to know how atoms emit light. The light is emitted when electrons in atoms lose energy – the energy they lose is carried away by light.

That is a simple version of what happens, and it does not explain why only certain wavelengths appear in the spectrum. Here is a deeper explanation:

- The electrons in an atom can only have certain values of energy. Scientists think of them as occupying points on a 'ladder' of **energy levels**.
- When an electron drops from one energy level to another, it loses energy.
- As it does so, it emits a single **photon** of light – that is, a packet of energy. The energy of the photon is equal to the difference between the two energy levels.

The greater the energy gap, the greater the energy of the photon. High-energy photons correspond to high-frequency, short-wavelength light.

In the simplified diagram of energy levels shown above, you can see that only three photon energies are possible. The most energetic photon comes from an electron that has dropped from the top level to the bottom level.

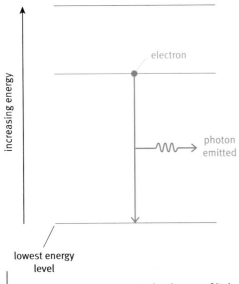

An electron gives out a single photon of light as it drops from one energy level to another.

Absorbing light

The same model can explain absorption spectra. The dark lines come about when electrons absorb energy from white light.

*   White light consists of photons with all possible values of energy.
*   An electron in a low energy level can only absorb a photon whose energy is just right to lift it up to a higher energy level. When it absorbs such a photon, it jumps to the higher level.
*   The white light is now missing photons that have been absorbed because their energies corresponded to the spacings in the ladder of energy levels. The 'missing' photons correspond to the dark lines in an absorption spectrum.

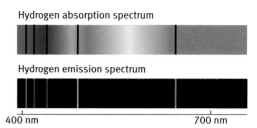

The missing frequencies in the absorption spectrum of hydrogen correspond exactly to the frequencies seen in its emission spectrum.

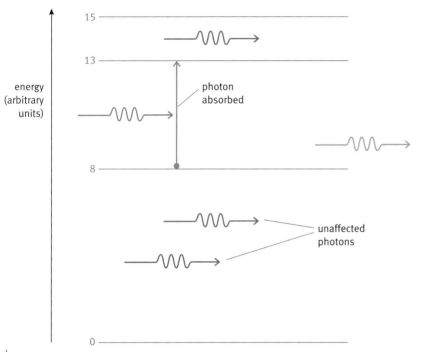

An electron jumps from one energy level to another when the atom absorbs a single photon of light.

The diagram above shows values of energy for each level (in arbitrary units). You can see that:

*   Photons of energies 2, 5, 7, 8, 13, and 15 would be absorbed.
*   Photons with other energies below 15 would not be absorbed.

A photon with sufficient energy can ionise an atom. An electron gains so much energy that it escapes the attractive force of the nucleus, and leaves the atom. As a result, the atom is left with net positive charge.

Questions

3   Which subatomic particles are associated with the emission and absorption of light?

4   For the energy-level diagram on this page:
    a   Explain how photons of energies 2, 5, and 8 would be absorbed.
    b   Give other energy values that would also be absorbed.
    c   Explain how an atom could emit a photon of energy 13 units.

Key words

✓   **energy levels**
✓   **photon**

Find out about

- ✔ **the nuclear reactions that power the Sun**

The mystery of the Sun

At the end of the 19th century, the source of the Sun's power was a matter of controversy. It had been thought that the Sun was a huge ball of burning coal or some other fuel, or perhaps it was heated by meteorites crashing into its surface. Another idea was that the Sun was shrinking under its own gravity, which would make it heat up.

But geological studies were revealing that the Earth was at least 300 million years old, and that life had evolved over that time. None of the ideas about the Sun's energy source could account for its output of light and heat over such a long time – there was nowhere near enough energy available.

Some influential physicists, including Lord Kelvin, argued that the geologists' and biologists' estimates of the Earth's age were wrong. Their arguments were so forceful that Darwin removed all mention of timescales from his book *On the Origin of Species* (1859).

Mystery solved

The turning point was the discovery of radioactivity and the realisation that radioactive decay could liberate enormous amounts of energy per atom. This led to the idea that nuclear fission and **fusion** reactions could be a source of energy. In 1920, the English astrophysicist Sir Arthur Eddington explained how fusion of hydrogen to produce helium could make the Sun shine for many *thousand* million years.

Nuclear fusion in the Sun

Nuclear fusion occurs when two atomic nuclei get so close together that the **strong nuclear force** makes them react to form a new nucleus. The nuclei's positive charges mean that they repel each other with an electrostatic force. Nuclei can only get close enough to fuse if they approach each other with very high energy. The interior of the Sun is very hot, so the particles are very energetic and nuclear fusion can take place.

Inside the Sun, hydrogen nuclei fuse to make helium. In a sequence of steps, four hydrogen nuclei (protons) make one helium nucleus.

Arthur Eddington, a British astrophysicist, explained how the Sun could be powered by nuclear fusion.

First, two hydrogen nuclei make a deuterium nucleus – the hydrogen isotope that has a proton and a neutron in its nucleus. As the proton decays to a neutron it releases a **positron**, a small positive particle similar to an electron.

$$^1_1H + {}^1_1H \longrightarrow 2\,{}^2_1H + {}^0_{+1}e^+$$

Notice that the nuclear equation balanced. The sum of the charges is the same both sides, and so is the sum of the atomic numbers. The whole process is shown in the diagram on the right. It can be summarised by the equation:

$$4\,{}^1_1H \longrightarrow {}^4_2He + 2\,{}^0_{+1}e^+ + 4\gamma$$

The total mass of the particles after the reaction is less than the total mass beforehand; there is a release of energy. This is described by Einstein's equation:

$$E = mc^2$$

$$\text{energy released} = \text{loss of mass} \times (\text{speed of light})^2$$

Overall, fusion of hydrogen to helium involves a mass loss of about 0.7%. Calculations show that hydrogen fusion releases enough energy to provide the Sun's radiation output from the time the Earth formed and for about as long again into the future.

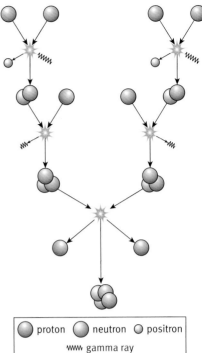

| proton | neutron | positron |
| ʌʌʌ gamma ray | | |

Fusion of hydrogen nuclei to make a helium nucleus involves several steps, with two nuclei fusing at each stage. This diagram shows one possible sequence of steps.

Questions

1 The second stage in the sequence shown in the diagram is:

$$^1_1H + {}^2_1H \longrightarrow {}^x_y Z$$

   a Work out the values of the mass number X and the charge Y of the new nucleus.

   b Is Z a nucleus of hydrogen or helium?

2 Write a balanced nuclear equation for the final stage shown in the diagram.

3 The Sun contains 1% oxygen nuclei. There are eight protons in an oxygen nucleus. Explain why oxygen nuclei are less likely to fuse together than hydrogen nuclei.

Key words

✓ **fusion**

✓ **strong nuclear force**

✓ **positron**

Find out about

- ✓ **using a Hertzsprung–Russell diagram to compare stars**
- ✓ **how stars are classified using their temperature and luminosity**
- ✓ **the raw materials for making stars**
- ✓ **the range of conditions found between stars**

Looking at the night sky, you see stars of different brightnesses and colours. By the beginning of the 20th century, astronomers had worked out how to make sense of this:

- Stars might be faint because they were a long way off. Knowing the distance to a faint star, they could work out its luminosity.
- Stars are different colours because they are different temperatures. Red is cool, blue is hot.

A Danish astronomer called Ejnar Hertzsprung set about finding if there was any connection between luminosity and temperature. He gathered together published data and drew up a chart, which he published in 1911.

An American, Henry Russell, came up with the same idea independently. He was unaware of Hertzsprung's chart, which had been published in a technical journal of photography. Today, the chart is known as the Hertzsprung–Russell diagram, or H–R diagram. A modern version is shown below.

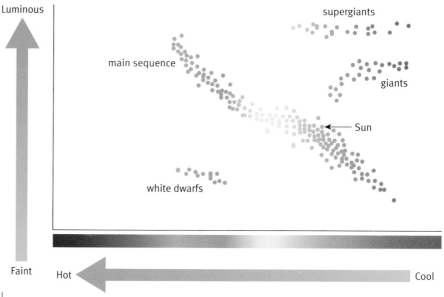

Data for stars – the H–R diagram.

Understanding the H–R diagram

This chart has luminosity on the vertical axis and temperature on the horizontal axis. It is usually drawn as shown, with temperature *decreasing* along the *x*-axis. The Sun is roughly at the middle of the chart.

By 1924, over 200 000 stars had been catalogued. When plotted on the H–R diagram, these stars fell into three groups:

- About 90% of stars (including the Sun) fell along a line running diagonally across the diagram. This is known as the **main sequence**.
- About 10% of stars were **white dwarfs**, small and hot.
- About 1% of stars were **red giants** or **supergiants**, much more luminous than main-sequence stars with the same temperatures.

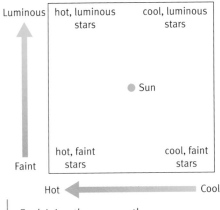

Explaining the axes on the Hertzsprung–Russell diagram.

What the H–R diagram reveals

The stars that appear on the H–R diagram are a representative selection of all stars. A first guess might be that there are simply three different, unrelated types of star. However, astronomers now believe that an individual star changes during its lifetime. They interpret the H–R diagram like this:

- Since most stars are on the main sequence, this suggests that an average star spends most of its lifetime as a main-sequence star.
- A star may spend a small part of its lifetime as a giant, and/or as a white dwarf.

With the exception of supernova explosions, astronomers cannot watch individual stars change through a lifetime because the process is much too slow to see. Instead, they link their observations of star populations to models of how stars work.

In the rest of this section, you will learn how astronomers think stars change, and how this is reflected in the H–R diagram.

Questions

1 List the colours of stars, from coolest to hottest.

2 If the Sun became dimmer and cooler, how would its position on the H–R diagram change?

3 A star in the bottom left-hand corner of the H–R diagram is dim but hot. Why does this suggest that it is small?

Key words

- ✔ **main sequence**
- ✔ **white dwarfs**
- ✔ **red giants**
- ✔ **supergiants**

What are stars made from?

The 'space' between stars is not empty. It is filled with very low density gas known as the **interstellar medium** (ISM). The gas is mostly hydrogen and helium, with small amounts of other elements. Under certain conditions, some of this gas collects together to make new stars. To tell the story of how stars form, we need to start with the ISM.

The ISM includes clouds of glowing gas such as planetary nebulae, supernova remnants (see page 244) and other hot nebulae. Here the temperature is typically 10 000 °C and there are about 1000 atoms and molecules per cm^3.

Some ISM regions have about a million particles per cm^3 and are sometimes known as 'dense' clouds. But they are not dense by our everyday standards. Normal air has about 10^{20} molecules per cm^3, and even 10^{15} molecules per cm^3 is considered a 'vacuum' on Earth.

'Dense' clouds are very cold, below −200 °C, and are only seen because they block the light from stars or glowing gas behind them.

Between the dense clouds and glowing nebulae is more ISM. Some of this gas is very cold (−100 to −200 °C) with 10−100 particles per cm^3. In other places there is less than one particle per cm^3 and temperatures can reach a million °C.

The Rosette nebula is a hot nebula in the ISM.

Key word
✔ interstellar medium

Questions

4 a Use the information on this page to make a table summarising conditions in various regions of the ISM.

Number of particles per cm^3	Temperature (°C)

b Very roughly, what is the relationship between the numbers in the two columns?

5 Suggest a reason why many hot parts of the ISM glow pink. (Hint: look at page 253.)

Great balls of fire

As you have seen, the Sun releases energy by fusing hydrogen nuclei to make helium nuclei. This process takes place in the very hot core of the Sun and most other stars. Between the stars is very thin gas that is mostly very cold. To understand how this gas forms into stars, and how stars get hot enough for nuclear fusion, you need to learn about gases in general.

Describing a gas

Think of a balloon. You blow it up, so it is filled with air. How can you describe the state of that air? What are its properties?

- **Volume** – the amount of space the gas occupies, in m^3.
- **Mass** – the amount of matter, in kg.
- **Pressure** – the force the gas exerts per unit area on the walls of its container, in Pa ($= N/m^2$).
- **Temperature** – how hot the gas is, in °C (or K – see page 264).

These are all measurable quantities that a physicist would use to describe the gas. Understanding how these properties change is important. For example, the engine of a car relies on the pressure of an expanding gas to provide the motive force that makes the car go.

Pressure and volume

Now picture squashing the balloon. You are trying to decrease its volume. Its pressure resists you. It is easier to understand what is happening by pressing on a gas syringe.

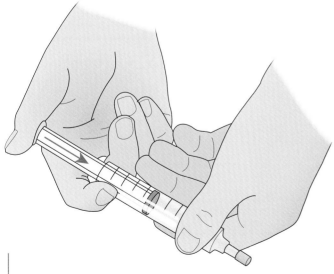

Compressing air in a syringe. This has a closed end so that it contains a fixed mass of air.

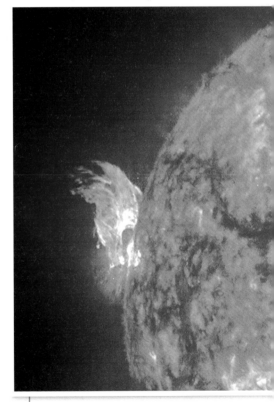

The Sun is a giant ball of hot gas, mostly hydrogen and helium.

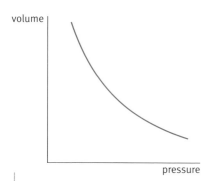

Increasing the pressure on a gas reduces its volume.

- It is easy to push the plunger in a little.
- The more you push on the plunger, the harder it gets to move it further.

This shows that the pressure of the air is increasing as you reduce its volume. If you reduce the force with which you press on the plunger, the air will push back and expand. The graph shows this relationship:

- When the volume of a gas is reduced, its pressure increases.
- The pressure of the gas is inversely proportional to the volume.

For a fixed mass of gas at constant temperature, we can express this relationship as:

$$\text{pressure} \times \text{volume} = \text{constant}$$

Worked example

The value of the constant depends on the amount of gas that you have. For example, suppose you have 100 cm^3 of gas in a container at normal atmospheric pressure (1×10^5 Pa). If you squash it with twice atmospheric pressure (2×10^5 Pa), its volume halves to 50 cm^3.

Before: pressure $\times$ volume = 1×10^5 Pa $\times$ 100 cm^3 = 100×10^5 (Pa cm^3)

After: pressure $\times$ volume = 2×10^5 Pa $\times$ 50 cm^3 = 100×10^5 (Pa cm^3)

Explaining pressure

The connection between the pressure and the volume of a gas was worked out before anyone was sure that gases were made of particles.

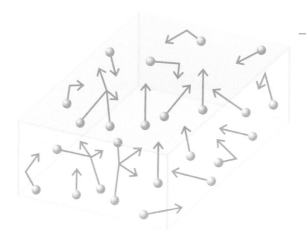

Particles of a gas collide with the walls of its container. This causes pressure.

Questions

1 Suppose you want to compress 300 cm^3 of gas at normal atmospheric pressure into a volume of 100 cm^3. How much pressure would you need to apply?

2 An inflated balloon has a volume of 2000 cm^3. When the air escapes it has a volume of 4000 cm^3 at normal atmospheric pressure. What was the pressure inside the balloon?

Yet you can use the **kinetic model** of matter to explain these findings. In this model, a gas consists of particles (atoms or molecules) that move around freely, and most of the volume of the gas is empty space.

- The particles of a gas move around freely. At room temperature, they have speeds around 450 m/s.

- As they move around, they bump into the walls of their container – see the diagram. (They also bump into each other.)
- Each collision with the walls causes a tiny force. Together, billions of collisions produce gas pressure.

Now think about what happens if the same gas is compressed into a smaller volume. The collisions with the walls will be more frequent, and so the pressure will be greater.

As cold as it gets

Now think about what happens when a gas gets cold. Blow up a balloon and put it in the freezer – it starts to shrink. Its pressure and volume have both decreased.

In an experiment to investigate this, it is best not to change one factor (temperature) and then to allow two others (pressure and volume) to both change. So experiments are designed to control one factor while the other is allowed to change. The picture on the right shows how a fixed volume of air (in a rigid flask) can be heated to change its temperature. The gauge shows how the pressure of the gas changes.

Heating up, cooling down

The graphs on the right show the results of experiments like this. Think about the effects of cooling down a fixed mass of gas.

- Fixed volume of gas: as the gas is cooled, its pressure decreases steadily.
- Fixed pressure of gas: as the gas is cooled, its volume decreases steadily.

Both of these graphs show the same pattern: the pressure and volume of the gas decrease as the temperature decreases, and both seem to be heading for a value of zero at a temperature well below 0°C. Whatever gas is used, the graph heads for the same temperature.

The point where a graph like this reaches zero is known as the **absolute zero** of temperature. In practice, all gases condense to form a liquid before they reach this point.

$$\text{absolute zero} = -273°C$$

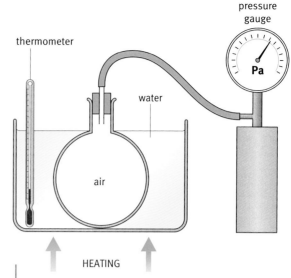

Because the flask is rigid, the volume of the air inside does not change as it is heated or cooled.

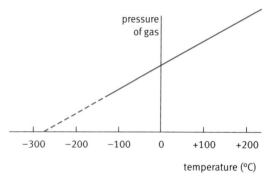

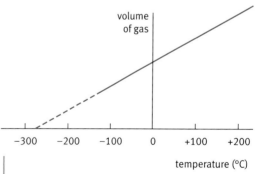

As a gas is cooled, its pressure and volume decrease.

Key words

- ✔ volume
- ✔ mass
- ✔ pressure
- ✔ temperature
- ✔ kinetic model
- ✔ absolute zero

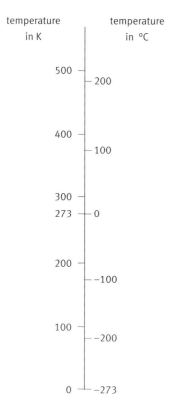

Comparing the Celsius and Kelvin scales of temperature.

Temperature scales

In everyday life, we use the Celsius scale of temperature. This has its zero, 0°C, at the temperature of pure melting ice. You can also define a scale that has its zero at absolute zero, the **Kelvin scale**. The individual divisions on the scale (degrees) are the same as on the Celsius scale, but the starting point is much lower. Because nothing can be colder than absolute zero, there are no negative temperatures on the Kelvin scale.

Temperatures on this scale are given in kelvin (K).

Here is how to convert from one scale to the other:
- temperature in K = temperature in °C + 273
- temperature in °C = temperature in K – 273

So, for example, suppose your body temperature is 37°C. What is this in K?
- Temperature in K = 37°C + 273 = 310 K.

A kinetic explanation

When a gas is cooled down, the particles of the gas lose energy, so they move more slowly.
- If the volume of the gas is fixed, each particle takes longer to reach a wall. So particles strike the walls less frequently. They also strike with less momentum. So the pressure decreases for these two reasons.
- If the pressure is to remain constant, the volume of the gas must decrease to compensate for the fact that the collisions are weaker and less frequent.

Eventually, you can picture the particles of the gas losing all of their kinetic energy, so that they do not collide with the walls at all. There is no pressure. This is absolute zero.

Questions

3 What are the values of the following temperatures on the Kelvin scale?
   a 0°C
   b 100°C
   c −100°C.

4 What are the values of the following temperatures on the Celsius scale?
   a 0K
   b 8K
   c 200K
   d 300K.

Dark clouds of gas and dust, such as the the Horsehead Nebula in Orion, can have temperatures as low as 8K.

Gas equations

We can redraw the graphs from page 263 using temperature in K. These graphs illustrate two equations that describe how gases behave.

For a fixed mass of gas at constant volume, the pressure is **proportional** to the temperature in kelvin.

$$\frac{\text{pressure}}{\text{temperature (in K)}} = \text{constant}$$

For a fixed mass of gas at constant pressure, the volume is proportional to the temperature in kelvin.

$$\frac{\text{volume}}{\text{temperature (in K)}} = \text{constant}$$

The value of the constant depends on how much gas there is.

For example, if you have a container with 600 cm^3 of gas at 300 K, and you heat it to 600 K (keeping it at the same pressure), the volume doubles to 1200 cm^3.

Before: $\dfrac{\text{volume}}{\text{temperature}} = \dfrac{600 \text{ cm}^3}{300 \text{ K}} = 2 \text{ cm}^3/\text{K}$

After: $\dfrac{\text{volume}}{\text{temperature}} = \dfrac{1200 \text{ cm}^3}{600 \text{ K}} = 2 \text{ cm}^3/\text{K}$

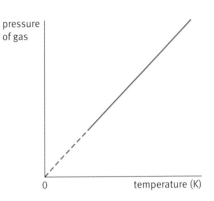

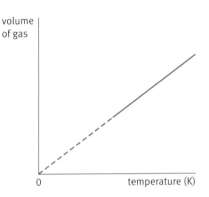

Questions

5 a 1000 cm^3 of gas is heated from 300 K to 400 K at constant pressure. What will the new volume be?

   b The gas is now heated from 300 K to 500 K in a container with a fixed volume. At the start its pressure was 1×10^5 Pa. What is its new pressure?

6 Suppose there are two gas clouds in space, and both have the same pressure but cloud A is much hotter than cloud B. What can you say about the density of the two clouds?

7 Imagine that a fixed mass of gas is compressed into half its original volume. The temperature remains constant. Which of the following statements are correct?

   a The pressure of the gas will increase.

   b The average separation of the particles of the gas will decrease.

   c A particle of the gas will strike the walls of the container with greater force.

   d A particle of the gas will strike the walls more frequently.

8 Use the kinetic model of matter to explain why the pressure of a fixed volume of gas increases as the temperature increases.

Key words

✓ **Kelvin scale**
✓ **proportional**

Find out about

- ✔ how stars and planetary systems form
- ✔ the structure of the Sun and other stars
- ✔ how energy is transferred within stars

How does a star form? The raw material of stars is hydrogen and helium, and there has been plenty of that since the early days of the Universe. Here is a simplified version of how astronomers think that stars form:

- A cold cloud of gas and dust starts to contract, pulled together by gravity. It breaks up into several smaller clouds and each continues to contract.
- Within a contracting cloud, each particle attracts every other particle, so that the cloud collapses towards its centre. It forms a rotating, swirling disc.
- As the gas particles are attracted towards the centre, they move faster, which means the gas gets hotter.
- Eventually, the temperature of this material is hot enough for fusion reactions to occur, and a star is born.
- Material further out in the disc clumps together to form planets.

So stars form in **clusters**, and planets form at the same time as the star that they orbit. In these early stages, as the star forms, it is known as a **protostar**. This stage in the Sun's life is thought to have lasted 100 000 to 1 million years.

A protostar at the centre of a new planetary system.

Getting warmer

Here are two ways to think about when a protostar gets hot enough for fusion to start.

- The *gas* idea. The star starts from a cloud of gas. When a gas is compressed, its temperature rises. In this case, the force doing the compressing is gravity.

- The *particle* idea. Every particle in the cloud attracts every other particle. As they 'fall' inwards, they move faster (gravitational potential energy is being converted to kinetic energy). The particles collide with each other, sharing their energy. The fastest particles are at the centre of the cloud (they have fallen furthest), and fast-moving particles mean a high temperature.

Note that these are *not* competing explanations. They are just different ways of describing what is going on.

Seek and find

Astronomers' ideas about star formation are based on what they can observe. For example, they usually observe protostars in clusters close to cold dark clouds (see the picture on page 211). They also use computer models to help test their ideas.

Computer models of star formation can help to explain why the (roughly) spherical material from which a star forms collapses to form a flattened disc. Such models suggest that we will always find that the planets orbiting a star lie in a plane, just as in the Solar System.

Some models of star formation predict that, as a protostar forms, it spins faster and faster. Eventually, it blows out giant jets of hot gas, at right angles to the planetary disc. Large telescopes now have sufficient resolution to allow us to see this going on, as shown in the photo on the right. Planets travelling around distant stars are generally too small to see directly, but the gas jets travel far out into space and can occasionally be spotted.

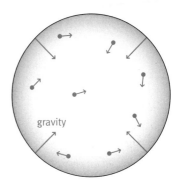

Explaining why a protostar gets hot.

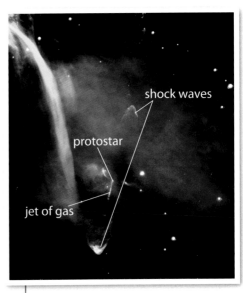

A protostar is forming at the centre of this image. One bright jet of gas can be seen coming downwards from it. Two symmetrical shock waves spread out in opposite directions. (Photo taken by the Very Large Telescope in Chile.)

Questions

1 From what materials does a protostar form?

2 If astronomers see a protostar glowing, does this indicate that nuclear fusion is taking place?

3 Imagine a sky-rocket exploding in the night sky. A small, hot explosion results in material being thrown outwards.
   a Describe the energy changes that are going on.
   b Now imagine the same scene, but in reverse. How is this similar to the formation of a protostar? How does it differ?

4 Suggest reasons why a *cold* cloud of gas is more likely to contract than a hot one.

Key words

✔ **clusters**
✔ **protostar**

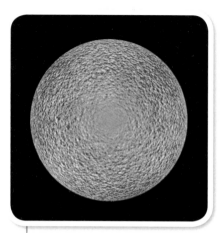

The surface of the Sun, photographed by the *SOHO* satellite, showing the granularity caused by the presence of convective cells.

Main-sequence stars

Spacecraft such as *SOHO* have allowed scientists to look in great detail at the surface of the Sun and to measure the rate at which it is pouring energy out into space. Its colour indicates that the surface temperature of the Sun is about 5800 K – which is far too 'cold' for nuclear fusion reactions to take place.

Modelling the Sun

You cannot tell exactly what is inside the Sun. However, there are some clues that can help physicists to make intelligent guesses:

- Nuclear fusion, the source of the Sun's energy, requires temperatures of millions of degrees.
- Energy leaves the Sun from its surface layer, the **photosphere**, whose temperature is about 5800 K.
- The photosphere has a granular appearance (see the photo), which is continually changing. Something is going on under the surface.
- A star like the Sun can burn steadily for billions of years, so it must radiate energy at the same rate that it generates it from fusion reactions.

Physicists can use these ideas to develop models of the inside of a star. The diagram below shows how they picture the internal structure of the Sun, based on such models.

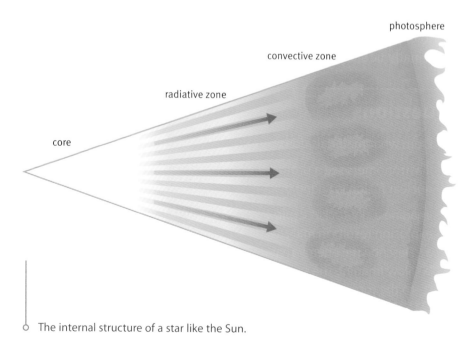

The internal structure of a star like the Sun.

Layer upon layer

- The **core** is the hottest part, with a temperature of the order of 14 million K. This is where nuclear fusion reactions occur. Hydrogen nuclei are fused together to form helium nuclei, releasing energy.

- **Radiation** (photons) travels outwards through the radiative zone.
- Close to the surface, temperatures fall to just 1 million K. Matter can flow quite readily, and **convection** currents are set up, carrying heat energy to the photosphere. This is the convective zone. It is the tops of the convective 'cells' that cause the granular appearance of the Sun's surface.
- Electromagnetic radiation is emitted by the photosphere and radiates outwards through the solar atmosphere.

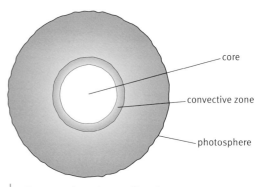

Cross-section of a star five times the mass of the Sun.

Other main-sequence stars

Other main-sequence stars can be modelled in the same way as the Sun. All main-sequence stars are fusing hydrogen in their cores to make helium. A main-sequence star has a steady luminosity and temperature for all the time that it is fusing hydrogen in its core – millions, or even billions, of years.

Differences between main-sequence stars are due to their different masses. The more massive the star, the hotter its core and the more rapidly it turns hydrogen into helium. The most massive main-sequence stars are also the hottest and the most luminous. The table below lists some typical values.

Mass of star	Luminosity	Surface temperature (K)
0.5 × Sun	0.03 × Sun	3800
1 × Sun	1 × Sun	5800
3 × Sun	60 × Sun	11 000
15 × Sun	17 000 × Sun	28 000

The lifetime of a star on the main sequence depends on its mass and the rate at which it turns hydrogen into helium.

Questions

5 Why does hydrogen fusion take place only in the *core* of a main-sequence star?

6 On a sketch copy of an H–R diagram (see page 258), label the ends of the main sequence to show the most massive and the least massive stars.

7 The helium made by a main-sequence star stays in its core. Look at the cross-section diagrams on these pages and put forward a reason for this.

8 The greater the mass of a star, the *shorter* the time it spends on the main sequence. Suggest an explanation for this.

Key words
- ✔ **photosphere**
- ✔ **core**
- ✔ **radiation**
- ✔ **convection**

Find out about

- ✓ **what happens when hydrogen fusion ends**
- ✓ **how a star's fate depends on its mass**
- ✓ **how a supernova leaves a neutron star or a black hole**
- ✓ **how elements made in stars become part of new stars and planets**

Many generations into the future, people can expect the Sun to keep releasing energy at a steady rate. Fusion reactions will continue in its core, as hydrogen is converted to helium.

But this cannot go on for ever, because eventually all of the hydrogen in the Sun's core will be used up. What happens then?

As fusion slows down in the core of any star, its core cools down and there is less pressure, so the core collapses. The star's outer layers, which contain hydrogen, fall inwards, becoming hot. This causes new fusion reactions, making the outer shell expand. At the same time, the surface temperature falls, so that the colour changes from yellow to red. This produces a red giant.

In the case of the Sun, calculations suggest that it may expand sufficiently to engulf the three nearest planets – Mercury, Venus, and Earth.

An artist's impression of the view from a planet when its star has become a red giant. A moon is also shown, for comparison.

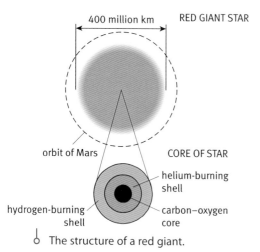

The structure of a red giant.

400 million km — RED GIANT STAR

orbit of Mars — CORE OF STAR

hydrogen-burning shell — helium-burning shell — carbon–oxygen core

Inside a red giant

While the outer layers of a red giant star are expanding, its core is contracting and heating up to 100 million K. This is hot enough for new fusion reactions to start. Helium nuclei have a bigger positive charge than hydrogen nuclei, so there is greater electrical repulsion between them. If they are to fuse, they need greater energy to overcome this repulsion. When helium nuclei do fuse, they form heavier elements such as carbon, nitrogen, and oxygen, releasing energy.

After a relatively short period (a few million years), the outer layers cool and drift off into space. The collapsed inner core remains as a white dwarf. No fusion occurs in a white dwarf so it gradually cools and fades.

Life of the Sun

Picture the life of a star like the Sun on the Hertzsprung–Russell diagram (page 258).

- Protostars are to the right of the main sequence. As it heats up, a protostar moves to a point on the main sequence, where it stays for billions of years.
- When it becomes a red giant, it moves above the main sequence.
- Finally, as a white dwarf, it appears below the main sequence.

More massive stars

The Sun is a relatively small star. Its core won't get hot enough to fuse elements beyond carbon. Bigger stars, greater than about 8 solar masses, also expand, to become supergiants. In these, core temperatures may exceed 3 billion degrees and more complex fusion reactions can occur, forming even heavier elements and releasing yet more energy. But this cannot go on forever; even massive stars do not make elements heavier than iron.

Beyond iron

When a star gets as far as making iron in its core, events take a dramatic turn.

So far, fusion of nuclei to make heavier ones has involved a release of energy. The star's core is heated, raising the pressure and stopping the star collapsing under its own gravity.

But when nuclei heavier than iron are made by fusing lighter nuclei, there is an overall increase in mass. This means that some input of energy is needed (remember: $E = mc^2$), rather than energy being released. Once iron is made in a star's core, there is no further release of energy.

Supernova explosion

What happens after the supergiant phase of a massive star is one of the most dramatic events in nature. A star of about 8 solar masses or more can get as far as making iron in its core. Iron nuclei absorb energy when they fuse, and there is no source of heating to keep up the pressure in the core. Now the drama starts.

The outer layers of the star are no longer held up by the pressure of the core, and they collapse inwards. The core has become very dense, and the outer material collides with the core and bounces off, flying outwards. The result is a huge explosion called a supernova.

Questions

1 At what point in its life does a star become a red giant?

2 What determines whether a star becomes a red giant or a supergiant?

3 How many helium-4 nuclei must fuse to give a nucleus of:
   a carbon-12?
   b oxygen-16?

In the course of the explosion, temperatures rise to 10 billion K, enough to cause the fusion of medium-weight elements and thus form the heaviest elements of all – up to uranium in the periodic table. For a few days, a supernova can outshine a whole galaxy.

The remnants of a supernova in the constellation of Cassiopeia. The cloud is about 5 parsecs across. This is a composite image, made using three telescopes to capture infrared, visible, and X-ray data.

Key words

- ✔ neutron star
- ✔ black hole

The next generation

The photograph above shows the remnants of a supernova that happened in about 1660. You can see the expanding sphere of dust and gas, formed from the star's outer layers. This material contains all of the elements of the periodic table. As it becomes distributed through space, it may become part of another contracting cloud of dust and gas. A protostar may form with new planets orbiting it, and the cycle starts over again.

Dense and denser

The core of an exploding supernova remains. If its mass is less than about 2.5 solar masses, this central remnant becomes a **neutron star**. This is made almost entirely of neutrons, compressed together like a giant atomic nucleus, perhaps 30 km across.

A more massive remnant collapses even further under the pull of its own gravity, to become a **black hole**. Within a black hole, the pull of gravity is so strong that not even light can escape from it.

Neutron stars are thought to explain the pulsars, discovered by Jocelyn Bell and Anthony Hewish (page 210). As the core of a star collapses to form a neutron star, it spins faster and faster. Its magnetic field becomes concentrated, and this results in a beam of radio waves coming out of its magnetic poles. As the neutron star spins round, this beam sweeps across space and might be detected as a regular series of pulses at an observatory on some small, distant planet.

Questions

4 On a sketch copy of an H–R diagram (page 258), draw and label a line tracing out the life of a Sun-like star from protostar to white dwarf.

5 Put these objects in order, from least dense to most dense:
    neutron star, protostar, supergiant, black hole, main-sequence star

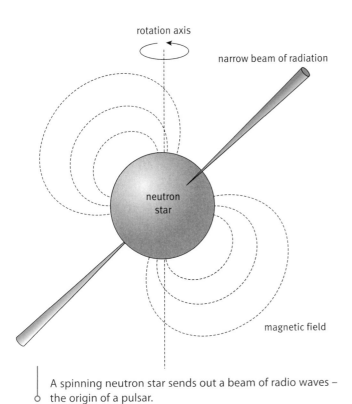

A spinning neutron star sends out a beam of radio waves – the origin of a pulsar.

The neutron star and the black hole shown here have the same mass as the Sun.

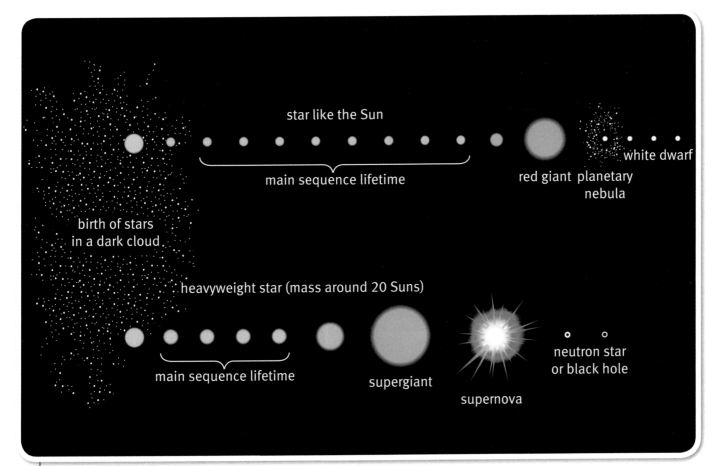

The life and death of a star mainly depends on its mass. The most massive stars have the shortest lives and most spectacular deaths.

Find out about

- ✓ planets around stars other than the Sun
- ✓ the search for extra-terrestrial intelligence

This module started with people making simple naked-eye observations of the sky, as they have done for thousands of years. It ends with a simple question about our place in the Universe – are we alone?

Life on other planets?

The story of star formation (pages 266–269) also explains how planets might be formed. Some of the gas and dust in a collapsing cloud orbits around the protostar rather than falling into it. Over time, this gas and dust gradually clumps together to make planets.

If the gas and dust includes some remnants of supernova explosions, then it will contain traces of elements from the whole periodic table, including those (such as carbon and oxygen) needed for life as we know it on Earth.

So there is an intriguing argument that goes like this:

- There are about 100 thousand million stars in the Milky Way, so it seems likely that at least some of them have planets.
- If there are planets round other stars, then maybe life has evolved on some of them. It might be possible to detect some living organisms by the effect they have on a planet.
- If life is present, some organisms might be intelligent. It might be possible to communicate with intelligent organisms on other planets. They might be sending out signals. Or they might have detected our presence on Earth.

Exoplanets

Towards the end of the 20th century, astronomers started to look for planets orbiting other stars, known as **exoplanets**. This search needs very sensitive telescopes with good resolving power. Between 1990 and 2010 astronomers found over 460 exoplanets and they are still finding more.

Astronomers detect exoplanets by clever techniques such as small dips in the brightness of a star as its planet passes in front of it, or by the wobbling motion of the star caused by the gravity of a planet. The image opposite shows a planet orbiting a star that is surrounded by a disc of dust. The star is about 25 light-years away.

So far, all exoplanets detected have been much more massive than Earth.

Key words

- ✓ exoplanets
- ✓ SETI

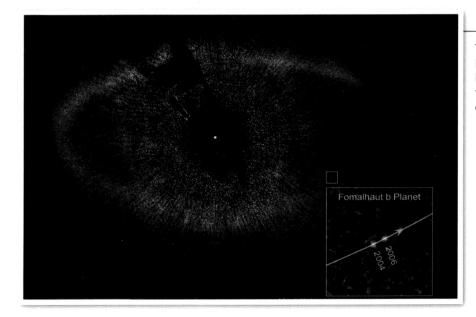

This image shows the exoplanet known as Fomalhaut b in 2004 and 2006. Astronomers have calculated that it takes 872 years to orbit the star, and its orbit is about 115 times the size of Earth's orbit.

SETI

As long ago as the 1950s, when the first satellites were launched into Earth orbit, scientists had the idea that it might be possible to detect radio signals sent by intelligent life elsewhere in the Universe. This marked the start of the Search for Extra-Terrestrial Intelligence (**SETI**). Since then, several SETI projects have taken place. One of the biggest is the SETI @home project, where some 50 000 people around the world use their home computers to process data from radio telescopes to see whether it contains any sign of 'intelligent' signals.

So far, there is no evidence of life elsewhere.

This vast radio telescope in Arecibo, Puerto Rico, has been used to scan the sky for evidence of 'intelligent' radio signals.

Questions

1 There may be intelligent life forms on exoplanets. What risks and benefits could there be in communicating with them?

2 The closest stars to our Sun are several light-years away. What problems might this cause if we wanted to communicate with life forms on planets orbiting other stars?

3 Suppose you are an alien on a planet 10 light-years from Earth. Describe any possible evidence you could have to suggest that the Earth exists and there is life on it.

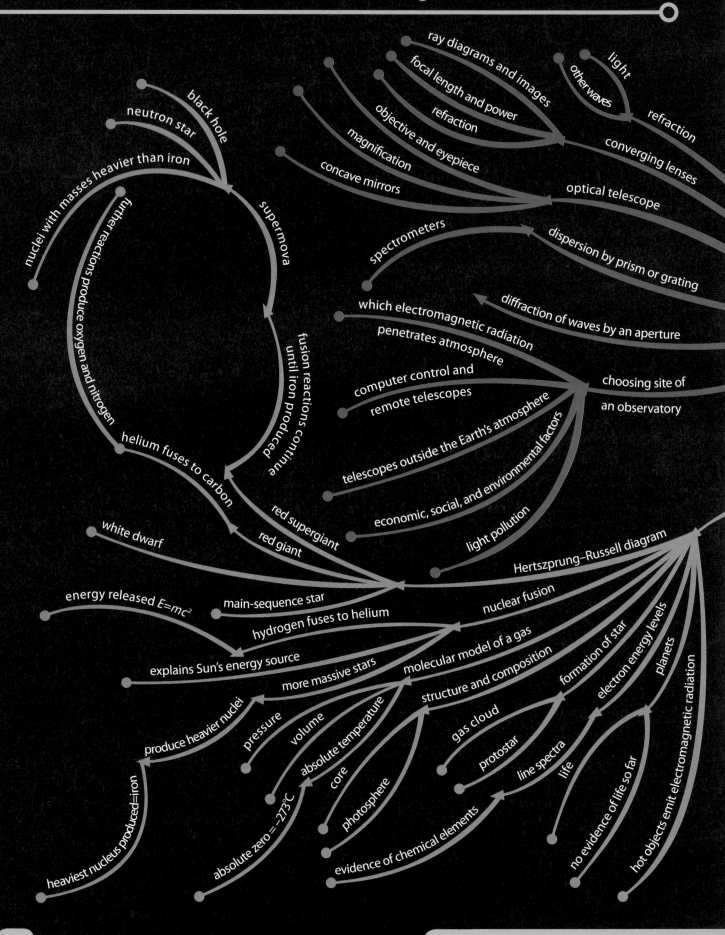

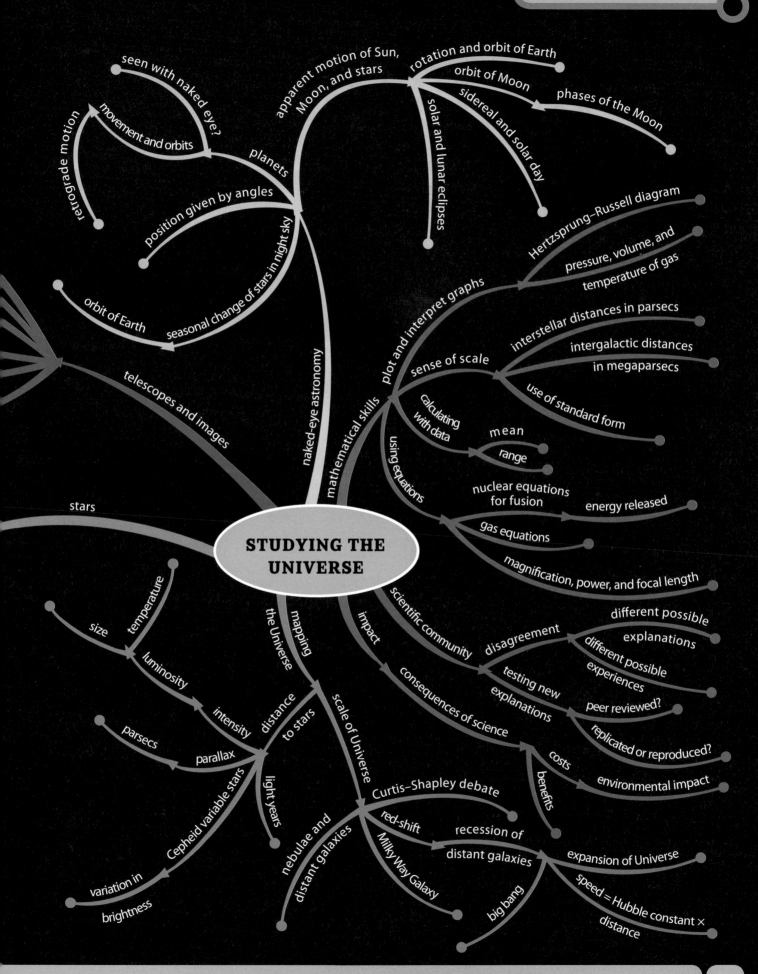

Science Explanations

Astronomy is a very ancient science. People have been observing and tracking the stars and planets for many hundreds of years to learn more about our Universe.

You should know:
- how the Sun, Moon, and stars appear to travel across the night sky
- how and why a sidereal day is different to a solar day
- about the way the Sun, Moon, planets, and stars appear to move because of their orbits and the rotation of the Earth
- how to explain, using the position of the Sun, Moon, and Earth:
  - the phases of the Moon
  - solar and lunar eclipses
- that the difference in tilt of the Earth's orbit around the Sun and the Moon's orbit around the Earth explains why eclipses do not occur more frequently
- that the position of astronomical objects seen from Earth is measured by angles
- that the different stars in the night sky at different times of year is explained by the movement of the Earth around the Sun
- which planets can be seen with the naked eye and that all the planets move against the background of stars
- that planets sometimes appear to move with retrograde motion (in the opposite direction to the stars) and how to explain why this happens.

Telescopes and images

A telescope makes distant objects appear larger and closer, so that more detail can be seen. It also allows fainter objects to be studied because a telescope has a larger aperture than the human eye and collects more light. Modern telescopes can produce lasting images using electronic detectors or photographic film.

You should know:
- about the refraction of light and other waves
- how converging (convex) lenses use refraction to form an image
- how to draw and interpret ray diagrams that show how converging lenses form images
- about the focal length and power of a lens and how to calculate them
- that an optical telescope has an objective lens, or mirror, and an eyepiece

- about optical telescopes, including how to calculate the magnification
- about dispersion of light by a prism, a grating, and spectrometers
- why most astronomical telescopes use mirrors
- how concave mirrors bring light to a focus
- about the diffraction of waves by an aperture, and how this affects telescopes
- which electromagnetic radiation can get through the atmosphere
- the effect of light pollution on astronomy
- the locations of major optical and infrared observatories on Earth
- the factors that influence the choice of site for major observatories
- how astronomers work with local and remote telescopes
- the advantages of computer-controlled telescopes
- the advantages and disadvantages of telescopes outside the Earth's atmosphere
- the advantages to the astronomy community of working together
- the economic, environmental, and social factors involved in planning, building, operating, and closing down an observatory.

Mapping the Universe

In order to understand and explain the Universe and the objects we see in it, we need to know how far away they are. Once an object's distance is known, then astronomers can work out other things, such as how big it is and how much energy it is giving out.

You should know:
- about the parallax effect and how it can be used to measure the distance to stars
- that the parsec and light-year are units of distance, and how they are defined
- that the luminosity of a star depends on its temperature and size
- why the intensity of light from a star depends on its luminosity and distance from Earth
- about Cepheid variable stars, how they vary in brightness, and how they can be used to measure distance from Earth
- about the role of Cepheid variable stars in showing the scale of the Universe and that most spiral nebulae are distant galaxies
- about the Curtis–Shapley debate
- that the Sun is a star in the Milky Way galaxy
- about Hubble's discovery of distant galaxies and about the red-shift in the electromagnetic radiation received from distant galaxies
- that the motion of galaxies suggests the Universe is expanding
- about the scale of the Universe, including that interstellar distances are measured in parsecs, and intergalactic distances in megaparsecs
- how to use the equation speed of recession = Hubble constant × distance
- that scientists believe the Universe began with a 'big bang' about 14 thousand million years ago.

Stars

Scientists study the star at the centre of the Solar System, the Sun, to understand more about other stars and about the Universe. The radiation produced by stars reveals their structure and composition and allows us to find out how they are formed and what will happen to them at the end of their life.

You should know:

- that hot objects emit a continuous range of electromagnetic radiation with luminosity and peak frequency that depends on temperature
- about electron energy levels in atoms and how these give rise to line spectra
- that specific spectral lines in the spectrum of a star provide evidence of the chemical elements present in it and how to use data to identify elements
- how, in the early 20th century, nuclear fusion explained the Sun's energy source, which, until then, had been a mystery
- that the nuclear fusion of hydrogen to form helium releases energy
- how to complete nuclear equations relating to fusion in stars (including positron emission) and be able to calculate the energy released using $E = mc^2$
- about the structure and composition of stars
- about the different stars found in different regions of the Hertzsprung–Russell diagram, which is a plot of star temperature against luminosity
- that more massive stars have hotter cores and create heavier nuclei, up to the mass of the iron nucleus
- how to explain, using a molecular model, that the volume of a gas is inversely proportional to its pressure at constant temperature
- that the absolute zero of temperature is –273ºC, which is 0 K, and how to convert between temperatures in ºC and temperatures in kelvin
- that gas pressure and volume are proportional to the absolute temperature
- how to calculate pressure, volume, and temperature using the gas equations
- how to explain the formation of a protostar, and a star, from a cloud of gas
- how to explain what happens to a star when its hydrogen runs out, including the formation of red giants, supergiants, white dwarfs, and supernovae
- that in red giants helium fuses to form carbon, followed by further reactions that produce heavier nuclei such as nitrogen and oxygen
- how to explain that supernovae form nuclei with masses heavier than iron and leave a neutron star or black hole
- that astronomers have evidence of hundreds of planets around nearby stars
- why many scientists think that life exists elsewhere in the Universe
- that no evidence of extraterrestrial life in the present or past has been detected.

Ideas about Science

In addition to developing an understanding of the composition of the Universe, it is important to understand how the scientific community works together and how decisions are made about science and technology.

Scientists use their knowledge and evidence to suggest explanations for their observations and discoveries. They share their results with the scientific community to see if other scientists agree with the explanations. You should be able to:

- describe the peer-review process in which new scientific claims are evaluated by other scientists; the Curtis–Shapley debate was an example of this; both Heber D. Curtis and Harlow Shapley presented their evidence to other astronomers
- recognise that new scientific claims that have not yet been evaluated by the scientific community are less reliable than well-established ones.
- identify the fact that a finding has not been reproduced by another scientist as a reason for questioning a scientific claim
- explain that scientists think it is important for results to be replicated, because if the same results are obtained by other scientists who are completely independent this rules out lots of reasons for doubting the results, for example, errors in technique, poor equipment, or a bias on the part of those doing the experiment
- show that you are aware that the same data may be interpreted in more than one way; for example, the data that showed galaxies were moving apart was interpreted by some scientists as showing that the Universe started from a small point – the big bang theory – but other scientists thought the data supported the steady-state theory in which galaxies moved apart and new ones appeared in the gaps
- suggest reasons why scientists may disagree, for example, their personal background, experience, or interests may influence their judgement
- discuss what may happen when new data disagrees with predictions using an accepted explanation; for example, at the end of the 19th century geological data showed the Earth to be at least 300 million years old – however, none of the possible accepted explanations for the Sun's energy source predicted that the Sun could last this long, so the age for the Earth was not accepted until a new theory for the energy source of the Sun – nuclear fusion – was suggested
- suggest reasons why scientists should not give up an accepted explanation immediately if new data appears to conflict with it; there may be another explanation. When the planet Uranus was observed to be in a different position from that predicted by its orbit around the Sun, instead of saying that Newton's laws of motion did not apply to Uranus, it was suggested that this might be due to the presence of another planet. This was later confirmed when Neptune was discovered.

In making decisions about science and technology, you should be able to:

- identify the groups affected and the main benefits and costs of a course of action for each group; for example, when an observatory is built in a remote location the main groups affected will be local people, the astronomers who may visit, and other people who may move to the area for jobs – you should be able to suggest benefits and costs for these groups
- suggest reasons why different decisions about choosing the site for an observatory might be appropriate in view of differences in social and economic context.

Review Questions

1 A star chart shows what can be seen in the night sky for a particular time and date and observation position on the Earth.

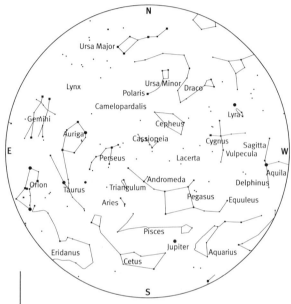

Star chart for 18th January 2011 at 18:00, observed from York, UK.

Describe and explain why the observations would look different from the chart shown for:

a observations of the stars made from York two hours later

b observations of Jupiter made from York two hours later

c observations of the stars made from York six months later

d observations of Jupiter one year later

e observations of the stars made from Australia on the same date.

2 Anna wants to make a telescope. The table shows some properties of the lenses that are available.

Lens	Diameter in mm	Focal length in mm
A	16.5	30
B	16.5	49
C	16.5	65
D	34.5	65
E	34.5	225

a Calculate the power in dioptres of lens **A**.

b Which lens would be the best lens for the eyepiece of a telescope? Explain your answer.

c Which lens would be the best lens for the objective lens? Explain your answer.

d Most astronomical telescopes have a concave mirror as the objective. Explain why a mirror is used instead of a lens.

3 Astronomers use various methods of measuring distances to stars.

a Explain why the parallax method is less precise for more distant stars.

b Explain why there is a problem with using the observed brightness of a star to estimate its distance.

c Explain the property of Cepheid variable stars that is used to measure their distance.

4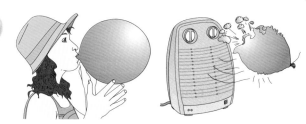

A balloon is inflated and a knot tied in the end to seal it. The balloon is placed near a heater and soon bursts.

Use the molecular model of a gas to explain why the balloon bursts.

5 A car tyre is inflated to a pressure of 200 kPa on a cold morning when the temperature is 7°C. Later in the day after a long car journey the temperature of the tyre rises to 27°C.

a Convert the two temperatures to values in K.

b Calculate the pressure of the air in the tyre when the temperature has risen to 27 °C.

c What assumption did you have to make to carry out your calculation?

6 The Hertzsprung–Russell diagram shows patterns in the properties of stars.

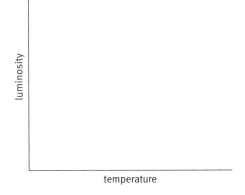

a Copy the axes and add labels to the axes:
- faint
- hot
- luminous
- cool

b Show the regions on the graph where each star appears:
- supergiant
- giant
- main sequence
- white dwarf

c Add the Sun to the diagram.

7 The European Southern Observatory (ESO) is a joint project between 14 European countries. The project carries out astronomical research using large optical telescopes placed in the Atacama desert high in the Andes in Chile. The headquarters of the organisation, where many of the scientists are based, are in Munich, Germany.

a Suggest some of the advantages of European countries carrying out a joint research project.

b Suggest and explain the advantages of having the headquarters of the organisation in Germany, but the telescopes in the mountains of Chile.

Glossary

absolute zero   Extrapolating from the behaviour of gases at different temperatures, absolute zero is the theoretically lowest possible temperature, –273°C. In practice, the lowest temperature achievable is about a degree above this.

absorb (radiation)   The radiation that hits an object and is not reflected, or transmitted through it, is absorbed (for example, black paper absorbs light). Its energy makes the object get a little hotter.

absorption spectrum (of a star)   Consists of dark lines superimposed on a continuous spectrum. It is created when light from the star passes through a cooler gas that absorbs photons of particular energies.

accuracy   How close a quantitative result is to the true or 'actual' value.

activation energy   The minimum energy needed in a collision between molecules if they are to react. The activation energy is the height of the energy barrier between reactants and products in a chemical change.

actual risk   Risk calculated from reliable data.

aerial   A wire, or arrangement of wires, that emits radio waves when there is an alternating current in it, and in which an alternating current is induced by passing radio waves. So it acts as a source or a receiver of radio waves.

alcohols   Alcohols are organic compounds containing the reactive group —OH. Ethanol is an alcohol. It has the formula C_2H_5OH.

algae   Simple green water plants.

algal bloom   Rapid growth of algae making the water green. It can be toxic.

alkane   Alkanes are hydrocarbons found in crude oil. All the C—C bonds in alkanes are single bonds. Ethane is an alkane. It has the formula C_2H_6.

alkene   Alkenes are hydrocarbons that contain a C—C double bond. Ethene is an alkene. It has the formula C_2H_4.

anaerobic   Without oxygen.

angular magnification (of a refracting telescope)   The ratio of the angle subtended by an object when seen through the telescope to the angle subtended by the same object when seen with the naked eye. It can be calculated as focal length of objective lens/ focal length of eyepiece lens.

antagonistic pair   Two muscles that work to move the same bone in opposite directions, for example, the biceps and triceps muscles.

antibiotic   Drugs that kill or stop the growth of bacteria and fungi.

aorta   The main artery that carries oxygenated blood away from the left ventricle of the heart.

aperture (of a telescope)   The light-gathering area of the objective lens or mirror.

aquaculture   Farming in water, such as fish farming.

aqueous   An aqueous solution is a solution in which water is the solvent.

asteroid   A dwarf rocky planet, generally orbiting the Sun between the orbits of Mars and Jupiter.

astrolabe   An instrument used for locating and predicting the positions of the Sun, Moon, planets, and stars, as well as navigating and telling the time.

atmosphere   The Earth's atmosphere is the layer of gases that surrounds the planet. It contains roughly 78% nitrogen and 21% oxygen, with trace amounts of other gases. The atmosphere protects life on Earth by absorbing ultraviolet solar radiation and reducing temperature extremes between day and night.

atom economy   A measure of the efficiency of a chemical process. The atom economy for a process shows the mass of product atoms as a percentage of the mass of reactant atoms.

atrium (plural atria)   One of the upper chambers in the heart. The two atria pump blood to the ventricles.

bacteriophage   A type of virus that infects bacteria.

bacterium (plural bacteria)   One type of single-celled microorganism. Bacteria do not have a nucleus. Some bacteria may cause disease.

baseline data   Data gathered at the start of a study or experiment so that patterns and trends can be established.

big bang   An explosion of a single mass of material. This is currently the accepted scientific explanation for the start of the Universe.

bioaccumulation   Build-up of chemicals in organisms as the chemicals travel through the food chain.

biodegradable   Able to be broken down by microorganisms, using enzymes.

biodiversity   The great variety of living things, both within a species and between different species.

biofuel   Fuel made from crops such as rape seed.

biomass   Plant material and animal waste that can be used as a fuel. A renewable energy source.

black hole   A mass so great that its gravity prevents anything escaping from it, including light. Some black holes are the collapsed remnants of massive stars.

blood pressure   The pressure exerted by blood pushing on the walls of a blood vessel.

body mass index   Your body mass index is calculated using the formula BMI=body mass (kg) / [height (m)]^2. Tables will tell you if your body mass is healthy for your size.

bond strength   A measure of how much energy is needed to break a covalent bond between two atoms. It is measured in joules.

bone   Strong, rigid tissues making up the skeleton of vertebrates.

bulk chemicals   Chemicals made by industry on a scale of thousands or millions of tonnes per year. Examples are sulfuric acid, nitric acid, sodium hydroxide, ethanol, and ethanoic acid.

burette   A graduated tube with taps or valves used to measure the volume of liquids or solutions during quantitative investigations such as titrations.

by-product   An unwanted product of chemical synthesis. By-products are formed by side-reactions that happen at the same time as the main reaction, thus reducing the yield of the product required.

cancer   A growth or tumour caused by abnormal and uncontrolled cell division.

capillary   Tiny blood vessels that are one cell thick. They carry blood through the tissues between the arteries and veins.

capillary bed   Large numbers of narrow blood vessels that pass through each organ in the body. Capillaries receive blood from arteries and return it to veins. Capillary walls are only one cell thick.

carbon sink   A system taking carbon dioxide from the air and storing it, for example, a growing forest.

carboxylic acid   Carboxylic acids are organic compounds containing the reactive group —COOH. Ethanoic acid (acetic acid) is an example. It has the formula CH_3COOH.

carrier gas   The mobile phase in gas chromatography.

cartilage   Tough, flexible tissue found at the end of bones and in joints. It protects the end of bones from rubbing together and becoming damaged.

catalyst   A chemical that speeds up a chemical reaction but is not used up in the process.

cellulose   The chemical that makes up most of the fibre in food. The human body cannot digest cellulose.

Cepheid variable   A star whose brightness varies regularly, over a period of days.

chemical species   The different chemical forms that an element can take. For example, chlorine has three chemical species: atom, molecule, and ion. Each of these forms has distinct properties.

chromatogram   The resulting record showing the separated chemicals at the end of a chromatography experiment.

chromatography   An analytical technique in which the components of a mixture are separated by the movement of a mobile phase through a stationary phase.

chymosin   Enzyme that breaks down proteins (a protease) found in calf stomachs. Fungi have been genetically modified to produce chymosin industrially for cheese-making.

closed-loop system   A system with no waste – everything is recycled.

cloud formation   Evaporation of water, for example, from a forest, condensing into clouds.

comet   A rocky lump, held together by frozen gases and water, that orbits the Sun.

constellation   A group of stars that form a pattern in the night sky. Patterns recognised are cultural and historical, and are not based on the actual positions of the stars in space.

convective zone (of a star)   The layer of a star above its radiative zone, where energy is transferred by convective currents in the plasma.

converging lens   A lens that changes the direction of light striking it, bringing the light together at a point.

core (of the body)   Central parts of the body where the body temperature is kept constant.

crop rotation   Changing the crop grown in a field each year to preserve fertility.

crude oil   Oil straight from an oil well, not refined into petrol or diesel.

dead organic matter   Any material that was once part of a living organism.

deforestation   Cutting down and clearing forests leaving bare ground.

dehydration   Drying out.

denatured   When the shape of an enzyme has been changed, usually as a result of external temperatures being too high or pH changes. The enzyme no longer works.

deoxygenated   Blood in which the haemoglobin is not bound to oxygen molecules.

desert   Very dry area where no plants can grow. The area can be cold or hot.

desertification   Turning to desert.

detector   Any device or instrument that shows the presence of radiation by absorbing it.

diabetes type 1   An illness where the level of sugar in the blood cannot be controlled. Type 1 diabetes starts suddenly, often when people are young. Cells in the pancreas stop producing insulin. Treatment is by regular insulin injections.

diabetes type 2   An illness where the level of sugar in the blood cannot be controlled. Type 2 diabetes develops in people with poor diets or who are obese. The cells in the body stop responding to insulin. Treatment is through careful diet and regular exercise.

differentiated   A differentiated cell has a specialised form suited to its function. It cannot change into another kind of cell.

diffraction   What happens when waves hit the edge of a barrier or pass through a gap in a barrier. They bend a little and spread into the region behind the barrier.

digestive enzyme   Biological catalysts that break down food.

dioptre   Unit of lens power, equivalent to a focal length of 1 m.

dioxin   Poisonous chemicals, for example, released when plastics burn.

direct drilling   Planting seeds directly into the soil without ploughing first.

dislocation   An injury where a bone is forced out of its joint.

dispersion   The splitting of white light into different colours (frequencies), for example, by a prism.

distillation   A method of separating a mixture of two or more substances with different boiling points.

DNA fingerprinting   A DNA fingerprint uses gene probes to identify particular sequences of DNA bases in a person's genetic make-up. The pattern produced in a DNA fingerprint can be used to identify family relationships.

DNA profiling   A DNA profile is produced in the same way as a DNA fingerprint, but fewer gene probes are used. DNA profiling is used in forensic science to test samples of DNA left at crime scenes.

double bond   A covalent bond between two atoms involving the sharing of two pairs of electrons. They are found in alkenes and unsaturated hydrocarbons.

double circulation   A circulatory system where the blood passes through the heart twice for every complete circulation of the body.

drying agent   A chemical used to remove water from moist liquids or gases. Anhydrous calcium chloride and anhydrous sodium sulfate are examples of drying agents.

dynamic equilibrium   Chemical equilibria are dynamic. At equilibrium the forward and backward reactions are still continuing but at equal rates so that there is no overall change.

ecosystem   Living organisms plus their non-living environment working together.

ecosystem services   Life-support systems that we depend on for our survival.

electromagnetic wave   A wave consisting of vibrating electric and magnetic fields, which can travel in a vacuum. Visible light is one example.

electron   A tiny, negatively charged particle that is part of an atom. Electrons are found outside the nucleus. Electrons have negligible mass and one unit of charge.

electrostatic attraction   The force of attraction between objects with opposite electric charges. A positive ion, for example, attracts a negative ion.

emission spectrum (of an element)   The electromagnetic frequencies emitted by an excited atom as electron energy levels fall.

end point   The point during a titration at which the reaction is just complete. For example, in an acid–alkali titration, the end point is reached when the indicator changes colour. This happens when exactly the right amount of acid has been added to react with all the alkali present at the start.

endothermic   An endothermic process takes in energy from its surroundings.

energy-level diagram   A diagram to show the difference in energy between the reactants and the products of a reaction.

enzyme   A protein that catalyses (speeds up) chemical reactions in living things.

equilibrium   A state of balance in a reversible reaction when neither the forward nor the backward reaction is complete. The reaction appears to have stopped. At equilibrium reactants and products are present and their concentrations are not changing.

erosion   The movement of solids at the Earth's surface (for example, soil, mud, rock) caused by wind, water, ice, and gravity, or living organisms.

ester   An organic compound made from a carboxylic acid and an alcohol. Ethyl ethanoate is an ester. It has the formula $CH_3COOC_2H_5$.

ethanol   Waste product from anaerobic respiration in plants and yeast.

ethical   Non-scientific, concerned with what is right or wrong.

eutrophication   Build-up of nutrients in water.

exoplanet   The planet of any star other than the Sun.

exothermic   An exothermic process gives out energy to its surroundings.

extended object   An astronomical object made up of many points, for example the Moon, or a galaxy. By contrast, a star is a single point.

extremities   Parts of the body away from the core, for example, fingers.

eyepiece lens (of an optical telescope)   The lens nearer the eye, which has a higher power. Often called a telescope 'eyepiece'.

fallow crop   Crop that is not harvested, allowing the field to regain nutrients

fat   Fats are esters of glycerol with long-chain carboxylic acids (fatty acids). The fatty acids in animal fats are mainly saturated compounds.

fatty acids   Another name for carboxylic acids.

feedstocks   A chemical, or mixture of chemicals, fed into a process in the chemical industry.

fermentation   Process that grows bacteria or fungi on a large scale. The microorganisms take in nutrients and make useful chemicals, including enzymes, other proteins, antibiotics, and other medicines.

fermenter   Large vessel in which microorganisms are grown to make a useful product.

fine chemicals   Chemicals made by industry in smaller quantities than bulk chemicals. Fine chemicals are used in products such as food additives, medicines, and pesticides.

fitness   State of health and strength of the body.

flowers   Reproductive structures in plants often containing both male and female reproductive structures.

fluorescent marker   Chemical attached to a DNA strand so it can be found or identified when separated from other strands in a gel.

focal length   The distance from the optical centre of a lens or mirror to its focus.

focus (of a lens or mirror)   The point at which rays arriving parallel to its principal axis cross each other. Also called the 'focal point'.

focusing   Adjusting the distance between lenses, or between the eyepiece lens and a photographic plate to obtain a sharp image of the object.

fossil fuel   Fuel made of the bodies of long-dead organisms.

fossil sunlight energy   Sunlight energy stored as chemical energy in fossil fuel.

fruit   Remaining parts of a flower containing seeds after fertilisation.

functional group   A reactive group of atoms in an organic molecule. The hydrocarbon chain making up the rest of the molecule is generally unreactive with common reagents such as acids and alkalis. Examples of functional groups are —OH in alcohols and —COOH in carboxylic acids.

fungus   A group of living things, including some microorganisms, that cannot make their own food.

galaxy   A collection of thousands of millions of stars held together by gravity.

gene probe   A short piece of single-stranded DNA used in a genetic test. The gene probe has complementary bases to the allele that is being tested for.

genetic modification (GM)   Altering the characteristics of an organism by introducing the genes of another organism into its DNA.

globular cluster   A cluster of hundreds of thousands of old stars.

glycerol   Glycerol is an alcohol with three —OH groups. Its chemical name is propan-1,2,3-triol. Its formula is CH_2OH—$CHOH$—CH_2OH.

Haber Process   The reaction between nitrogen and hydrogen gas used to make ammonia on an industrial scale.

haemoglobin   The protein molecule in red blood cells. Haemoglobin binds to oxygen and carries it around the body. It also gives blood its red colour.

heart disease   A range of potentially serious illnesses that affect the heart.

heat under reflux   Heating a reaction mixture in a flask fitted with a vertical condenser. Vapours escaping from the flask condense and flow back into the reaction mixture.

heavy metals   Metals such as lead and mercury, which are toxic in small concentrations.

herbicide   Chemical that kills plants, usually plants that are weeds in crops or gardens.

hormone   A chemical messenger secreted by specialised cells in animals and plants. Hormones bring about changes in cells or tissues in different parts of the animal or plant.

Hubble constant   The ratio of the speed of recession of galaxies to their distance, with a value of about 72 km/s per Mpc.

hydrocarbon   A compound of hydrogen and carbon only. Ethane, C_2H_6, is a hydrocarbon.

hypothalamus   The part of the brain that controls many different functions, for example, body temperature.

insulin   A hormone produced by the pancreas. It is a chemical that helps to control the level of sugar (glucose) in the blood.

intensity (of light in a star's spectrum)   The amount of a star's energy gathered by a telescope every second, per unit area of its aperture.

intensive agriculture   Farming with high inputs of fertiliser and pesticides and high productivity.

interference   What happens when two waves meet. If the waves have the same frequency, an interference pattern is formed. In some places, crests add to crests, forming bigger crests; in other places, crests and troughs cancel each other out.

intermediates   The chemicals formed in a chemical reaction that then go on to react further to produce the final product.

intrinsic brightness (of a star)   A measure of the light that would reach a telescope if a star were at a standard distance from the Earth.

inverted image   An image that is upside down compared to the object.

irreversible change   A chemical change that can only go in one direction, for example, changes involving combustion.

joint   A point where two or more bones meet.

Kelvin scale   A scale of temperature in which O K is absolute zero, and the triple point of water (where solid, liquid, and gas phases co-exist) is 273 K.

kinetic model of matter   The idea that a gas consists of particles (atoms or molecules) that move around freely, colliding with each other and with the walls of any container, with most of the volume of gas being empty space.

Le Chatelier's principle   The principle that the position of an equilibrium will respond to oppose a change in the reaction conditions.

lifestyle history   The way you have been living, taking regular exercise, eating healthily, and so on.

ligament   Tissue that joins two or more bones together.

light pollution   Light created by humans, for example, street lighting, that prevents city dwellers from seeing more than a few bright stars. It also cause problems for astronomers.

light-year   The distance travelled by light in a year.

lignocellulase   Enzyme that can break down the woody fibres in plant material (lignin) and the cellulose of plant cell walls.

limiting factor   The factor that prevents the rate of growth of living things.

linear system   A system based on the take–make–dump model.

locating agent   A chemical used to show up colourless spots on a chromatogram.

luminosity (of a star)   The amount of energy radiated into space every second. This can be measured in watts, but astronomers usually compare a star's luminosity to the Sun's luminosity.

lunar eclipse   When the Earth comes between the Moon and the Sun, and totally or partially covers the Moon in the Earth's shadow as seen from the Earth's surface.

magnification (of an optical instrument)   The process of making something appear closer than it really is.

measurement uncertainty   Variations in analytical results owing to factors that the analyst cannot control. Measurement uncertainty arises from both systematic and random errors.

medical history Health or health problems in the past.

medication Any pharmaceutical drug used to treat or prevent an illness.

megaparsec (Mpc) A million parsecs.

microorganism Living organisms that can only be seen by looking through a microscope. They include bacteria, viruses, and fungi.

microwaves Radio waves of the highest frequency (shortest wavelength), used for mobile phones and satellite TV.

Milky Way The galaxy in which the Sun and its planets including Earth are located. It is seen from the Earth as an irregular, faintly luminous band across the night sky.

minisatellite Sections of DNA made up of repeats of sequences about 30 base pairs long.

mobile phase The solvent that carries chemicals from a sample through a chromatographic column or sheet.

muscle Muscles move parts of the skeleton for movement. There is also muscle tissue in other parts of the body, for example, in the walls of arteries.

nanometre A unit of measurement (abbreviation nm). A millimetre is the same as 1 million nanometres. 1 nm = 1 m $\times$ 10^{-9} m)

nanotechnology Technology based on particles that are less than about 100 nm in one size.

native species Organisms naturally occurring in an area – not introduced by humans.

neutron star The collapsed remnant of a massive star, after a supernova explosion. Made almost entirely of neutrons, they are extremely dense.

nitrogen cycle The continual cycling of nitrogen, which is one of the elements that is essential for life. By being converted to different chemical forms, nitrogen is able to cycle between the atmosphere, lithosphere, hydrosphere, and biosphere.

nitrogen fixation The conversion of nitrogen gas into compounds either industrially or by natural means.

nitrogenase The enzyme system that catalyses the reduction of nitrogen gas to ammonia.

nitrogen-fixing bacteria Bacteria taking nitrogen gas from the air, living in the roots of some plants.

noise Unwanted electrical signals that get added on to radio waves during transmission, causing additional modulation. Sometimes called 'interference'.

non-aqueous A solution in which a liquid other than water is the solvent.

non-biodegradable Waste materials that microorganisms cannot break down.

normal An imaginary line drawn at right angles to the point at which a ray strikes the boundary between one medium and another. Used to define the angle of the ray that strikes or emerges from the boundary.

nuclear fusion The process in which two small nuclei combine toform a larger one, releasing energy. An example is hydrogen combining to form helium. This happens in stars, including the Sun.

obesity A medical condition where the increase in body fat poses a serious threat to health. A body mass index over 30 kg/m^2.

objective lens (of an optical telescope) The lens nearer the object, which has a lower power. Often called a telescope 'objective'.

observed brightness (of a star) A measure of the light reaching a telescope from a star.

organ Part of a plant or animal made up of different tissues.

organic chemistry The study of carbon compounds. This includes all of the natural carbon compounds from living things and synthetic carbon compounds.

overgrazing Too many grazing animals, such as goats, damaging the environment.

oxygenated Blood in which the haemoglobin is bound to oxygen molecules (oxyhaemoglobin).

pancreas An organ in the body that produces some hormones and digestive enzymes. The hormone insulin is made here.

parallax The apparent shift of an object against a more distant background, as the position of the observer changes. The further away an object is, the less it appears to shift. This can be used to measure how far away an object is, for example, to measure the distance to stars.

parallax angle When observed at an interval of six months, a star will appear to move against the background of much more distant stars. Half of its apparent angular motion is called its parallax angle.

parsec (pc) A unit of astronomical distance, defined as the distance of a star that has a parallax angle of one arcsecond. Equivalent to 3.1×10^{12} km.

peer review The process whereby scientists who are experts in their field critically evaluate a scientific paper or idea before and after publication.

penumbra An area of partial darkness in a shadow, for example, places in the Moon's path where the Earth only partially blocks off sunlight. Some sunlight still reaches these places because the Sun has such a large diameter.

percentage yield A measure of the efficiency of a chemical synthesis.

petrochemical Chemicals made from crude oil (petroleum) or natural gas.

phagocytosis Engulfing and digestion of microorganisms and other foreign matter by white blood cells.

phases (of the Moon) Changing appearance, due to the relative positions of the Earth, Sun, and Moon.

photons Tiny 'packets' of electromagnetic radiation. All electromagnetic waves are emitted and absorbed as photons. The energy of a photon is proportional to the frequency of the radiation.

photosphere The visible surface of a star, which emits electromagnetic radiation.

pipette A pipette is used to measure small volumes of liquids or solutions accurately. A pipette can be used to deliver the same fixed volume of solution again and again during a series of titrations.

planet A very large, spherical object that orbits the Sun, or other star.

plasma The clear straw-coloured fluid part of blood.

plasmids Small circle of DNA found in bacteria. Plasmids are not part of a bacterium's main chromosome.

platelets Cell fragments found in blood. Platelets play a role in the clotting process.

pollen Plant reproductive structures containing a male gamete.

pollinators Animals, such as bees, that transfer pollen from anther to stigma.

precision A measure of the spread of quantitative results. If the measurements are precise all the results are very close in value.

pressure (of a gas) The force a gas exerts per unit area on the walls of its container.

primary forest A forest that has never been felled or logged.

principal axis An imaginary line perpendicular to the centre of a lens or mirror surface.

proton A positively charged particle found in the nucleus of atoms. The relative mass of a proton is one and it has one unit of charge.

protostar The early stages in the formation of a new star, before the onset of nuclear fusion in the core.

pulmonary artery The artery that carries deoxygenated blood to the lungs. The artery leaves the right ventricle of the heart.

pulmonary vein The vein that carries oxygenated blood from the lungs to the left atrium of the heart.

qualitative Qualitative analysis is any method of identifying the chemicals in a sample. Thin-layer chromatography is an example of a qualitative method of analysis.

quantitative Quantitative analysis is any method of determining the amount of a chemical in a sample. An acid–base titration is an example of quantitative analysis.

quota Agreed total amount that can be taken or harvested per year.

radiation A flow of information and energy from a source. Light and infrared are examples. Radiation spreads out from its source, and may be absorbed or reflected by objects in its path. It may also go (be transmitted) through them.

radiative zone (of a star) The layer of a star surrounding its core, where energy is transferred by photons to the convective zone.

radio waves Electromagnetic waves of a much lower frequency than visible light. They can be made to carry signals and are widely used for communications.

ray diagram A way of representing how a lens or telescope affects the light that it gathers, by drawing the rays (which can be thought of as very narrow beams of light) as straight lines.

recovery period The time for you to recover after taking exercise and for your heart rate to return to its resting rate.

red blood cells Blood cells containing haemoglobin, which binds to oxygen so that it can be carried around the body by the bloodstream.

reference materials Known chemicals used in analysis for comparison with unknown chemicals.

reflection What happen when a wave hits a barrier and bounces back off it. If you draw a line at right angles to the barrier, the reflected wave has the same angle to this line as the incoming wave. For example, light is reflected by a mirror.

reflector A telescope that has a mirror as its objective. Also called a reflecting telescope.

refraction Waves change their wavelength if they travel from one medium to another in which their speed is different. For example, when travelling into shallower water, waves have a smaller wavelength as they slow down.

refractor A telescope that has a lens as its objective, rather than a mirror.

reject How a body might react to foreign material introduced in a transplant.

reliability How trustworthy data is.

renewable resource Resources that can be replaced as quickly as they are used. An example is wood from the growth of trees.

replicate sample Two or more samples taken from the same material. Replicate samples should be as similar as possible and analysed by the same procedure to help judge the precision of the analysis.

representative sample A sample of a material that is as nearly identical as possible in its chemical composition to that of the larger bulk of material sampled.

resolving power The ability of a telescope to measure the angular separation of different points in the object that is being viewed. Resolving power is limited by diffraction of the electromagnetic waves being collected.

respiration A series of chemical reactions in cells that release energy for the cell to use.

retardation factor A retardation factor, R_f, is a ratio used in paper or thin-layer chromatography. If the conditions are kept the same, each chemical in a mixture will move a fixed fraction of the distance moved by the solvent front. The R_f value is a measure of this fraction.

retention time In chromatography, the time it takes for a component in a mixture to pass through the stationary phase.

retrograde motion An apparent reversal in a planet's usual direction of motion, as seen from the Earth against the background of fixed stars. This happens periodically with all planets beyond the Earth's orbit.

RICE RICE stands for rest, ice, compression, elevation. This is the treatment for a sprain.

risk A measure of the size of a potential danger. It is calculated by combining a measure of a hazard with the chance of it happening.

sample A small portion collected from a larger bulk of material for laboratory analysis (such as a water sample or a soil sample).

saturated In the molecules of a saturated compound, all of the bonds are single bonds. The fatty acids in animal fats are all saturated compounds.

selective absorption Some materials absorb some forms of electromagnetic radiation but not others. For example, glass absorbs infrared but is transparent to visible light.

selective breeding Choosing parent organisms with certain characteristics and mating them to try to produce offspring that have these characteristics.

shivering Very quick muscle contractions. Releases more energy from muscle cells to raise body temperature.

sidereal day The time taken for the Earth to rotate 360°: 23 hours and 56 minutes.

silting of rivers Eroded soil making the water muddy and settling on the river bed.

single-celled protein (SCP) A microorganism grown as a source of food protein. Most single-celled protein is used in animal feed, but one type is used in food for humans.

skeleton The bones that form a framework for the body. The skeleton supports and protects the internal organs, and provides a system of levers that allow the body to move. Some bones also make red blood cells.

soil erosion Soil removal by wind or rain into rivers or the sea.

solar day The time taken for the Earth to rotate so that it fully faces the Sun again: exactly 24 hours.

solar eclipse When the Moon comes between the Earth and the Sun, and totally or partially blocks the view of the Sun as seen from the Earth's surface.

Solar System The Sun and objects that orbit around it – planets and their moons, comets, and asteroids.

solvent front The furthest position reached by the solvent during paper or thin-layer chromatography.

source An object that produces radiation.

spectrometer An instrument that divides a beam of light into a spectrum and enables the relative brightness of each part of the spectrum to be measured.

spectrophotometer An instrument that can measure the intensities of each colour or wavelength present in the optical spectrum. It can be used to convert thin-layer chromatography into a quantitative technique.

spectrum One example is the continuous band of colours, from violet to red, produced by shining white light through a prism. Passing light from a flame test through a prism produces a line spectrum.

speed of light 300 000 kilometres per second – the speed of all electromagnetic waves in a vacuum.

speed of recession The speed at which a galaxy is moving away from us.

sprain An injury where ligaments are located.

stable ecosystem An ecosystem that renews itself and does not change.

standard solution A solution whose concentration is accurately known. They are used in titrations.

star life cycle All stars have a beginning and an end. Physical processes in a star change throughout its life, affecting its appearance.

stationary phase The medium through which the mobile phase passes in chromatography.

stem cells Unspecialised animal cells that can divide and develop into specialised cells.

strong acid A strong acid is fully ionised to produce hydrogen ions when it dissolves in water.

Sun The star nearest Earth. Fusion of hydrogen in the Sun releases energy, which makes life on Earth possible.

supernova A dying star that explodes violently, producing an extremely bright astronomical object for weeks or months.

sustainable Using the Earth's resources in a way that can continue in future, rather than destroying them.

sustainable development A plan for meeting people's present needs without spoiling the environment for the future.

symptom What a person has when they have a particular illness, for example, a rash, high temperature, and sore throat.

synovial fluid Fluid found in the cavity of a joint. The fluid lubricates and nourishes the joint, and prevents two bones from rubbing against each other.

tap funnel A funnel with a tap to allow the controlled release of a liquid.

telescope (from Greek, meaning 'far-seeing') An instrument that gathers electromagnetic radiation, to form an image or to map data, from astronomical objects such as stars and galaxies. It makes visible things that cannot be seen with the naked eye.

tendon Tissue that joins muscle to a bone.

tissue Group of specialised cells of the same type working together to do a particular job.

tissue fluid Plasma that is forced out of the blood as it passes through a capillary network. Tissue fluid carries dissolved chemicals from the blood to cells.

titration An analytical technique used to find the exact volumes of solutions that react with each other.

torn ligament An injury of the elastic tissues that hold bones together, a common sports injury of the knee. For treatment see 'RICE'.

torn tendon An injury of the inelastic tissues that connect muscles to bones. For treatment see 'RICE'.

toxic Poisonous.

triple bond A covalent bond between the two atoms involving the sharing of three pairs of electrons, for example, nitrogen gas. It makes the molecule very stable and unreactive.

umbra An area of total darkness in a shadow, for example, places in the Moon's path where the Earth completely blocks off sunlight.

Universe All things (including the Earth and everything else in space).

unsaturated There are double bonds in the molecules of unsaturated compounds. There is no spare bonding. The fatty acids in vegetable oils include a high proportion of unsaturated compounds.

unstable The nucleus in radioactive isotopes is not stable. It is liable to change, emitting one of several types of radiation. If it emits alpha or beta radiation, a new element is formed.

valves Flaps of tissue that act like one-way gates, only letting blood flow in one direction around the body. Valves are found in the heart and in veins.

vasoconstriction Narrowing of blood vessels.

vasodilation Widening of blood vessels.

vector A method of transfer. Vectors are used to transfer genes from one organism to another.

vegetable oil Vegetable oils are esters of glycerol with fatty acids (long-chain carboxylic acids). More of the fatty acids in vegetable oils are unsaturated when compared with the fatty acids in animal fats.

vein Blood vessels that carry blood towards the heart.

vena cava The main vein that returns deoxygenated blood to the right atrium of the heart.

ventricle One of the lower chambers of the heart. The right ventricle pumps blood to the lungs. The left ventricle pumps blood to the rest of the body.

vinegar A sour-tasting liquid used as a flavouring and to preserve foods. It is a dilute acetic (ethanoic) acid made by fermenting beer, wine, or cider.

virus Microorganisms that can only live and reproduce inside living cells.

weak acids Weak acids are only slightly ionised to produce hydrogen ions when they dissolve in water.

white blood cells Cells in the blood that fight microorganisms. Some white blood cells digest invading microorganisms. Others produce antibodies.

X-rays Electromagnetic waves with high frequency, well above that of visible light.

Index

Appendices

Useful relationships, units, and data

Relationships

You will need to be able to carry out calculations using these mathematical relationships.

B7 Further biology

$$\text{BMI} = \frac{\text{body mass (kg)}}{[\text{height (m)}]^2}$$

C7 Further chemistry

$$\text{concentration of a solution} = \frac{\text{mass of solute}}{\text{volume of solution}}$$

$$\text{percentage yield} = \frac{\text{actual yield}}{\text{theoretical yield}} \times 100\%$$

$$\text{chromatography: retardation factor } (R_f) = \frac{\text{distance travelled by solute}}{\text{distance travelled by solvent}}$$

P7 Studying the Universe

$$\text{power of a lens} = \frac{1}{\text{focal length}}$$

$$\text{magnification of a telescope} = \frac{\text{focal length of objective lens}}{\text{focal length of eyepiece lens}}$$

Hubble equation: speed of recession = Hubble constant × distance

Einstein's equation: $E = mc^2$ where E is the energy produced, m is the mass lost and c is the speed of light in a vacuum

For a fixed mass of gas:

pressure × volume = constant *at constant temperature*

$$\frac{\text{pressure}}{\text{temperature}} = \text{constant } \textit{for constant volume}$$

$$\frac{\text{volume}}{\text{temperature}} = \text{constant } \textit{at constant pressure}$$

Units that might be used in the Physics course

length: metres (m), kilometres (km), centimetres (cm), millimetres (mm), micrometres (μm), nanometres (nm)

mass: kilograms (kg), grams (g), milligrams (mg)

time: seconds (s), milliseconds (ms)

temperature: degrees Celsius (°C); Kelvin (K)

area: cm^2, m^2

volume: cm^3, dm^3, m^3, litres (l), millilitres (ml)

speed and velocity: m/s, km/s, km/h

force: newtons (N)

energy/work: joules (J), kilojoules (kJ), megajoules (MJ), kilowatt-hours (kWh), megawatt-hours (MWh)

distance (astronomy): parsecs (pc)

power of a lens: dioptres (D)

Prefixes for units

nano	micro	milli	kilo	mega	giga	tera
one thousand millionth	one millionth	one thousandth	× thousand	× million	× thousand million	× million million
0.000000001	0.000001	0.001	1000	1000 000	1000 000 000	1000 000 000 000
10^{-9}	10^{-6}	10^{-3}	$\times 10^3$	$\times 10^6$	$\times 10^9$	$\times 10^{12}$

Useful Data

P7 Studying the Universe

solar day = 24 hours

sidereal day = 23 hours 56 minutes

age of the Universe: approximately 14 thousand million years

absolute zero of temperature , 0 K = −273 °C

Chemical Formulae

C7 Further Chemistry

methanol CH_3OH, ethanol C_2H_5OH

methanoic acid HCOOH, ethanoic acid CH_3COOH

Periodic table

																		4 **He** helium 2
1	**2**											**3**	**4**	**5**	**6**	**7**	**0**	

Key: relative atomic mass / atomic symbol / name / atomic (proton) number

1 **H** hydrogen 1

1	2											3	4	5	6	7	0
7 **Li** lithium 3	9 **Be** beryllium 4											11 **B** boron 5	12 **C** carbon 6	14 **N** nitrogen 7	16 **O** oxygen 8	19 **F** fluorine 9	20 **Ne** neon 10
23 **Na** sodium 11	24 **Mg** magnesium 12											27 **Al** aluminium 13	28 **Si** silicon 14	31 **P** phosphorus 15	32 **S** sulfur 16	35.5 **Cl** chlorine 17	40 **Ar** argon 18
39 **K** potassium 19	40 **Ca** calcium 20	45 **Sc** scandium 21	48 **Ti** titanium 22	51 **V** vanadium 23	52 **Cr** chromium 24	55 **Mn** manganese 25	56 **Fe** iron 26	59 **Co** cobalt 27	59 **Ni** nickel 28	63.5 **Cu** copper 29	65 **Zn** zinc 30	70 **Ga** gallium 31	73 **Ge** germanium 32	75 **As** arsenic 33	79 **Se** selenium 34	80 **Br** bromine 35	84 **Kr** krypton 36
85 **Rb** rubidium 37	88 **Sr** strontium 38	89 **Y** yttrium 39	91 **Zr** zirconium 40	93 **Nb** niobium 41	96 **Mo** molybdenum 42	98 **Tc** technetium 43	101 **Ru** ruthenium 44	103 **Rh** rhodium 45	106 **Pd** palladium 46	108 **Ag** silver 47	112 **Cd** cadmium 48	115 **In** indium 49	119 **Sn** tin 50	122 **Sb** antimony 51	128 **Te** tellurium 52	127 **I** iodine 53	131 **Xe** xenon 54
133 **Cs** caesium 55	137 **Ba** barium 56	139 **La★** lanthanum 57	178 **Hf** hafnium 72	181 **Ta** tantalum 73	184 **W** tungsten 74	186 **Re** rhenium 75	190 **Os** osmium 76	192 **Ir** iridium 77	195 **Pt** platinum 78	197 **Au** gold 79	201 **Hg** mercury 80	204 **Tl** thallium 81	207 **Pb** lead 82	209 **Bi** bismuth 83	209 **Po** polonium 84	210 **At** astatine 85	222 **Rn** radon 86
223 **Fr** francium 87	226 **Ra** radium 88	227 **Ac★** actinium 89	261 **Rf** rutherfordium 104	262 **Db** dubnium 105	266 **Sg** seaborgium 106	264 **Bh** bohrium 107	277 **Hs** hassium 108	268 **Mt** meitnerium 109	271 **Ds** darmstadtium 110	272 **Rg** roentgenium 111							

Elements with atomic numbers 112–116 have been reported but not fully authenticated

- The lanthanoids (atomic numbers 58–71) and the actinoids (atomic numbers 90–103) have been omitted.
- The relative atomic masses of copper and chlorine have not been rounded to the nearest whole number.

OXFORD
UNIVERSITY PRESS

Great Clarendon Street, Oxford OX2 6DP

Oxford University Press is a department of the University of Oxford. It furthers the University's objective of excellence in research, scholarship, and education by publishing worldwide in

Oxford   New York

Auckland   Cape Town   Dar es Salaam   Hong Kong   Karachi
Kuala Lumpur   Madrid   Melbourne   Mexico City   Nairobi
New Delhi   Shanghai   Taipei   Toronto

With offices in
Argentina   Austria   Brazil   Chile   Czech Republic   France   Greece
Guatemala   Hungary   Italy   Japan   Poland   Portugal   Singapore
South Korea   Switzerland   Thailand   Turkey   Ukraine   Vietnam

Oxford is a registered trade mark of Oxford University Press in the UK and in certain other countries.

© University of York and the Nuffield Foundation 2011.

The moral rights of the authors have been asserted.

Database right Oxford University Press (maker).

First published 2011.

British Library Cataloguing in Publication Data.

Data available.

ISBN 978-0-19-913847-0

10 9 8 7 6 5 4 3 2 1

Printed in Spain by Cayfosa-Impresia Ibérica.

Paper used in the production of this book is a natural, recyclable product made from wood grown in sustainable forests. The manufacturing process conforms to the environmental regulations of the country of origin.

Acknowledgements
The publisher and authors would like to thank the following for their permission to reproduce photographs and other copyright material:
P13: Andrew Lambert Photography/Science Photo Library; **P16:** Greg Epperson/Shutterstock; **P18tl:** Ingram Publishing/Photolibrary; **P18tr:** Juniors Bildarchiv/Photolibrary; **P18ml:** BSIP Medical/Photolibrary; **P18mr:** Dan Suzio/Science Photo Library; **P18bl:** Manfred Grebler/Photolibrary; **P18br:** Urban Zone/Alamy; **P19:** Firefly Productions/Corbis UK ltd.; **P22t:** Ian Hooton/Science Photo Library; **P22b:** DJ Mattaar/Shutterstock, **P23:** Jim DeLillo/Istockphoto; **P24l:** Widmann Widmann/Photolibrary; **P24r:** Adam van Bunnens/Alamy; **P27t:** Times Newspapers/Rex Features; **P27m:** Clive Brunskill/Getty Images Sports/Getty Images; **P28-29:** DJ Mattaar/Shutterstock; **P28:** Banana Stock/Photolibrary; **P31b:** Biophoto Associates/Science Photo Library; **P34r:** Klaus Guldbrandsen/Science Photo Library; **P35:** Martin Dohrn/Royal College Of Surgeons/Science Photo Library; **P36:** Pasieka/Science Photo Library; **P38:** Dave Bartruff/Corbis, **P39:** John Cleare Mountain Camera; **P40tl:** Lynne Harty Photography/Alamy; **P40tm:** Corbis UK Ltd.; **P40tr:** Wartenberg/Picture Press/Corbis; **P40bl:** Francesco Ridolfi/Shutterstock; **P40bm:** David Stoecklein/Corbis; **P40br:** Owen Franken/Corbis; **P41:** Mark Clarke/Science Photo Library; **P42:** Mark Clarke/Science Photo Library; **P43t:** Samuel Ashfield/Science Photo Library; **P43bl:** Steve Meddle/Rex Features, Alina555/Istockphoto, Tomasz Zajaczkowski/Istockphoto, Charlotte Allen/Istockphoto, Elena Schweitzer/Istockphoto, Lauri Patterson/Istockphoto; **P43br:** Hulton Archive/Getty Images; **P44t:** Paul Harizan/Getty Images; **P44m:** Construction Photography/Corbis; **P44b:** ITV/Rex Features; **P46t:** Patrick Robert/Sygma/Corbis; **P46b:** Bettmann/Corbis; **P47t:** Janie Airey/Cancer Research UK; **P47b:** Moodboard/Corbis; **P48:** Ivonne Wierink/Shutterstock; **P49:** NatureOnline/Alamy; **P52t:** David M Dennis/Photolibrary; **P53:** Sergio/Pitamitz/Robert Harding/Rex Features; **P54t:** Mpemberton/Dreamstime; **P54b:** Hugh Clark/FLPA; **P56tl:** S & D & K Maslowski/FLPA; **P56b:** Rodger Klein/Photolibrary; **P57l:** Ken Griffiths/NHPA; **P57r:** Mary Terriberry/Shutterstock; **P58:** Edward Webb/Rex Features;

P59: No-till On The Plains; **P60:** Sean Gladwell/Shutterstock; **P62:** Tusia/Shutterstock; **P63t:** fazon1/Istockphoto; **P63b:** Dr Jeremy Burgess/Science Photo Library; **P64:** Thomas Winz/Photolibrary; **P65:** Moodboard RF/Photolibrary; **P66t:** Mark Edwards/Photolibrary; **P66b:** © RBG Kew; **P67tl:** Larissa Siebicke/Photolibrary; **P67tr:** ImageBroker/Imagebroker/FLPA; **P67b:** Food and Agriculture Organisation of the United Nations; **P68:** Stasvolik/Dreamstime; **P69t:** Adrian Arbib/Photolibrary; **P69m:** Fletcher & Baylis/Science Photo Library; **P69b:** Francois Savigny/Nature Picture Library; **P71:** Conservation International; **P73:** Ashley Cooper, Visuals Unlimited/Science Photo Library; **P74t:** Sue Darlow/Photolibrary; **P74b:** Ruddy Gold/Photolibrary; **P84:** Jerry Mason/Science Photo Library; **P85:** Bill Barksdale/Agstockusa/Science Photo Library; **P57t:** T Philippe Plailly/Science Photo Library; **P87b:** Yoav Levy/Photolibrary; **P88:** Eloy Alonso/Reuters; **P90t:** Steve Gschmeissner/Science Photo Library; **P90m:** Keys; **P90b:** Net Resources International; **P91:** Picsfive/Shutterstock; **P92t:** Pasieka/Science Photo Library; **P92b:** Mauro Fermariello/Science Photo Library; **P93:** Henrik Jonsson/Istockphoto; **P95tl:** Steve Allen/Science Photo Library; **P95tr:** BSIP, Raguet H/Science Photo Library; **P95bl:** David Leah/Science Photo Library; **P95br:** Hank Morgan/Science Photo Library; **P104:** Y.Beaulieu, Publiphoto Diffusion/Science Photo Library; **P106:** Maximilian Stock Ltd./Science Photo Library; **P107:** R Estall/Robert Harding Picture Library Ltd/Alamy; **P108:** Steve Bicknell/The Steve Bicknell Style Library/Alamy; **P109t:** Mark Thomas/Science Photo Library; **P109b:** William Taufic/Corbis; **P110l:** Laurance B. Aiuppy/Stock Connection/Alamy; **P111:** Du Pont (UK) Ltd; **P112t:** Martyn F. Chillmaid/Science Photo Library; **P112b:** chas53/Fotolia; **P114:** Nigel Cattlin/Hot Studios International; **P115:** Alamy; **P117:** Leslie Garland/Leslie Garland Picture Library/Alamy; **P118:** Fred Hendriks/Shutterstock; **P120t:** Christine Osborne/Corbis; **P120b:** Corbis UK Ltd.; **P121:** Nina Towndrow/Nuffield Curriculum Centre; **P122:** Andrew Lambert Photography/Science Photo Library; **P124:** Nina Towndrow/Nuffield Curriculum Centre; **P126t:** Alex Bartel/Science Photo Library; **P126b:** David R. Frazier/Science Photo Library; **P127:** Jamie Jones/Rex Features; **P128t:** North Dakota Department of Commerce Division of Community Services; **P128b:** Kathy Collins/Getty Images; **P129:** Patrick Wallet/Eurelios/Science Photo Library; **P130t:** Imagebroker/Alamy; **P130b:** Helene Rogers/Art Directors & Trip Photo Library; **P131:** Nina Towndrow/Nuffield Curriculum Centre; **P132:** Nina Towndrow/Nuffield Curriculum Centre; **P134-135:** Fred Hendriks/Shutterstock; **P136:** Nina Towndrow/Nuffield Curriculum Centre; **P138:** Zooid Pictures; **P138-139:** Fred Hendriks/Shutterstock; **P140t:** The Metropolitan Council; **P140b:** Crown Copyright Health & Safety Laboratory/Science Photo Library; **P141:** Getty Images; **P147:** Fred Hendriks/Shutterstock; **P148t:** Fred Hendriks/Shutterstock; **P148b:** Charles D. Winters/Science Photo Library; **P149:** Eulenblau/Istockphoto; **P151:** Science Photo Library; **P156:** Emilio Segre Visual Archives/American Institute Of Physics/Science Photo Library; **P158:** Dr Jeremy Burgess/Science Photo Library; **P161t:** Clive Freeman, The Royal Institution/Science Photo Library; **P161b:** Laguna Design/Science Photo Library; **P162t:** HR Bramaz, ISM/Science Photo Library; **P162b:** Photo courtesy of LGC; **P163t:** Pullman; **P163b:** Nick laham/Getty Images; **P164:** Bayer AG; **P165:** www.ars.usda.gov; **P166:** Zooid Pictures; **P167t:** Adrian Arbib/Corbis; **P167b:** Zooid Pictures; **P168:** Environmental Health Department, London Borough of Camden/Oxford University Press; **P168-169:** Fred Hendriks/Shutterstock; **P169l:** BBC Photograph Library; **P169r:** David Stoecklein/Corbis; **P171:** Maximilian Stock Ltd/Science Photo Library; **P172:** Analtech Inc.; **P173:** Analtech Inc.; **P174:** Wellcome Trust; **P175:** James Holmes/Thomson Laboratories/Science Photo Library; **P176-177:** Fred Hendriks/Shutterstock; **P180:** Anna Grayson; **P180-181:** Fred Hendriks/Shutterstock; **P181t:** Anna Grayson; **P182t:** Anna Grayson, **P182b:** Fred Hendriks/Shutterstock; **P196t:** Adam Hart-Davis/Science Photo Library; **P196b:** Detlev Van Ravensway/Science Photo Library; **P197bl:** Jerry Lodriguss/Science Photo Library; **P197br:** AFP; **P198t:** Dr Juerg Alean/Science Photo Library; **P199t:** Herman Heyn/Science Photo Library; **P199b:** The British Library Board; **P202t:** NASA; **P202b:** Royal Astronomical Society/Science Photo Library; **P203:** Victor Habbick Visions/Science Photo Library; **P206t:** Dr Fred Espenak/Science Photo Library; **P206b:** George Bernard/Science Photo Library; **P207b:** Dr Fred Espenak/Science Photo Library; **P208l:** Royal Astronomical Society/Science Photo Library; **P208r:** D.A. Calvert, Royal Greenwich Observatory/Science Photo Library; **P209m:** NASA; **P209bl:** Eckhard Slawik/Science Photo Library; **P209br:** X-ray: NASA/UIUC/Y.Chu et al., Optical: NASA/HST; **P211tl:** Detlev Van Ravensway/Science Photo Library; **P211tr:** Nasa/Science Photo Library; **P211bl:** Image courtesy of NRAO/AUI; **P211br:** NASA/JPL-Caltech/Science Photo Library; **P212:** Arthur S. Aubry/Riser/Getty Images; **P213:** Justin Quinnell/NASA; **P218r:** Science Photo Library; **P220:** David Parker/Science Photo Library; **P223l:** Dr Juerg Alean/Science Photo Library; **P223r:** Konstantin Remizov/Shutterstock; **P225:** Dr Seth Shostak/Science Photo Library; **P226t:** **P227t:** NRAO/AUI/NSF/Science Photo Library; **P227b:** MRAO; **P228:** NASA; **P230:** ESO/G.Hüdepoh; **P231tl:** ESO/Jose Francisco Salgado; **P231tr:** ESO/H.H.Heyer; **P231b:** ESO/H.H.Heyer; **P234t:** NASA; **P234b:** NASA; **P235tl:** NASA/ESA/STSCI/AURA/A. Evans (University Of Virginia, Charlottesville; NRAO Stony Brook University)/Science Photo Library; **P235tr:** NASA/ESA/Hubble Heritage Team/STSCI/Science Photo Library; **P237:** European Space Agency/Science Photo Library; **P239:** NASA/ESA/H. Richer, UBC/STSCI/Science Photo Library; **P241:** Harvard College Observatory/Science Photo Library; **P244t:** Richard J. Wainscoat, Peter Arnold Inc./Science Photo Library; **P244m:** JAXA/NASA; **P244bl:** NASA/ESA/STSCI/A. Fruchter, Ero Team/Science Photo Library; **P244bm:** Nasa/Esa/Jpl/Arizona State University; **P244br:** Nasa/Esa/Stsci/J.

Bahcall, Princeton Ias/Science Photo Library; **P245:** Noao/Science Photo Library; **P246:** Emilio Segre Visual Archives/American Institute Of Physics/Science Photo Library; **P248:** NASA/Science Photo Library; **P249m:** Physics Dept., Imperial College/Science Photo Library; **P249b:** European Space Agency/Science Photo Library; **P250t:** Royal Observatory, Edinburgh/Aao/Science Photo Library; **P250b:** Dr Juerg Alean/Science Photo Library; **P256:** Segre Collection/American Institute Of Physics/Science Photo Library; **P260:** Robert Gendler/NASA; **P261:** SOHO/ESA/NASA/Science Photo Library; **P264:** European Southern Observatory/Science Photo Library; **P268:** European Space Agency/Science Photo Library; **P270:** David A. Hardy, Futures: 50 Years In Space/Science Photo Library; **P272:** NASA/Science Photo Library; **P275b:** David Parker/Science Photo Library. **P281:** NASA.

Illustrations by IFA Design, Plymouth, UK, Clive Goodyer, and Q2A Media.

The publisher and authors are grateful for permission to reprint the following copyright material:
Although we have made every effort to trace and contact all copyright holders before publication this has not been possible in all cases. If notified, the publisher will rectify any errors or omissions at the earliest opportunity.

Project Team acknowledgements
These resources have been developed to support teachers and students undertaking the OCR suite of specifications *GCSE Science* Twenty First Century Science. They have been developed from the 2006 edition of the resources. We would like to thank David Curnow and Alistair Moore and the examining team at OCR who produced the specifications for the Twenty First Century Science course.

Authors and editors of the first edition
Jenifer Burden, Peter Campbell, Simon Carson, Anna Grayson, Angela Hall, Andrew Hunt, Pam Large, Robin Millar, John Miller, Michael Reiss, David Sang, Elizabeth Swinbank, Carol Tear, Charles Tracy
Many people from schools, colleges, universities, industry and the professions contributed to the production of the first edition of these resources. We also acknowledge the invaluable contribution of the teachers and students in the Pilot Centres.
The first edition of Twenty First Century Science was developed with support from the Nuffield Foundation, The Salters Institute and the Wellcome Trust. A full list of contributors can be found in the Teacher and technician resources.

The continued development of *Twenty First Century Science* is made possible by generous support from:
• The Nuffield Foundation
• The Salters' Institute